A Chuukese Theory of Personhood

The Concepts Body, Mind, Soul and Spirit
on the Islands of Chuuk (Micronesia)

An Ethnolinguistic Study

Lothar Käser

VTR
Publications

Bibliographic Information Published by the Deutsche Nationalbibliothek
The Deutsche Nationalbibliothek lists this publication in the Deutsche
Nationalbibliografie; detailed bibliographic data are available in the Internet
at http://dnb.d-nb.de.

ISBN 978-3-95776-116-3

VTR Publications
Gogolstr. 33, 90475 Nürnberg, Germany, http://www.vtr-online.com

Translated from German by Geoffrey Sutton and
Derek Cheeseman of MissionAssist (http://www.missionassist.org.uk)

Cover photo: © Ulrike and Klaus W. Müller

It is on the long road and within humble lodgings
that one learns to know one's companions
(Chinese proverb)

for Gisela, Matthias, Beate and Oliver

Contents

Part 2
The Concept of Body

Part 3
The Concepts of Soul, Mind and Spirit

Foreword

The circumstances which led to this study of the notions of body and soul as reflected in the language and thinking of the Chuuk Islanders of Micronesia are rather unusual. When I arrived in Chuuk in September 1969 I had no thoughts of ever tackling this. The stimulus came from Thomas S. Barthel (now deceased), who was at that time Professor of Ethnology at the University of Tübingen. I visited him in the summer of 1972 during a short stay in Germany, for he had invited me to discuss at length the plans for my future ethnological studies. Looking back I admire the way he took for granted that he could entrust me with the investigation of such a difficult topic, for at that time my studies in ethnology were not at all advanced.

The material presented here is based on two studies, my dissertation (Käser 1977), towards which Barthel had pointed me, and which was eventually supervised by Rolf Herzog (formerly Professor at the Institute of Ethnology at the University of Freiburg im Breisgau), and my professorial thesis (Käser 1989).

In the years that have since passed it has become evident that the material in this volume, interpreted somewhat differently (than in 1989) could throw light on an issue which is (still) noted for considerable gaps in research and is the cause of serious difficulties of understanding especially among those involved in aid projects and church work in the so-called third world (doctors, nurses, teachers, missionaries). This has to do with the concept of man that other societies have with regard to themselves, which is shown to be strictly shaped by their culture, is only visible in fragmentary form, and is to a large extent encrypted in their language. In fact it is almost exclusively the language material which makes it possible to grasp their notions of what man is, where he comes from, and where he is heading. What I have described in the following chapters is one particular form among the many concepts of man which have emerged from human cultures both past and present.

It should be mentioned that my research would have been inconceivable without the pioneering work of my colleague Hans Fischer (1965). His results were also a determining factor in the detailed investigations of Horst Cain (1979) on the concept of man of the Samoans, a study which I would strongly recommend to my readers.

Goodenough has also evaluated my research data in his dictionary (Goodenough/Sugita 1980:IX) and in his broadly conceived presentation of the religious traditions of the Chuuk Islanders (2002).

Finally I should mention two researchers who made studies on the same subject. The first one is my former student and present colleague Robert Badenberg, who has ventured to make use of my research in Oceania in his investigation of the concept of man held by an African ethnic group, the Bemba of Zambia. In the process he arrived at some surprising insights by applying the method of doubting derived from the French thinker Descartes, using it as the basis of questions put to his Zambian informant. The result is a parallel study of great significance. His findings on the Bemba concept of man are available in Badenberg 1999 and 2004. The second one is Oliver Venz. His outstanding doctoral dissertation of 2012 (a) contains meticulously researched information about Benuaq concepts of body, mind, soul and spirit. The Benuaq are an ethnic group on Borneo whose language is Austronesian.

A series of further parallel studies would be necessary in order to achieve a comparative investigation of a variety of concepts of man, leading to new and important knowledge with regard to their basic structures. Here I would appeal to my readers to get to work themselves, addressing myself particularly to those with experience of mission. Hardly anyone apart from them fulfils, almost ideally, the two basic requirements for such work: experience of living with an ethnic group for a lengthy period of time, and self-evident expertise in the language.

In conclusion I am grateful to all those who may in future draw my attention to current studies on the theme concepts of man.

Schallstadt, Summer 2015
Lothar Käser

Part 1
Introduction

Chapter 1
The Territory and Environment of Chuuk

1.1 Geographical Terminology

Anyone dealing with the ethnological writings on Micronesian societies has to be aware of a problem of terminology. Until about 1990 these groups of islands, belonging mainly to the Carolines, bore the geographical names they had acquired through the Europeans in the age of discovery and colonisation. With the development of national independence since the 1970s, leading to the formation of the Federated States of Micronesia, the islands were given indigenous names, i.e. the modern form reflects the phonology of the local languages. Thus "Truk" became the modern form "Chuuk", and "Ponape", the group of islands to the east of Chuuk, was modernised to "Pohnpei".

These changes present difficulties in accessing the literature, especially by computer and internet research. It is therefore best to use both forms as search terms.

1.2 Geographical Position and Climate

Chuuk is situated more or less in the centre of the Caroline archipelago, about 7° latitude and 152° longitude. Until the beginning of the 1970s Chuuk, with its wreath of islands around Pwolowót (formerly "Puluwat") in the west, the Mortlock Islands in the south-east (indigenous names Mwochunong, Mwóchunók or Nómwun Kuu) and the Hall Islands to the north (indigenous names Nómwun Soomá, Nómwun Paafeng, Fánáápi, Ennefen or Nóórowanú), formed one of the six administrative districts of the Trust Territory of the Pacific Islands, which after the end of the second world war was governed by the USA on behalf of UNO.

Chuuk itself is one of the largest atolls on the planet. Its lagoon is formed by a reef more than 200 km long, and contains 17 so-called high islands of volcanic origin, divided into an eastern group (Nómwoneyas) and a western one (Fááyichuk).

The name "Chuuk" means "mountains". The islands of the atoll, being high ones, are different from all the others of the region, which are formed of coral and rise to only 3 metres above sea level. The highest of the former is Winipwéét on Toon, ca. 450 m.

Chuuk's tropical ocean climate is characterised by high humidity (over 80%), relatively heavy rainfall (over 3000 mm annually) and small variations in temperature (32°-26° Celsius). Malaria is unknown.

The periodic trade winds give rise to two seasons in the year. The months from July to October are calm or only occasionally slightly affected by the trade winds of the southern hemisphere. During this time the rain is more frequent. From November to May the northern trade winds blow steadily. This means that there is less rain in January and February, which can cause a shortage of water. Occasionally the islands are hit by typhoons.

1.3   Economy

The ground of Chuuk's high islands, which is of volcanic origin, reveals four zones of vegetation: 1. a belt of mangrove swamp at the water's edge; 2. a strip close to the edge, producing coconut palms, breadfruit trees, screw pine, bananas, various species of taro etc., and there are also settlements; 3. the slopes of the hills behind, also with coconut palms, breadfruit trees and occasionally fields of sweet potatoes; and 4. a pathless belt overgrown with bush, reaching up to the peaks.

In comparison the fauna on land is lacking in variety. There is no game for hunting. The most important domestic animals are dogs, pigs and hens, all of which serve for food. The population derives most of its protein from the sea. The extensive coral reefs provide rich fishing grounds.

1.4   Population

In 2002, according to the local census office, the total population of all the islands which comprise the state of Chuuk was about 53,000. Of this, somewhat more than 75% live on the islands of the Chuuk lagoon itself. In general the people are of strong physical build. Their hair, which is dark brown to black, is grown long, the skin colour is light to dark brown. Their appearance is similar to that of the Polynesians.

1.5   History

The Spanish navigator Alvaro Saavedra was probably the first European to sight Chuuk, in 1529. Another Spaniard, Alonso de Arellano, visited Chuuk in 1565.

During the second half of the 19th century Spanish influence in the Carolines intensified, but was comparatively minor on Chuuk. After Spain lost its war against the USA in 1898 and had got into financial difficulties, it sold the Carolines and the Marianas (apart from Guam, which already belonged to the USA) to the German Empire in 1899, which had thus begun to build up a colonial empire following the model of its European neighbours. In 1903 the German Jaluit Company opened a trading post on Chuuk

(Tonowas). In 1904 a naval action (by the German patrol cruiser S.M.S. Condor) forced the islanders to hand over their weapons. This put an end to the feuds which the individual islands had till then continually waged against each other. Production of copra (the dried meat of the coconut) began to develop.

As part of the Südsee-Expedition 1908-1910 (Hamburg South Pacific Expedition) Augustin Krämer, his wife Elisabeth, and Ernst Sarfert spent some time in the Chuuk region carrying out ethnological studies.

In 1914 Japan declared war on Germany, occupied most of the islands of Micronesia provisionally and was given the mandate over them in 1920 by the League of Nations.

Under Japanese rule the economic development experienced an enormous boost. With its monopoly the Nanyo Boeki Trading Company enjoyed a decisive share. It had originated from a number of Japanese firms and had already been active on Chuuk during the German colonial period (1905).

However, the Japanese development of agriculture and fishing on the islands of Micronesia was not aimed primarily at benefiting the indigenous population. Japan planned to integrate them complete under its empirical rule. Contrary to the terms of the mandate agreement it set up military installations, made Japanese the obligatory foreign language in the schools and infiltrated the indigenous population with immigrants from Japan, Korea and Okinawa to such an extent that in 1945 there were 35,000 foreigners living on Chuuk, but only about 9,000 local people, corresponding to a ratio of four to one.

Following the capitulation of Japan the USA took over the administration of these islands under the auspices of the United Nations. This marked the beginning of a development which was to lead to the creation of economically and politically modern conditions on the islands of Micronesia.

Since then Chuuk has become one of the four "Federated States of Micronesia", gaining a certain degree of independence, but still not detached from close political and economic relations with the USA.

1.6 Christianisation

The "opening up to mission", as Jaspers (1972) described the process, is of considerable significance in the history of Chuuk. The first Christian (Catholic) missionaries arrived occasionally from Pohnpei during the Spanish period. In 1873 an islander from Pohnpei was the first Protestant missionary to come, living for some time on the Mortlock islands. From there, working with the American Robert Logan, he began the Christianisation of Chuuk. During the German period the first permanently resident

Catholic missionaries (Capuchins) arrived on Chuuk (from 1905). On the Protestant side missionaries from the Liebenzell Mission replaced the Americans (from 1907).

Under the mandate agreement Japan was expressly obligated to permit missionary activity. Hence for some time there were even Japanese missionaries on Chuuk. By contrast the work of Buddhist and Shintoist priests limited itself to the pastoral care of Japanese immigrants. These religions have left no trace on Chuuk.

The number of missionaries working on Chuuk between 1879 and the present day (Kohl 1971, Müller 1989, 2014) has (along with other factors) resulted in a relatively intensive Christianisation. Today almost without exception the population adheres to some form of Christian belief. The investigation below will aim to reveal to what extent this has affected the separate elements of their concept of man. As far as the social structure of the islanders is concerned, it appears to be of no significance (Goodenough 1951:26).

This is a survey painted in broad strokes. A detailed presentation of the history of mission on the islands around Chuuk can be found in Crawford (1967), Müller (1989, 2014), Hezel (1991), and numerous others.

1.7   Bibliographical Resources

In Germany Micronesia is somewhat on the fringes as a subject for ethnological research, and so the relevant literature, even the more and most recent, is not very well known, and also not easily accessed, so that is a good reason for providing details here.

Chuuk, its population and history, have been set out in detail in Goodenough (1951 and 1966), Gladwin/Sarason (1953) and Fischer/Fischer (1970).

The first noteworthy detailed biographical material on Chuuk can be found in the volumes published by Georg Thilenius, containing the results of the Südsee-Expedition 1908-1910 (Hamburg South Pacific Expedition): Hambruch/Sarfert (Damm) (1935); Krämer (1932, 1935).

Damm (1932/35) records the relevant studies from 1928 onwards, but only covering a fairly short time span.

Utinomi's Bibliography of Micronesia, appearing for the last time in 1952, goes as far as 1944 and contains mainly scientific publications, including in its ethnological section particularly Japanese authors.

Publications from 1944-1974 are contained in Marshall/Nason (1975), years 1975-1987 in Goetzfrid/Wuerch (1989). In addition there are two bibliographies tapping particularly into studies and dissertations for master's degrees: Dickson/Dossor (1970) and Coppell (1980).

The little known Bibliotheca Missionum by Streit/Dindinger (1955, 1963 and 1964) is significant for its handling of themes relating to ethnology and religion. This is a multi-volume work even including in detail essays in scarcely known missionary periodicals (up to the date of publication in each case). The material on Oceania is contained in volumes 21 to 23.

Finally, as far as more recent bibliographical sources are concerned, there is the excellent account of the research by Kiste/Marshall (1998) with its comprehensive bibliography of studies on Micronesia up to 1988, and the bibliographies contained in Hiery (2001) and Goodenough (2002).

Chapter 2
Body, Mind, Soul and Spirit as the Basic Components Underlying Concepts of Man in Different Societies and Cultures

2.1 What is a Concept of Man?

It is not easy to describe in simple terms what is meant by a concept of man. Wolters defines it as: "... beliefs regarding the being and place of man in the cosmos, society, nation and family, together with the meaning and purpose of his life and actions ..." (1999:96).

In fairly abstract terms this comprehensive definition certainly does justice to the concept, but at the same time creates a problem of perception by producing the impression that particular conceptual weight is to be placed on the second part ("place of man in the cosmos ..."). In so doing the first part ("being of man ...") involving for example such elementary things as the anatomy and physiology of the body, as perceived by a particular society and culture, are viewed as peripheral or even lost from view in the process of debate. It is clear from the example of the Chuuk Islanders that their concept of man is imbued in a very particular way with their notions of the body, without knowledge of which their ideas on the place of man in the cosmos etc. cannot be comprehensively grasped.

It is evident that all societies and cultures, both past and present[1], even the so-called pre-literate ones, lay claim to a concept of man in the sense described above, and for reasons which are simply to do with everyday life. In all societies children have to be encultured, i.e. shaped in such a way that they behave in the way expected of them by the other members of that society. Only when that goal is attained can they regard themselves as adults, equipped with the strategies for coping with existence which are in tune with their environment, and only in this way can they themselves be accepted as members of their society. Hence concepts of man contain notions of goals towards which educative considerations and procedures are directed. Thus they provide normative models for "true human existence", also playing a part in daily living together, by establishing, among other things, what constitutes cooperative behaviour.

---

[1] Present cultures, as opposed to those only accessible to archaeologists, are those which are still practised by people alive today.

Such normative models with their notions of the purpose of authentic human existence often constitute only one of a number of aspects which concepts of man can reveal in addition, although it is an important one. Wolters (1999:96) distinguishes four types: 1. artistic, 2. metaphysical, theological and ideological, 3. concepts of man based on the combined experiences of everyday life, and 4. scientific concepts of man.

It is fairly clear that the Chuuk Islanders' concept of man belongs, as will be shown, to type 3 ("based on the combined experiences of everyday life"), which does not, however, exclude definite elements of type 2 ("metaphysical, theological and ideological").

Europeans who want to research and learn to understand the concepts of man of other, unfamiliar societies must be absolutely clear about the basic structure of their own concept of man, because the latter can decisively determine in advance one's perception of unfamiliar concepts. The history of research into the concept of man provides clear evidence of this.

2.2   The Features of the European/Western Concept of Man

The European/Western concept of man, reflecting also the corresponding notions of the English-speaking societies of North America, Australia etc., is characteristically tri-partite: man consists of body, soul and spirit.

This relatively simple formula is suitable neither as the foundation of a scientific concept of man, nor is it of use in modern psychology and psychiatry. It forms in fact the conceptual underlying structure of a view of man which I would describe as "popular", "of the everyday man in the street", a concept of man proposed by Wolters as type 3, prevalent in the non-reflective thought and speech of the members of societies and cultures of Europe and the West. It enables one to make simple judgments about the nature of man, but with the limitation that perceptions and statements based on this simple formula result in only a very rough or ill-defined picture of man.

The problem has been pointed out particularly in connection with the term "soul". Haekel writes, " … that there is no unified Western concept of the soul which can be used as a basis for comparison, it varies according to each philosophical orientation and world view … often it is simply a commonly popular or "vulgar" concept of the soul which the ethnographer uses as a guide …" (1971:81). However, Haekel does not give any further details about what he understands as a "vulgar" concept of the soul. H. Fischer expresses similar thoughts when referring to the difficulties associated with trying to arrive at a clear definition (1965:52 ff.). The same is also true of the term "spirit".

The concept of man which I understand in this way as being typical of Europe and the West is also basic to New Testament notions of man, expressed e.g. in 1 Thessalonians 5:23 (King James version "… your whole spirit, soul and body …").

Looking more closely at the three parts of this simple formula, it is apparent that the term "body" presents no particular difficulties of understanding for Europeans and other Westerners who speak Indo-European languages. By contrast the terms "soul" and "spirit" are hard to understand and cannot be defined in few words. The reasons for this are as follows:

Both concepts[2] are characterised by two very different constituent aspects. In the cultural environment of Europe and the West the soul is on the one hand the centre or seat of a person's psychological capacities and processes, i.e. the place in the body where joy, fear and numerous other emotions are located, and on the other hand the soul is the being which survives the death of the person (of the body) and perpetuates his personality.

By contrast in Germany the spirit (Geist) is understood to be on the one hand the seat of one's intellectual abilities and processes, i.e. the place in the body where thought, memory and numerous other mental activities are located, and on the other hand a being that usually remains invisible and hence exists not in physical form but in "spirit-like" form, e.g. as a fairy, guardian angel, elf, ghost, demon etc. In English the latter part of this definition remains true, but as regards the former the concept of the spirit is more closely related to the soul, referring to the animating force within living beings, the non-material essence of a person. Activities associated with the intellect, thought and memory etc. are located in the mind rather than the spirit, which thus adds a further concept to the overall problem! These definitions form the background to the contents of this study, from which the ensuing hypothesis with regard to the Chuuk Islanders' concept of man can be deduced.

The fact that both soul and spirit contain two very different semantic[3] properties has given rise to countless controversies and debates both past and present, as to how these terms should be understood. These discussions have produced a rich cascade of literature, not least in theology. However, a solution is not in sight and is probably not even possible, for the two

---

[2] A concept is an object, event, process or quality in abstract form, i.e. a mental image of an element (perceived or imagined) of reality, usually indicated and comprehended by a word in the language (noun, verb, adjective etc.).

[3] Semantics is the study of the meaning of the words of a language. A semantic property is a characteristic aspect of meaning. Example: the word "cow" has three basic semantic properties: 1. bovine animal (e.g. in contrast to horse), 2. female (as opposed to bull), 3. mature (as opposed to calf).

semantic properties of the terms "soul" and "spirit" are too far apart for them to be of any help in providing conceptual clarity.

Finally, the problem is accentuated by the fact that both terms occasionally mean much the same, and not just in relevant passages in the New Testament (e.g. Luther's translation of Philippians 1:27 " … that you stand in one spirit and one soul …"). Even in ethnological publications vagueness about the concept can creep in, derived from the (Indo-European influenced) semantic structure. Thus in Hirschberg's Dictionary of Ethnology we find the phrase "… of spirits of the dead (the souls of the deceased) …" (1965:143).

In the final analysis the difficulties over the semantic properties of "soul" and "spirit" are shown to be insurmountable when the (theological and basic human) question is to be answered concerning what happens to both when the person dies. In what form does one imagine one's after-death existence? As some kind of dual being? How else? One solution to the problem may lie in the recognition that two different linguistic terms may not necessarily have to represent two different meanings.

One of the consequences of this difficult smorgasbord of concepts is the fact that "soul" and "spirit", with their characteristic European/Western semantic properties, are not, or only in a very limited way, suitable as a starting-point and basis of comparison for researching and understanding the concepts of man of other, unfamiliar societies. However, because the formula "body, soul and spirit" is to begin with the only point of contact for someone beginning to work in one of these societies and cultures, the foreigner, whether teacher, doctor, church worker or ethnographer, has no option but to fall back on this formula. An essential requirement is to be thoroughly clear about the basic structure of one's own concept of man because, as I have already pointed out, this can decisively pre-determine one's perception of unfamiliar concepts.

2.3 The Concept of Man of Non-European/Western Cultures in Ethnological Research

Previous attempts to tackle the subject of the concept of man and to research it are to be found mainly in the area of philosophy, Christian theology and literature on the languages and cultures of European and Near-Eastern antiquity, the accessible written texts of which reveal a lot of information about correlative concepts.

The quest for what notions of man other societies have, especially societies which were until recently pre-literate, is admittedly as old as ethnology as an independent science, which has meanwhile also compiled comprehensive ethnographic material to provide answers. However, titles of ethnographic publications dealing with the whole person of man are rare and of recent date, e.g. Laufer 1957, or their presentations are only illustrative and figurative, such as Heintze 1973. An exception is the collective work of Müller 1983, containing examples of Wolters' type 3, including extensive material on notions of the body of a great variety of pre-literate societies.

By contrast if you look for corresponding information in comprehensive descriptions of individual pre-literate cultures you will make rich finds in the chapters dealing with aspects of the concept of man such as body, soul, spirit, and also death, veneration of ancestors etc.

It is interesting that in this material the term "soul" plays a much more significant role than the terms "body" and "spirit". This imbalance could have been caused by the fact that notions about that which, in Europe and the West, is termed the soul are found much more clearly in some form among all known ethnic groups than phenomena which we would describe in terms of spirit, mind, or intellect.[4] It is also noteworthy that researchers have paid rather less attention to notions of the body, and when they have done so they have scarcely at all related them to notions of soul and spirit, but described them separately. In consequence their descriptions of how man is perceived were one-sided and incomplete, hindering their integration into the corresponding world view and often preventing any further deductions. I hope that my contributions will rectify the situation, at least with regard to Chuuk.

There are already frequent examples in older literature of ethnological research into other cultures where notions of the body were investigated without integrating them into the overall concept of man. The best survey can be found in Blacking 1977.

It can also be deduced from the ethnographic source material that the concept of the "soul" can consist of a great variety of individual notions, not all of which are simultaneously evident in any single concept of man, with the result that there are considerable differences from one ethnic group to the next. Hence ethnologists felt compelled, on the basis of particular characteristic and frequently re-occurring features in the source material, to group the various notions of the soul into types, so that comparative work can be done.

Hirschberg (1965, also partly 1988) proposes the following types: external soul, image soul, bisexual soul, ego soul, free soul, function soul,

---

[4] This is my own extension of a sentence in its original form in Haekel 1971:80.

breath soul, bone soul, body soul, organ soul, shadow soul, dream soul, vital soul, and growth soul. In drawing up this list of concepts of the soul there is clearly a factor at work which is also disturbingly evident in the primary sources: the characteristic concept of the soul of Europe and the West with its two very different semantic properties.

In their desire to comprehend the concept of man belonging to different societies and cultures the ethnographers mostly proceeded according to the following scheme. They started from the features defining their own concept of man, including particularly their own concept of the soul, and looked for comparable elements in the culture they studied. In this way they did indeed find material which when pieced together produced something which had similarities with their own concept of man. But they were for the most part, at least at first, blind to the features which defined over and above that the unfamiliar notions of man. They discovered many things quite by accident. At all events they were in danger of overlooking essential areas of the foreign perceptions, all the more since the time they had available for compiling their findings was scrimped and their knowledge of the language limited. Often the result was a description containing serious gaps, possible only contributing non-essentials, falsely evaluating essentials, and in extreme cases leading to the conclusion that the foreign concept of body, soul and spirit was identical with that of Europe and the West. Only with difficulty can any particular typology of the soul having some validity be acquired on the basis of such sources.

2.4   The Concept of Man of Oceanic Cultures in Ethnological Research

The fact that ethnographers used features of the concept of man and of the soul belonging to Europe and the West as their starting point, looked for similarities in the foreign culture, and so only arrived at an incomplete picture of the object of their research, is very apparent in the above-mentioned study of the relevant sources on Oceanic cultures by H. Fischer (1965). Here are two examples:

European and Western notions of the soul sometimes reveal a connection with the concept of breath, for example in the idea that it is with the final breath of a person that the soul leaves the body. In Oceania this connection is so rare that if it does occur somewhere it must be viewed as untypical. Even so many ethnographers have attempted to prove the existence of this connection in Oceanic societies (H. Fischer 1965:314-320).

It would also seem that a further feature of the European and Western concept of the soul has brought about a distinctive gap in research in the area of notions of the soul and hence of the concept of man in Oceanic cultures. For Europeans the soul is not only the being that survives the death of the body but is also the seat of its emotions.

In Oceania (and evidently also in many other regions) these two notions are for the most part separate or connected with each other in a totally different way. It follows that any attempt to comprehend the notions of the soul as the seat of the emotions in the European/Western sense must come to nothing. Fischer comes to the conclusion: "The investigation of this topic, the Oceanic peoples' own psychology, is still for the time being the most poorly studied area. [...]. To do comparative work here requires precise philological study of the relevant languages and/or a fairly keen interest in the ethnographic field research into these questions" (1965:324).

His challenge still holds (even decades later).

In order to place his typology concerning Oceanic notions of the soul on as sound a basis as possible H. Fischer has selected 39 primary sources from the plethora of relevant material (well over 400 individual publications in the bibliography), from which it can be assumed that they would surely contain more data than that which only reflects the European/Western concept of the soul. According to his research there are in Oceania four fairly broad areas of perception with some correspondence to the European/Western concept: 1. the spirit-like double or dream ego, 2. the spirit of the dead, 3. the life force and 4. the centre of psychic abilities.

In addition the work contains a detailed survey of ethnological and religious publications on the concept of the soul, from Adolf Bastian to Carl August Schmitz.

A long time ago Barthel insisted emphatically that the concept of the body and the way the language reflects its symbolism in the original religions of Oceania plays an essential role (1964:920-926). Although his essay is limited to the situation in Polynesia I am convinced that his statements (mutatis mutandis) are also pertinent for Micronesia. First, he points to the possibility of "identifying cultural models more closely using ethnolinguistic methods" (1964:920). After a brief note on the problems associated with determining the meanings of words from language data consisting purely of lexical items, he addresses to researchers the following challenges, objectives and proposals for procedural methods for acquiring useable data (my italics): "... A truly comprehensive and critically probing study should [...] as far as possible analyse indigenous texts in order to grasp all semasiological nuances (including mood content and connotations) *in the medium of the language itself*" (924). " [...] What we are looking for are [...] particular cognitive models and culture-specific prevalent

examples rooted *in the language* [...] How can one discover a way of classifying symbolism in Polynesia? A technique for this would need to follow
the rules of onomastics – i.e. the way words and names and their origins
are classified. This would involve collecting particular vocabulary groups
(e.g. *parts of the body*)" (925).

Barthel then sets out the (admittedly provisional) framework within
which, in his opinion, one could expect results from research, which he
entitles "main principles of Polynesian symbol formation". He begins with
"biomorphic models" representing "anthropomorphic symbolism", i.e. the
"figurative meaning of 'conception, birth, growth, maturity and death', derived from the vocabulary of both anatomy and physiology..." (925-926).

In his summary Barthel envisages "as the provisional key features of
the trends in Polynesian symbolism [...] a triangle with the three corners
representing 'body', 'plant', 'boat' ..." and establishes that "only by means
of a larger series of future detailed studies [...] " can "the overall richness
and also finally a kind of hierarchy of symbol formation in the language
and culture of Polynesia be compiled and broadened" (926).

2.5   The Concept of Man in the Ethnological Literature on Chuuk

The deficiencies with regard to the concept of the soul in the literature
on Oceania as revealed in H. Fischer's professorial thesis are also found in
reports and studies on the culture of the Chuuk Islanders. The only material
about the soul consists mostly of the occasional brief section embedded in
the description of the religion. Exceptions are the studies by Bollig (1927)
und Goodenough (1963:132-140), but these also only contain a summary
of the most important aspects.

Various reasons can be assumed for the sparseness of material about the
concept of the soul in the records of studies made before 1945. Here also
one of the most far-reaching would appear to have been the various Euro-
pean/Western notions of the soul. This is e.g. the only way to explain the
remarkable fact that the concept of the spirit double of objects ("souls of
objects"), absent in the cognitive framework of Europe and the West, is
only given a brief mention, even in detailed descriptions such as that of
Bollig (1927). The reason I find this remarkable is because among the
Chuuk Islanders it is precisely the notions of the nature of objects which
constitutes the actual foundation of a whole area of their perceptions concerning the soul, and hence also of their concept of man, without which
they cannot be meaningfully explained and understood.

Moreover it is apparent that in the studies in question the soul as the centre of psychic qualities ("seat of the emotions") is only mentioned in passing, such as in the text of a song, or not at all. This could be because this essential aspect of the European/Western concept of the soul has such a different form among the Chuuk Islanders that it must for a long time remain untapped by any questioning emanating from a European/Western outlook. Then there is the professional and philosophical perspective of the authors of earlier reports. They were zoologists or doctors (even Kubary (1980) had begun medical studies), or they were missionaries imbued with the New Testament concept of man as they understood it.

In addition insufficient knowledge of the Chuukese language impeded the efforts of the ethnographers to understand such an intuitively inaccessible area of the culture as the concept of man and the associated notions of the soul. They had no phonologically based system of writing at their disposal, a fact which must have concealed from them a whole series of linguistic categories which the islanders employed to frame the concepts of their world. Usually there was not enough time for intensive investigation, particularly evident with regard to Oceania in the Ergebnisse der Südsee-Expedition [5] 1908-1919 (Krämer 1932, 1935; Hambruch, Sarfert, [Damm] 1935).

The first findings concerning the notions of the soul were recorded by Kubary (1880), who for many years headed up the ethnological involvement of the Hamburg Trading Company Godeffroy in Micronesia. The Mortlock Islands, which were the focus of his reports, are very closely related to Chuuk, both in language and culture.

Kubary's findings were extended by Finsch (1893). His (mistaken) view that soul and shadow were identical notions because they were given the same term is typical of the older reports about notions of the soul among the Chuuk Islanders (1893:321,[559]). Finsch was a zoologist and ethnologist. He spent several years in various parts of Oceania. He only visited the Carolines briefly.

One of the earliest important sources is Girschner (1911). He makes various references to a "soul of objects" (1911:144) and has many detailed descriptions about what he was able to learn concerning the religion. Of foremost importance are his findings about the "spirit mediums" and their practices. The main lack of clarity in his statements relates to the connections between the souls of the living and the spirits of the dead. Girschner, who was the official medical practitioner on Pohnpei for a while, obtained

---

[5] Results of the Südsee-Expedition 1908-1910 (South Pacific Expedition).

his information from inhabitants of the Mortlock Islands to the south of Chuuk. Although the cultures of Chuuk and Pohnpei are related, Girschner's awareness of Chuuk culture must have been limited. Nevertheless the material contained in his report is impressive.

The most extensive and hence the most important source of the notions of the soul held by the Chuuk Islanders is the work of Bollig (1927). H. Fischer included it in his 39 primary sources. It deals mainly with religion and language. Here for the first time the presence on Chuuk of the notion of persons having two souls is discussed in detail and linked with notions of the life beyond. However, the author only makes a brief mention of the spirit double of objects, and notions of the soul as the centre of the psychic abilities are completely missing. According to Krämer (1932: preface) Bollig worked from 1912 till 1914 (according to Kohl [1971] till 1919) as a Catholic missionary on Chuuk and owing to the political situation in the years afterwards was not able to publish his material until 1927.

Krämer, Hambruch and Sarfert (1932, 1935) experienced similar delays in publishing their work. Krämer was a naval doctor and in later years a well-known ethnologist and spent time on Chuuk before Bollig (1906-1907). His account of the notions of the soul is somewhat fragmentary and hence unsystematic. An important addition to Bollig's findings is his illustrative material, together with descriptions of indigenous medical procedures for the recovery of escaped souls.

During the Japanese colonial rule on the Carolines (1914-1945) only a small amount of ethnographic work on Chuuk was accomplished. Japanese sources are difficult to access unless they have been published in a European language. However, relevant bibliographies (Utinomi 1952) reveal no indications of any Japanese research on the concept of the soul among the Chuuk Islanders.

In 1937 the studies named so far were compared and evaluated by Böhme together with similar accounts from other island groups in Micronesia. Böhme also established time and again that the findings for Chuuk and the other regions were in significant areas unsatisfactory, making it very difficult to draw conclusions. Particularly problematic for him was the sparse amount of information on the relationship of body and soul (1937:25). The conclusions which he nevertheless tried to draw have led to a whole series of errors. The cause of this may well lie in the fact that he reckoned on finding the notion of the "living corpse" in Micronesia (1937:101). This is unlikely, and for Chuuk out of the question.

During the first half of the 20th century the published material on the Chuuk Islanders' concepts of the body was limited to word lists and dictionary entries, with occasional added notes on physiological processes.

Girschner's work on Namoluk (Nómwuluuk), an island with a similar culture and language to Chuuk, contains a word list of body parts (1913:183-86), similarly Krämer's reports for Chuuk (1932:313-15) and the surrounding islands (1935: on various pages).

After the end of the Second World War American anthropologists began a systematic research into the island cultures of Micronesia. The CIMA project (Coordinated Investigation of Micronesian Anthropology) 1947 to 1948 involved a total of 42 scientists and brought a team from Yale to Chuuk, led by George Peter Murdock. The results of this research were set out in various dissertations, some of which were published. The most important are the studies by Goodenough on the social structure (1951, 1966), Gladwin/Sarason on the relationship between culture and personality (1953), the work of LeBar on the material culture (1964) and the grammar by Dyen (1965).

More detailed material on the vocabulary of the body is provided by the (first published) dictionary of the Chuukese language (Elbert 1947), but not using a phonemically systematic orthography. The latter was developed by Goodenough and Sugita (1951, 1980 and 1990) at the beginning of the 1950s, based on the preparatory work of Dyen (not published till 1965).

Goodenough's essay on taboo words in the Chuukese language (1975:263-273) has a list of ca. 115 expressions, but mainly limited to the genital and anal regions.

By far the most comprehensive compilation of words on the anatomy and physiology of the human body is contained in the dictionary by Goodenough/Sugita (1980 and 1990).

Work done after 1950 is based on findings obtained using modern methods of ethnological and linguistic field research, emphasising the necessity of adequate knowledge of the language (especially Goodenough 1951, 1966). Nevertheless, even in these works, notions of the soul are only dealt with in passing.

The above-mentioned summary of the notions of the two "souls" of man published by Goodenough in another connection (1963:132-140), forms an exception. It does not contain detailed information on the spirit double of objects and the concept of the soul as the centre of psychic abilities.

The essay by Ushijima (Japanese with English summary) which appeared in 1967 deals with the Micronesians' concepts of the afterlife, comparing them with those of Southern Asia, and also incorporating concepts of the soul. However, this study also relies on the known older sources and not on the author's own field research.

Another significant contribution to understanding the Chuuk Islanders' concepts of the soul is provided by the (unpublished) dissertation by Mahony (1970) on their concepts of disease and medicine. The main features of these are based on the assumption that diseases are caused by spirit beings. The nature of such spirit beings, which Mahony investigates and describes with extensive knowledge both of the topic and the language, is appropriate for clarifying and comprehending the main aspects of concepts of the spirit double of objects and of the human soul. The following observations owe much of their thinking to Mahony's research and hence reference is often made to it.

Chapter 3
Objectives, Methods of Gathering Data,
and the Course of the Field Research

3.1 Prerequisites

H. Fischer's professorial thesis and the perusal of currently available ethnographic studies of the concept of man and in particular the concept of "soul" among the Chuuk Islanders had revealed significant gaps in research. My field research aimed to produce the data to fill these gaps, while at the same time paying special attention to Fischer's demand for "more precise philological study". (Today one would talk of linguistic or simply language study rather than philological study.)

The language material which was collected and which will be analysed below is also probably making a valuable contribution to reducing a research deficit of a regional kind. In Marshall/Nason's bibliography Chuuk (and the Marshall Islands) are described as "the two districts with the largest remaining number of unstudied islands" (1975:31), and in the list of "inhabited Micronesian islands and atolls that have not been researched anthropologically or linguistically during the period 1944-1974..." There is also the name of the island of Tol (Toon), where the material forming the basis of this study originates.

The selection of Chuukese language vocabulary that has been collected should, at least as far as Chuuk is concerned, throw some light on the issue mentioned in Caughey's dissertation (1977): the problem of cultural variants within an overall cultural entity. It would appear that ethnographers are too quick to propose that the statements provided by their own (few!) informants are representative of the whole culture or of its members. Thus Goodenough writes in the preface to Caughey's dissertation: "...Anthropologists have paid relatively little attention to the problem of local cultural or social-psychological differences within the ethnic or tribal units they selected for study purposes. They usually regarded the specific community they studied as representative of the larger unit ..." (1977:III).

Caughey himself regards this as fully confirmed in the case of Chuuk: "With Truk, as elsewhere, the anthropological literature implicitly assumes that the culture of one local group can be taken as representative of the wider society as a whole." By contrast he considers that: "In fact it is more likely that the similarity among local groups masks a great deal of variation in cultural emphasis and detail" (1977:2).

I find myself in agreement with this. Comparisons of the vocabulary of the body in the lexicon of Goodenough/Sugita (1980) taken from the island of Romónum and from Toon indeed reveal a lot of commonalities, but also considerable differences, both in pronunciation and in meaning, although the two islands are only separated by a few kilometres.

It is, however, the following aspect which seems to me to be the most important. During my field research the impression had already been confirmed that the investigation of terms such as "body" and "soul" in emic categories, i.e. those which belong to the culture and language being investigated, are sometimes particularly appropriate for verifying theories about the history of settlements in a region such as Micronesia. All the more so as these two conceptual areas revealed structures which were shown to be so unexpected, so specific to the culture, and so difficult to transfer, that presumably they would only be found again in those cultures which shared a common origin. In other words, the structures were so characteristic in form that parallels in other cultures could not arise by chance. Hence I am of the view that their spread might well provide a more reliable key to the reconstruction of the history of the settlements of Micronesia than the elements of the material culture used up till now (Käser 1989).

3.2   Field Research

In September 1969 I had arrived in Chuuk in order to work first of all for three years as a teacher in a secondary school (Junior High School according to the American system) run by the Evangelical Church of Chuuk. During this time I learned the local language, which I also had to use alongside English in adult classes.

The field research itself for recording the notions of body, soul and spirit began in September 1972 and finished in May 1974. So there were about 18 months available. During this time part of my work was also involved with translating parts of the Old Testament into the Chuukese language. This task and the field research complemented each other excellently.

Although I was officially working under the auspices of an indigenous church, linked with a German church-based development aid organisation (Dienste in Übersee) and the Liebenzell Mission, as a teacher (*sense*) I was not regarded by the local people as a missionary. Also my role could not be connected with any government operation which might give rise to fears that I could perhaps be passing on information to official quarters for the purpose of raising taxes (Freilich 1970). I had a kind of neutral status. Although this made my ethnographic interests somewhat hard to understand they appeared to be without suspicion and at the same time guaranteed easy access to valuable informants[6].

3.3   Characteristics and Problems Associated with Researching Body, Soul and Spirit

Notions of the body on the one hand, and of the soul as the centre or seat of a person's psychic abilities and processes on the other, are part of the conceptual areas of daily life on Chuuk, thus requiring no special knowledge, and can therefore be presumed to belong to the general awareness of any average intelligent islander and to be open to enquiry. Nevertheless informants for this area need to fulfil certain prerequisites: interest in their language and its connections with their conceptual world which can be comprehended via the language; in addition the ability to recognise that the various overtones of the concepts which appear obvious to them may not be obvious to the ethnographer, and vice versa.

It is different with the concepts of the soul as the being that survives the death of the person and perpetuates his personality. Clearly the islanders can only have some general knowledge, in broad outline, of the vocabulary and other associations. For the most part they understand this area of knowledge as *wuruwo*, a term embracing what we can understand as the lore (Goodenough 1951, 1966:53) of the culture. This includes mythology, the nature of the world, explanations of physical phenomena, the (mythical and actual) history of the individual islands, family trees etc. The knowledge contained therein is only known to a few specialists, and they are the only ones qualified to be competent informants. However, engaging them for this task is hedged around with considerable difficulties.

3.4   Informants

Those who preside over this kind of knowledge enjoy considerable esteem, signifying prestige for their social group. Since the islanders have an interest in such prestige, this knowledge is also of material value. It is regarded as the possession of the whole group and can only be passed on for payment or some other compensation. As a rule it is not discussed in front of groups of strangers. Informants who might actually be willing to communicate their knowledge to the ethnographer sometimes feel exposed to

---

[6] Informants are members of a society who are questioned by ethnographers in order to find out about its culture.

considerable pressure from their group to demand something of appropriate value in return. As far as the participants were concerned the interest I showed in this knowledge during my field research could only mean that I would profit materially from it after returning to Germany.

This imputation became all the more apparent when it involved areas of knowledge which the islanders classified as "medical", e.g. in the case of treating symptoms which could be evoked by the absence of the soul (the good spirit double) from the body, phenomena which are known in anthropology as the consequences of "soul loss". In addition to that, such knowledge is considered to have been acquired via mediums from the beyond, as will be shown later, and so informants hesitate to pass on information about methods of making contact with spirit beings in the beyond who are able to convey this knowledge. During the time of my field research divulging details was always bound up with the fear that groups of strangers could have the opportunity of getting hold of this knowledge themselves. This in turn would have signified a loss for the group to which the informant belonged, both materially and in terms of prestige. (An in-depth description of the issues relating to this kind of property, "incorporeal property", can be found in Goodenough 1951, 1966:52-56).

The only people qualified to be competent informants for the various aspects of the concept of the soul as the being that survives the death of the body are those who are designated by the islanders as *waatawa, wáátawa, wáán énú, wáánaanú, sowuyawarawar* and *móngupwi*.

Waatawa, wáátawa, wáán énú, wáánaanú, or *sowuyawarawar* are the terms used for men and women who, as opposed to ordinary people, can perceive and converse with spirit beings (*ngúún* and *énú*) not only in dreams but also when awake. In certain situations they are able to get a particular group among these spirit beings (*énú* as good spirits of the dead) to talk to ordinary people. These are the mediums. A precise description will follow later.

Móngupwi are men and women who, in contrast to ordinary people, are able to perceive exclusively those spirit beings termed *ngúún*, or more precisely *ngúnúyééch*, both in dreams and when awake, but are not able to speak with them nor get them to talk to ordinary people. The *móngupwi* is not a medium but a kind of "seer".

All my data was provided essentially by four men: by *Wupwiini*, presumed to be 80 to 90 years old and formerly holder of the highest title (*samwoon nap*) on the island of Toon, who provided detailed descriptions and interpretations of religious practices from the period before the Christianisation of Chuuk, and was regarded as a seer (*móngupwi*); by *Apenis*,

presumed to be only a little younger, a former medium in the village of
Chukiyénú, and indeed the local expert in the area of notions of the soul as
the being that survives the death of the person; by *Namiyo*, about 50 years
old, and *Mwékút*, 25 years old, both of whom worked mainly on the concepts of the body, and in addition on general issues of language, and on
checking the information provided by the other informants.

3.5 Preliminary Considerations and Procedures for Eliciting Data (Techniques of Questioning)

The terms "body" and "soul" (of necessity at first European/Western)
formed my starting point. For obvious reasons – notions of the body are
easy to put into concrete terms – I began by collecting the vocabulary for
the anatomy and physiology of the human body, including that of animals
and plants ("bodies of objects").

My first recourse was to what I already knew, i.e. I perused the literature
available to me at the start of my field research for relevant material in
order to be able put the statements they contained into question form and
review them, a kind of doubting method introduced into European philosophical thought by the French philosopher René Descartes (1596-1650)
(and recommended to me by Ward Hunt Goodenough).

The language material referring to the body which I found in the ethnological literature about Chuuk had been systematically put into alphabetical order by the authors. Collections of language material classified in this
way certainly do have their scientific value. Depending on how comprehensive they are one can appreciate the various nuances in how the ethnic
group using this vocabulary understands the concepts of the world of reality to which this vocabulary belongs. Also word lists and lexical entries
sometimes provide suitable starting points for drawing up questionnaires
as the basis of making recordings in the field with the help of informants.
However, they always prove to be significantly lacking.

Wordlists operate with the so-called word comparison approach. A term
in the target language is usually matched with only one German (English
etc.) word. This ignores the fact that words can often delineate a whole
series of objects and situations that can be perceived in a variety of ways.
If these are not listed as well, and in both columns of the lexical comparison, conclusions derived from them can hardly lay claim to validity, or
only in a limited way. Here is an example: matching *pwásuk* with "knee"
neither shows that *pwásuk*, apart from "knee," also describes the elbow as
well as the knots of grass blades or bamboo stems, nor does it answer the

question whether it may also refer to the "knee" or bend of a river or the shaft of an adze that is bent like a knee[7].

Lexical entries in dictionaries offer a much more exact impression of the breadth of meaning of a term as well as any other conceptual aspects it may contain within its setting in the culture. But here also the need for brevity prevails, so that e.g. the words for the human body cannot include any information about notions of physiological processes, let alone any overtones of mood or metaphorical usage in which the body is involved. This can only be achieved by descriptions that select a manageable terminological area, in order to record it linguistically as closely as possible and examine it as to its structure.

I expected that by means of the material collected and analysed in this way as to its semantic structures I would gain important knowledge for making comparisons. In the meantime one has become aware that the range of linguistic nuances revealed by a particular area of existence, in this case the body, is an indicator of the interest that this area holds for that society, and that this interest is in turn an indicator that within that culture there is a need or a necessity to be more precise about how the language contains the concepts of that area within its structures. In addition the way pre-literate people think about the body can be compared with the approach of so-called scientific thinking, leading to insights into the connection between language, thought and reality, as will have to be demonstrated later.

With regard to the term "soul" I had already reckoned from the start on the probability that for the islanders its two main features (the person's centre of psychic faculties and processes, and the being that survives the death of the body and perpetuates the personality) would be divided into two separate conceptual areas. If this assumption was correct, there should then be the possibility of initially gaining some understanding of both areas from the linguistic perspective, i.e., to find terms for them that could be used as starting points for the particular notions of each of these conceptual areas to be examined.

After these terms (*neetip* and *neenuuk*; *ngúún*) had been found, the European/Western term "soul" was to remain excluded as far as possible. In order to guarantee this, interviews among the informants were to be based principally on a term from their own language. In this way, their statements always remained related to a term of their own thinking and they were not

---

[7] An adze is an axe-like tool, used for dressing timber roughly, with a curved steel head mounted at an oblique angle to the shaft.

forced to express their views within the framework of an alien concept with its correspondingly formulated questions.

I usually met with my informants daily for conversations lasting (rarely longer than) one and a half hours. Numbered questions, written out beforehand, formed the basis for these conversations, with correspondingly numbered answer pages, separately for each of the two informants. As a rule, a starting point for recording, e.g., notions of the body, was some part of the body, i.e. the vocabulary belonging to it.

Essentially, my collection of data was built up with the help of the following three questions:

1. **What is the particular body part called?** (Result: a word in the local idiom.)

2. **What other meaning(s) does the word have?** (Result: all objects and situations belonging to the term described by this word. N.B.: In this way, informants express their understanding of a concept of their own thinking, not of a concept belonging to the ethnographer.)

3. **What kind of thing(s) and situation(s) is this about?** (Result: the generic term, without which it would be impossible to recognize the setting of individual terms within their respective semantic fields and how they are assigned to each other.)

I recorded the statements of the informants in the Chuukese language and in phonemic orthography. In this way, again and again, I came across terms whose existence was unexpected in certain contexts, or that led to the recognition of new connections between terms (frequently in totally unexpected places) which, in turn, became the starting points for further questioning.

This process of eliciting is the methodological principle which was initially called the "ethno-scientific approach" (described by Tyler, 1969, in numerous examples) in American ethnology (cultural anthropology). In the meantime it has become the standard procedure for cognitive ethnology (cognitive anthropology) (Renner 1980, 1983; D'Andrade 1995). In time, the extensive data collection that came about with the help of this procedure formed an increasingly tighter network of terms (categories), ultimately resulting in a theory of body and soul concepts among the islanders of Chuuk from their own point of view.

This data collection is characterized by two features. It contains statements about human beings that are broadly free of any dependence on corresponding European/Western concepts, and it contains these statements within the categories of the language used by my informants.

3.6   The Role of the Language as a Research Instrument

Ethnological research is indeed well aware of difficulties and dangers that could lead to serious misjudgements in the process of examining such a hard to describe cultural area as the concepts of the soul. H. Fischer is "of the opinion that the area of culture dealt with here is altogether the most difficult for any ethnographer to investigate. **Without exact knowledge of the language under consideration and without a lengthy stay in the region to be examined, the results can only be fragments that are either not understood or misunderstood"** (1965:X, emphasis mine). This means, one must always ask the question whether such ethnographers are giving "an undistorted picture of what the people really think and feel" (Haekel 1971:81).

3.7   Safeguarding the Results

I believe that the following three perspectives have kept the influence of these difficulties and dangers with regard to my investigation to a minimum.

1. Before starting work on this topic, there was a three-year period, in which I busied myself exclusively with the language of the region to be investigated. For the field research on the topic itself, I had 18 months at my disposal.

2. This period allowed me to go over the whole area of investigation three times. At the end, the number of questions alone that were asked of the informants and recorded in writing amounted to 20,000 in round numbers. Working out the taxonomic structure of the terms for emotional and mental (psychological) aspects (Table 2; cf. 16.3: Dispositions of the SEIC) proved to be especially time-consuming and laborious.

3. Another perspective where I consider my statements to be relevant, is my endeavour to pay attention to the demand that the field researcher should "report (in the sense of 'ethno-science' and 'cognitive anthropology') that which he learns about what the people believe in general, including the soul concept in particular, recording it in the thought categories and ways of expression as found in the particular culture, at the same time freeing himself from European/Western opinions and forms of expression" (Haekel 1971:81).

The very nature of the topic obliged me to observe this principle in my field work, especially as it concerned the recording of what was, in part, totally intangible, being purely conceptional. In most cases the only way of accessing these concepts was by means of the corresponding language terms. Many behaviour patterns among the islanders that, in earlier times, had been connected with their notions of the soul (sacrifices, communication of mediums with spirit beings), are no longer accessible to the participating observer today, after their acceptance of the Christian faith.

3.8   Difficulties in Description

Despite the advantages of being guided in one's field research by the "thought patterns and ways of expression of the culture" (Haekel 1971:81) the editing and presentation of the material proved to be extremely difficult. There is a lot of headache involved, especially in overcoming problems of terminology, when trying to describe in a typical European language ways of thinking for which there are no existing categories. However, this observation should not deter anyone working in an unfamiliar society from getting down to work. Despite all the difficulties, concepts of man are well worth researching, and understanding them will enable one to get better acquainted with the people in one's area of work, be it as a physician, teacher, farmer, engineer, or church worker of any kind.

3.9   The Chuukese Language and Its Written Form

It belongs to the Austronesian language group (Dyen, 1949 etc.). Dialects related to the Chuukese language are spoken all the way to Ulithi and the southern islands of the Palauan group on the extreme western side of the Caroline Archipelago. The most important latest publications in this respect are the grammar by Dyen (1965) and the dictionary by Goodenough/Sugita (1980, 1990). According to it (XIV–XVII), the language reveals the following phonemes (simplified):

a   a low, central unrounded vowel (like the *a* of English *father*): *fan* "go aground," *faan* "break open (as a boil)."

á   a low, front, unrounded vowel (like the *a* of English *hat*): *már* "move, be shifted," *máár* "grow (as a plant)."

e   a mid, front, unrounded vowel (like the e of English *set*): *wen* "straight," *ween* "well."

é   a mid, central, unrounded vowel (close to the *u* of English *but*): *té* "crawl," *téé* "uninhabited island."

i   a high, front, unrounded vowel (between the *i* of English *fit* and the *ee* of English *feet*): *it* "emptied," *iit* "name."

o   a mid, back, rounded vowel (like the *o* of English *note*): *rong* "hear," *roong* "magic."

ó   a low, back rounded vowel, (like the *aw* of English *law*): *pwór* "curved," *pwóór* "box."

u   a high, back rounded vowel (between the *u* of English *put* and the *oo* of English *boot*): *num* "be bailed," *nuum* "bailer."

ú   a high, central, unrounded vowel (not encountered in standard English): *kú* "be kindled," *kúú* "louse."

f   a voiceless labiodental spirant (like English *f*): *faat* "shallow water," *ffaat* "be strung (as fish)," *afat* "reveal," *affat* "be made clear," *ááf* "fire."

s   a voiceless, dental spirant (like English *s*): *son* "be deceived," *sson* "damsel fish," *ását* "sword grass," *ássát* "cause to split lengthwise," *maas* "face, eye."

k   a velar, voiceless stop, unaspirated, voiced (unless double) between vowels (like English *k* and *g*) and pronounced with lip rounding if preceded or followed by a back rounded vowel: *kóón* "corn," *kkóón* "lie down," *ika* "if," *ikka* "here they are," *taak* "needle fish."

m   a voiced, bilabial, nasal continuant (like English *m*) pronounced without accompanying velar constriction or lip rounding, even when preceded or followed by a back, rounded vowel, and tending (unless double) to be denasalized between vowels, where it approaches a bilabial flap: *mas* "be well joined," *mmas* "opened, bloomed," *amasa* "cause to be joined," *ammasa* "cause to be opened," *reem* "for us."

mw   a voiced, bilabial nasal, pronounced with accompanying velar constriction but with lip rounding only when preceded or followed by a back, rounded vowel, and tending (unless double) to be denasalized between vowels: *mwáán* "man," *mwmwáán* "err," *omwusa* "release him," *omwmwusa* "make him vomit," *reemw* "for you."

n   a voiced, dental or alveolar, nasal continuant, (like English *n*), tending (unless double) to be denasalized between vowels, where it sounds more like an alveolar flap: *num* "be bailed," *nnum* "be creased, folded," *anaw* "cordia tree," *annaw* "display platform," *maan* "be adrift."

ng   a voiced, velar, nasal continuant (like the *ng* of English *singer*), tending (unless double) to be partially denasalized between vowels, where it approaches a velar flap: *ngút* "be congested," *ngngút* "be flexible," *nengi* "welsh onion," *nengngin* "girl," *nááng* "sky."

p   a voiceless, bilabial stop, unaspirated (like English *p* and *b*), voiced (unless double) between vowels and pronounced without accompanying velar constriction or lip rounding, even when preceded or followed by a back, rounded vowel: *pan* "be tilted," *ppan* "hillside, steep slope," *apach* "be fastened," *appach* "glue," *sap* "be caught."

pw   a voiceless, bilabial stop, unaspirated, voiced (unless double) between vowels and pronounced with accompanying velar constriction but with lip rounding only when preceded or followed by a back, rounded vowel: *pwó* "be pampered," *pwpwó* "a medicine," *apwang* "channel through mangrove," *apwpwang* "hole cut in a tree trunk for water catchment," *sapw* "not."

r   an alveolar trill, voiced between vowels and tending to be voiceless before or after pause: *rusi* "gather it," *rrus* "be gathered," *kúrúr* "slipping to and fro (as a zipper)," *rúrrúr* "slip, become loose," *iir* "they."

ch   a voiceless, usually retroflex, affricate, voiced (unless double) between vowels. For some speakers it is an alveo-palatal affricate (like English *ch* and *j*), and for some it is an alveolar affricate. It is pronounced more like the English *sh* in Mortlockese: *chú* "extracted," *chchú* "wooden comb," *achawa* "squirrel fish," *achchawa* "make slow," *faach* "pandanus."

t   a voiceles, dental or alveolar stop, unaspirated (like English *t* and *d*), voiced (unless double) between vowels: *taf* "be gathered, picked," *ttaf*, "be combed," *metip* "be lonely," *mettip* "spit out," *maat* "brave."

w   a bilabial glide, unrounded except when preceded or followed by a back rounded vowel in Chuukese, but always rounded in Mortlockese: *waa* "canoe," *sáwá* "fishing basket," *aaw* "mouth."

y   an alveo-palatal glide, unrounded (not written at the beginning of a word, where it is phonetically absent in some dialects): *éé* (*yéé*) "fishhook," *ááyá* (*yááyá*) "liver," *mááy* or *maay* "breadfruit."

Length and shortness of vowels and consonants make for distinct changes in meaning. They are depicted by single or double spelling.

Local terms in the text indicate the language form of the island of *Toon* in the western region of Chuuk.

Part 2
The Concept of Body

Chapter 4
The Body as a Whole

4.1 The Term *inis*

The term *inis* describes the body of human beings (*aramas*) and animals (*maan*). Among the animals, as a rule, only those that belong to the category of *ménúmanaw* (living beings) possess a body.

Certain animals living on coral reefs like sponges (*farawa, ammat, sopwusopw*) and coral itself, are not considered to be *ménúmanaw*. Plants (*irá*), too, are not counted as such, although they are said to be *manaw* (living). Coral may occasionally be described as *féwúmanaw* (living stones).

In the case of crustaceans and snails, only their soft tissues are understood to be *inis*. When it comes to turtles and tortoises, however, the carapace is also reckoned as part of the body.

Bodies in the sense of geometrical figures are not covered by the term *inis*. They are either *mettóóch* or *meen* (lifeless things). There are a few lifeless things that may be described as having an *inis*, if they bear a resemblance to human or animal body forms (bottle, watercraft, airplane, shirt). In any case, the term is also always used for things when their material form of existence (*inis*) is contrasted with its spirit counterpart (*ngúún*). Thus it is said of a food offering, whose spirit counterpart was consumed by an ancestral spirit (*énú*): *inisin chék aa nómw* (only its material substance is left).

Spirit beings of the *énú* and *ngúún* category do not possess a body in the sense of *inis*, only a form (*napanap*).

In the narrower sense, with regard to the human body, *inis* describes the torso in contrast to the limbs or, in certain cases, only the upper body. One context that certainly suggests this meaning is the statement: *aa aaya raweses, nge aa ekinissow inisin* (he wears pants, but his upper body is naked).

The term for body is used remarkably often for the human ego or self. Thus it is said of an egotist: *aa ekiyekiiy feyiyéchchún wóón inisin chék* (he only thinks of himself, is egocentric).

4.2 Rough Divisions of the Body

The body of humans or animals is essentially made up of the three components of bones (*chúú*), flesh (*fituk*) and skin (*siin, wúnúúch* et al.); (cf. Mahony 1970:203).

Flesh and muscles (with the exception of biceps and calf muscles) are not given different terms; *fituk* is used for both. Besides that, *fituk* also means flesh or meat in its raw or cooked form as food for humans and animals. (For the meaning of "blood relative" [in the form of *futuk*] see Goodenough 1951:102–103.)

The components of the human body are grouped under the following terminology: *mékúr* (head), *wúú* (neck), *paaw* or *péwún* (arms), and *peche* (legs). They are also described as such in the bodies of animals and lifeless things, though in a less differentiated but largely corresponding way.

These five parts of the body are then further subdivided into areas and organs; e.g., the head in face, the back of the head etc.; the face in nose, mouth, eyes etc. In this manner, the parts of the human body form, conceptually speaking, a hierarchy on whose lowest level all the terms are parts of a term on the next higher level etc., up to the highest level where we find the term *inis*. But it must be remembered that the terms of one level are exclusively parts of a term on the next higher level. Their own subordinate terms are not.

The structure on which this hierarchy is based shows (very simplified) the following form of a tree diagram:

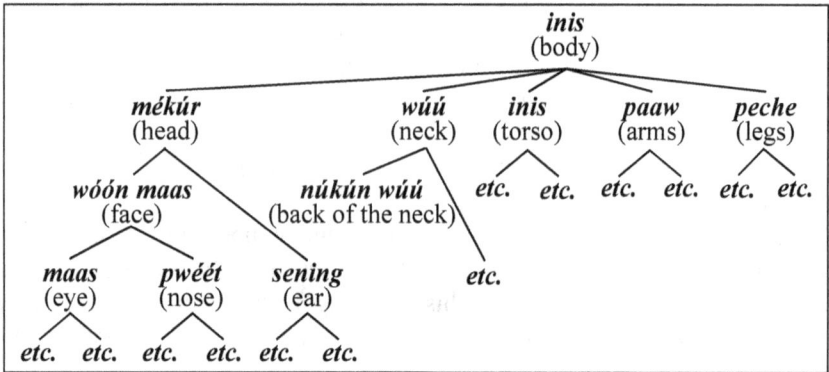

Table 1: Terminological Structure of the Body

The diagram shows the more important terms for individual body parts, like the head (*mékúr*), in greater taxonomical depth, i.e. resulting in branching out over more levels than, e.g., the neck (*wúú*). The fact that *inis* (body) occurs on two levels, is due to the possibility of using this term not only for the whole body but also for the torso in a more restricted sense.

It should be noted that not all terms of one level are necessarily also parts of a term on the immediately next higher level. Thus, e.g., the nose (*pwéét*) is only part of the head via the intermediate level of face (*wóón maas*), itself a part of the head (*mékúr*); whereas the ear (*sening*) skips, so to speak, the level of the face and is directly assigned to the head.

Every part of the body can also be called *kúkkún inis* or *kifetin inis* (something like a small part of the body), apart from its affiliation to a superordinate area of the body. In relation to the tree diagram this means that every term contained within this system may be substituted by either of the above-mentioned terms, quite aside from its affiliation with a certain level. Exception: On the highest level there is no substitute for *inis*.

Remark concerning personal interviews: The informant is asked about all things one may call "body" in one's own (Indo-European) mother tongue. This results in parallels, e.g., in the case of the human body, but also in differences, e.g., in the case of geometrical bodies like cube, pyramid etc., which the informant may not be able to describe as "bodies."

It is also important to take note of individual descriptions, not only by themselves, but register them in the context of a sentence, as expressed by the informant. Many word meanings can really only be recognized in context.

Anyone wanting to do systematic ethnological field research on the concepts of body, mind, soul and spirit (in any society) should use Badenberg' s excellent guide:

Badenberg, Robert: The Concept of Man in Non-Western Cultures. A Guide for One's Own Research. Handbook to Lothar Käser's Textbook: Animism – A Cognitive Approach. Nürnberg 2014.

Chapter 5
The Head

5.1 The Term *mékúr*

In the conceptual thinking of the islanders the head is of conspicuously low significance. Its most important position in the framework of the hierarchy of body parts is really only based on the fact that it happens to be "on top" of everything. Where other languages possess a plethora of metaphorical expressions to describe important things as "head," one finds mostly anything else but the term *mékúr* (e.g., *maas*, eye). The reason for this is obviously that the head is not regarded as the actual centre of thinking (more details in a later chapter).

The chief (*samwoon*) may, under certain circumstances, be metaphorically referred to as *mékúren fénú* (head of the country or island), but this is much less in connection with the characteristics of his personality and intellectual capacities than by reason of his position at the very top of the hierarchy.

Concerning the head, two large areas are differentiated: the face (*wóón maas*), and the remaining parts of the head that are only named individually.

5.2 The Face (*wóón maas*)

This comprises the whole frontal section of the head from the chin up to the hairline, but expressly without the ears. The face gets its name from the eye (*maas*), which plays an especially important role conceptually among the organs and the parts of the head.

The compound *wóón maas* literally means "upper-ness of the eye"; *wóón* expresses a local position (on top or above). However, it does not just fulfill a prepositional function but behaves formally and syntactically like the words for objects, i.e., like a noun: thus, *wóón chuuk* may mean "on top of the mountain" as well as "summit" or "mountain peak." *Faan* or *fáán* (underneath, "below-ness of"), also *nóón* (inside, "inside-ness of"), *núkún* (outside, "outside-ness of"; beside, "beside-ness of"), *neefiinen* (between, "between-ness of"), etc., all of which play a role in describing the body.

Regarding *wóón maas* as part of the construction of a house (a roof joist) see LeBar, 1964:112 and 115. The forms of *maas* with a possessive suffix (*mesey, mesomw*, etc.) may also refer to the facial area, and even more generally the appearance, without *wóón: aa siiwin mesan* (his face is changed), *kaa mesen soope* (you look like a ghost), *meseyééch* (pretty), *mesemesekkis* (diverse), *mesekin, mesemaama, mesesááw* (shy, embarrassed), *mesemaaw* (bold, provocative), etc.

The face is divided into eight subsections. The description of these sections begins with the one that is conceptually most important.

5.3 The Eye (*maas*)

The significance of the eye as a concept is shown in the abundance of things that can be described with the word *maas*: 1. a pointed end of an object: *mesen chúúfén* (point of a nail), *mesen piin* (point of a pencil), *mesaapwech* (a spear with several white prongs for fishing), etc. Pointed body parts: *mesen pwéét* (tip of the nose), *mesen aaw* (tip of a bird's beak), *mesen tténnaaw* (tip of the tongue), *mesen owupw* (breast nipple), *mesen kooch* or *ruumw* (tip of the glans), *mesen éwút* (tip of the finger and/or toe). 2. Position or point in time, which is regarded as coming ahead of another. Position: *niin etenimes* (front row of teeth, incisors), *fáán mesey* (ahead of me; euphemistically also for genitals). Point in time: *meseféépwún* (stage in a person's age – "almost young woman"), *meseeres* (time shortly before harvesting breadfruit). 3. Direction: *mesen ásápwáán* (wind direction), *meseeráán* (east, literally "eye of the day"). 4. Certain perforations: *mesen ttikek* (eye of a needle), *mesen taka* (the two smaller sprouting holes of the coconut), *mesen epino* (mesh hole in a fishing net), *meseyiset* (an eddy or whirlpool in sea water), etc. 5. Tiny things: *mesen mmak* (letter of the alphabet, literally "eye of script"). 6. Important location, centre: *mesen fénú* (residence of the chief, police station, location of a government office, literally "eye of the island").

The eye as a whole appears conceptually in two different forms – on the one hand as the externally visible eye including its surrounding area, i.e. as part of the face, and, on the other, as the eyeball (*féwún maas*). The former is classified as an elongated object, the latter as a round one.

The Chuukese language groups things classified according to their form: elongated, flat, round etc. As *féwún maas* (eyeball) the eye belongs to an extensive class of things considered to be round. The stem base *féwú-* describes any kind of plant seed and fruit, including underground bulbs, grains of sand, stones etc.

Concerning the grammatical concept of the base see Dyen, 1965:32; for the problem of classification see Elbert, 1947:22 ff. and Goodenough/Sugita, 1980:XXXIX ff. (cf. 5.8).

Besides the eyeball, other things also belong to the class of round things, e.g., the larynx (*féwún tiyor* or *chiyor*), the heart (*féwún ngasangas*), the testicles (*féwún wuun*), the buttocks (*féwún niwiit*), etc. The classification of the external eye as something elongated is not quite unambiguous. For more details on this see below concerning the external corner of the eye.

Both eyelids bear the same description (*épwpwén, épwpwénún*, lid), apart from differentiating between the upper and lower eyelids (*épwpwénún wóón* or *faan*). It is noteworthy that the lower eyelid (as in English, but unlike German) is also represented as a "lid."

The two corners of the eye, in contrast, have different descriptions. The outer one, next to the temple, is called *neesópwun*, the inner one *neepitik*.

The term *neesópwun* for the outer corner of the eye indicates that the eye is classified as something elongated. The inner corner of the eye (*neepitik*) gets its name from the secretion (*pitik*) that accumulates here during sleep and when the conjunctiva is infected; *pitik* is also the term for the germ of the coconut as it becomes visible in one of the sprouting holes.

The prefix *nee-* is very versatile in its usage. It changes the description of things in such a way that they appear as locations in space or time. Besides numerous words for parts and sections of the body, land place names also frequently contain this prefix (see examples in Goodenough, 1966:100 ff.).

Conceptually, eyelashes (*mátár, mátárin maas*) are differentiated from other body hair, since *mátár* can only be used to describe the eyelashes. Numerals in connection with the eyelashes, however, contain the classification suffix -*wún* for body hair.

Apart from the eyelashes, *mátár* and its adjectival form *mátáttár* also describe the frayed fringes of banana leaves and clothing, the feathery outgrowth of fish gills, a carelessly plucked chicken, etc.

For very precise information in connection with the visible part of the eye, *fáán owuren maas* can refer to the place immediately underneath the lower eyelid.

Because of its characteristic colouration, the visible part of the eyeball can be divided into the two sections of *pwechepwech, pwechepwechen maas* ("the white") and *chóchchón, chóchchónun maas* "the black," iris). Even when referring to races with a totally different colouration of the iris it is still called *chóchchón*. The centre, with the pupil, is the place connected with the process of seeing (*wereweren* or *cheweren maas*). The background of the eye has nothing to do with it, for the pupil is not considered to be an opening. For the same reason the function of the vitreous body of the eye (*mongomong*) is unknown.

The Chuukese language understands several aspects of seeing. The transitive verb *kúna* means to see in the sense of "discovering with the eye," "perceiving," or "finding something looked for." The morpheme *nne-* with its numerous suffixes like *nnengeni* etc. means "to look with a purpose," "to have a look at (something)." The stem *were-*, as in *wereweren maas*, seems to mean the process of becoming visible, making visible, and the sensory impression of seeing: A searchlight is thus *naam ewerewer* ("lamp causing to see"), binoculars are *mesewerewer*.

For the grammatical term of the stem see Dyen, 1965:32, and Goodenough/Sugita, 1980:XIX ff.

For the vitreous body of the eye, because of its composition, the expression *mongomong, mongomongen nóón maas* (slimy mass inside the eyeball) is used; *moong* or *mongomong* describe, moreover, the composition of the nasal secretion, semen, resin, etc.

The dilating and contracting of the pupil, according to some informants, is not seen as a consequence of the intensity of light, but is thought of as an individual physical characteristic: some people basically have narrow pupils, others have wider ones.

Myopia and hyperopia are seen as having the same cause as above. The reason for having blurred vision is said to be an opacity or clouding-over (*topwutopw*) of the pupil. A steamed-up mirror is said to be *topwutopw*, so is haze in the atmosphere etc. Clouding of the eye that is externally visible is called *wukowuk*.

Blindness is *chuun, mesechuun*. In case of a circulatory collapse, a hit on the head, etc., a person becomes *masaroch* (unconscious, literally "eyes dark"); *rochopwaak, rochokkich, kkiroch*, etc. are expressions for darkness. However, *masaroch* can only be used for one's own experience. To say of someone else that he or she is unconscious would be the same as making the verbal statement that the person is dead (*má*). A further meaning of *masaroch*: to be blinded (by overly bright light).

Tears, or the lacrymal liquid (*chchénún maas*), is a "juice" secreted inside the eyeball through the inner corner of the eye (*neepitik*). It tastes salty (*kken*) and has the task to keep the eye clean.

The strong secretion of lachrymal liquid when the emotions are stirred is inexplicable; the existence of a tear duct between the eye and nose is unknown. Weeping (*kkechiw*) for any length of time is caused by an increase of the secretion (*mongomong*) of the nasal mucous membrane. There is no concept of lachrymal glands.

The term *chchénún* means all plant juices as, e.g., the drinkable contents of the coconut (*chchénún núú*); but also bodily secretions: saliva (*chchénún aaw*), mother's milk (*chchénún owupw*), bile (*chchénún maras*), perspiration and prostatic secretion (*chchénúfaak*), urine (*achchénún*), etc.

5.4 The Eyebrows (*féét*)

… expressly belong neither to the eye nor the forehead, but are an independent conceptual entity. They start above the inner corner of the eye. This observation is important in that the place above the outer eye corner (*neesópwun*), where they end, is called by a different name from their beginning (*neepwopwun, neewoon*). This is the location where a person frowns in anger, not the forehead.

The expression is *aa apwpwacha neewoon fétún* (literally, "he knits the beginning of his eyebrows"); *neewoon* does not only refer to the beginning of the eyebrows but especially to the area lying between them; another possibility of denoting it would be to say *neefiinen féét* (between, "between-ness").

The terms *neewo* and *neepwopwun* mean descent, ancestry, but also places where tree trunks and similar plant parts come out of the ground, as well as where body parts start, e.g., the root of the nose (*neewoon* or *neepwopwun pwéét*), the base of the fingers (*neewoon* or *neepwopwun éwút*), the beginning of the thigh (*neewoon* or *neepwopwun peche*).

The hairs of the eyebrows are called *wúnen féét, wúnéwúnen féét, téréwúnen féét* or *méréwúnen féét* and belong conceptually to the hair covering of the body.

The eyebrows play a certain role in communication. Instead of just saying "yes" (*ewer, wúú*), affirmation to statements in a conversation can also be indicated by briefly, but clearly, lifting the eyebrows. This gestural movement is called *werifét ngeni emén*. For me, it was at first rather confusing, since it is deceptively similar to the facial expression members of societies in Europe and the West use to imply that they do not understand what the other person is saying.

The term *féét* is also used for the islanders' traditional cudgel weapon (*nifétúfét*), whose head end is reminiscent of eyebrows; see illustration by LeBar, 1964:177, fig. 113. The bird *nifétúkaraw*, which I was unable to identify, takes its name from a conspicuous area of the eyes and forehead.

5.5 The Forehead (*chaamw*)

It is delineated below by the eyebrows, above by the hairline (*meeten mékúr*), and to the left and right by the temples. All fairly large land animals, birds, and fish possess *chaamw*. The word plays an important role as a euphemism for the genital area.

When two islanders, during a meal, divide a fish vertically in the middle, the one may perhaps say *wúpwe mwéngé chamwan* (I will eat the half, where the head is); the other one then gets the part with the tail (*wúkún*). In addition *chaamw* denotes the cap of a mushroom (*chamwen seningen énú*), the peak of a cap (*chamwen akkaw*), the head of a nail (*chamwen chúúfén*), the nose of an airplane (*chamwen sepeniin*), etc.

5.6 The Temples (*esen mwéngé*)

... are delineated at the sides and the top by the forehead and the hairline. Below, they go over into the cheeks (*saap*). They are considered to be especially vulnerable. Injuries of the temples are regarded as life threatening.

As such, they belong to a group of areas of the head subsumed under the generic term of *neeniyen ennemá*. More about this in connection with the back of the head (*epinikú*, cf. 5.20).

The analysis of the meaning of the two-part designation *esen mwéngé* poses difficulties; *mwéngé* means to eat as well as anything generally edible. In this connection, informants point out that the area of the temples moves during eating; they explain *esen* as a variant of *asen* (above of), which sounds somewhat plausible. It may possibly be an attempt to deduce the meaning of a compound word form from the meanings of its parts (popular etymology).

5.7 The Cheeks (*saap*)

... are the side areas of the face between ear, temple, eye, nose, mouth, and chin. All the fairly large land animals have *saap*. With fish it refers to the plates of the gills. According to the linguistic diagnosis, if someone gets boxed on the ears, it is not so much the ears that are hit, but the cheeks (*péésapeey*, to slap a person). The side areas at the end of an outrigger canoe are called *neesapen waa*, the same applies to bigger boats and ships.

5.8 The Nose (*pwéét*)

In the area of the nose, seven places are designated: the root of the nose (*neepwopwun* or *neewoon pwéét*), the rhinion (the slightly thickened place of the junction of the nasal bone and cartillage, *náttipwo*), the bridge of the nose (*wóón pwéét*), the tip of the nose (*mesen pwéét*), the nostrils (*pwangen pwéét*), the alar wings of the nose (*kúwáách*), and the nasal septum (*wúréwúren pwéét*).

Regarding the root of the nose: *neepwopwun* and *neewoon* signify the beginning of something perceived as elongated. Regarding the thickened part of the rhinion: (*náttipwo*): *pwo* means swelling, inflation, pregnancy (*pwoopwo*). The initial part of the word cannot be analysed further. Regarding the bridge of the nose: *wóón* means above or "above-ness" of something. Regarding the tip of the nose: the conceptual connection between something pointed and the eye (*maas*) is obvious. Regarding the nostrils: *pwaang* means hole, bodily orifice; *ngaat* is also a possible term (*ngaten pwéét*). Regarding the alar wings: *kúwáách* does not indicate any conceptual connection to a wing (*paaw* or *péwún*). Regarding the septum (the nasal dividing wall): it is not really perceived as a wall but rather as something like a pillar; *wúúr* are the four corner posts of a house construction (LeBar, 1964:112 ff.).

The islanders make a distinction between the following nasal forms: there are people with a pointed nose (*pwéétúkken*), a blunted nose (*pwéétúkkopw*), and those with a crooked nose (*pwéétúpwpwór*). These expressions are also found in the terminology for the construction of a building. The gable girder (*pwéét*) is the "nose" of the house; houses with pointed gables are *pwéétúkken*; those with only a slightly slanted roof are said to be *mii mwoch pwéétúúr*. The trunk of an elephant likewise belongs to the category of things designated as *pwéét*.

The hair-growth of the nasal mucous membrane (*wúnéwúnen*, *téréwúnen*, or *méréwúnen nóón pwéét*) is conceptually the same as that of the other body hair. The nasal secretion belongs to a list of viscous body secretions (*moong, mongomong*). In case of a cold, a person is *mongopwéét* ("slimy nosed"); to blow one's nose is called *fongopwéét*.

Besides its role in breathing, the nose has the function of sensing smells. In this, the Chuukese language differentiates exactly between "smelling" as perceiving scents (*tini*) with one's nose, and "smelling" as giving off an odour.

Smells are frequently expressed with the help of combinations from the word form *pwoon* or *pwonnen* ("smell of") and the term for the thing itself that gives off this smell, e.g., *pwoon wuuch* (banana smell), *pwonnen ngaas* (scent of perfume oil), etc. A series of smell descriptions consists of the morpheme *pwoo-* or *pwo-* and an addition, e.g., *pwooyééch, pwokkus* (fragrant). Exception: *pwooniik* ("smell of fish") is a gull-like bird whose presence indicates where a shoal of fish may be found.

Smells do not count as sensory perceptions in the sense of *meefi*, a generic term (which will be dealt with later) for all other physical or psychological senses (apart from taste sensations). They also have a rather simple semantic field structure. They are (*pwooyééch*), neutral (without generic designation), or unpleasant (*pwongngaw*). This classification, however, is not clear-cut.

Sensory smell impressions are subjective. What may be a pleasant aroma to someone, may be perceived as an unpleasant odour by others.

5.9 The Mouth (*aaw*)

With all living beings, the orifice where nourishment is taken in is called *aaw*, even with birds. Things that have an opening for filling also have it, e.g. a bottle, a bag, a pocket, etc. In the case of a cave, the entrance is called *aaw* or *awan*; with knives, saws, and axes it is sometimes the cutting edge; with picking poles (*iyas*) it is the end; and with the coconut it is the bigger of the three sprouting holes. (See the image of an *iyas* by LeBar, 1964:21, fig. 15.)

The externally visible parts of the mouth form something perceived as elongated: the corners of the mouth (*neesópwun aaw*) are its "ends." On the lips (*ttuumw, ttumwun aaw*), the externally visible red-coloured area (with the islanders rather dark brown) (*ápárenaaw*) is differentiated from the generic term for "lips;" this applies also to animals. The labial frenulum (mucous membrane) between lips and gums is called *senin ttumwun aaw*.

Regarding *ttuumw, ttumwun aaw* (lips): The term may likewise be used for the labia, just as *aaw* may stand for the female genitalia as a whole. Regarding *ápárenaaw* (*ápáren aaw*?): The explanation of this designation poses a bit of a problem. Its stem reads *ápáre-*. In addition, there is the stem *ápári-*. Both mean something like "environment, surroundings, home, habitat" (e.g., in the phrase *ápárin Namiyo Chukiyénú*, Namiyo's home is Ch.). Informants point out that these, though obviously of similar congruencies ("surrounding"), are two different conceptual terms. Regarding *senin ttumwun aaw*: *sáán* or *senin* is any kind of cord, up to a ship's rope or a chain (*senimáchá*). The lingual frenum, analogously, is called *senin tténnaaw*.

The centre of the upper lip, between nose and mouth, is called *kusuwa*, although the term is actually only used in connection with the bone located beneath it (*chúún kusuwa*).

5.10 The Oral Cavity (*nóón aaw*) and Its Organs (*pisekin nóón aaw*)

Regarding the terms for the oral cavity and its organs: *Nóón aaw* literally means "inside-ness of the mouth." For the concept of "cavity" or "cave" the islanders use the terms *féyiimw* or *féwúwimw*, which do not apply to body parts. *Pisek*, as a rule, denotes objects of value in one's possession (Goodenough, 1951:40 "movable goods"); *pisekisek* (wealthy); *pisekin angaang* (tool or implement).

5.11   The Palate (*fáán fóngóóch*)

… and the velum palatinum or soft palate (*chechchen nóón aaw*) do not belong together conceptually. There is no term to be found for the uvula. Informants are of the opinion that it performs important functions in the process of swallowing and during speaking. Loss of the uvula would lead to a speech impediment: articulation and intelligibility would become bad (*newenewengngaw*).

Regarding the palate: *Fáán fóngóóch* ("underneath-ness of the concave") is a remarkable linguistic solution. It creates the impression as if the palate were not really present conceptually but only in the form of one of its characteristics. The use of *fóngóóch* by itself is not possible.

Regarding the velum or soft palate: *Chcheech* means anything cloth-like and flat, like a tablecloth (*chechchen cheepen*), draperies (*chechchen asam mwacho*), the cover of a pillow (*chechchen pinnu*), etc. The eardrum (tympanum) is called *chechchen nóón sening*. The term for the soft palate is, however, rather a circumscription than a common expression.

As with the uvula, there is no linguistic term for the tonsils. One informant speaking another dialect (the Hall Islands north of Chuuk) termed them *or*, which is also used to mean the gills of fish (*oren iik*).

5.12   The Tongue (*tténnaaw, chénnaaw, chéén mwéngé*)

… likewise plays an essential part in speaking. In the process of chewing (*núúnú*) it moves the food and conveys the sense of taste. The terms *chénnaaw* and *chéén mwéngé* indicate that the tongue is perceived as something leaf-like; *chéén irá* (leaf of a plant); *chéén tóropwe* ("leaf" or sheet of paper). The lingual frenum is called *senin tténnaaw* (cf. what is said about the labial frenum, 5.9).

Taste perception is frequently described with words containing the morpheme *nne-* (taste, as a noun) as prefix or infix: *nneni* (to taste), *nneyééch* (tasty), *nnengngaw* (its opposite), etc. The more rarely found term *chénnékan* for the tongue probably fits in here, too. Besides this, there is always the possibility to express taste perception with the help of combinations with the term *nennen* ("taste of") and the word for the item in question that has this taste: *nennen pweteeto* (potato taste) etc.

Taste perceptions, like smell sensations, are not counted as perceptions in the sense of *meefi*. Like those, they reveal a simple semantic field structure: pleasant taste (*nneyééch*), neutral (without generic designation) and unpleasant taste (*nnengngaw*). This differentiation also, like that of smells, turns out to be subjectively different, according to preference. Because of this, the following vocabulary for smell sensations has not been listed according to these aspects but in alphabetical order.

Further, the terms for perceptions of taste indicates synaesthetic traits. The words for hot (*pwichikkar*) and cold (*patapat*), e.g., also mean spicy and not spicy. Food containing salt tastes *kken* (hot or spicy). Salted food is altogether accorded special importance in the vocabulary for taste sensations.

For salt in its solid form, the Chuukese language has adopted the English word in the form of *sóón*. As a generic term for all kinds of liquids containing salt, like sauces, soups, etc., the term for sea water (*sáát*) is used. This term is also present in terms for taste like *nnesetirú* (brackish), *nneset, nnesesset, nenneset* (salty).

Unlike with smells (characteristic morpheme *pwoo-* or *pwo-*), the range of terms to do with taste has a larger number which do not contain the characteristic morpheme *nne-*.

The terms for taste perceptions individually:

araar: sweet; also *ngar, ngarangar*; opposites: *kken, kkipwin, maras, pwáánu.*

iwi: fatty, taste of fat.

kká: taste of the kind of taro having the same name (Lat. *alocasia macrorhiza*).

kken: salty, salted, oversalted; also *nnekken, nnekeniken*; with objects *kken* means sharpened, sharp edged, pointed; opposites: *patapat, nnepatapat, araar.*

kkipwin: bitter; synonyms: *maras, pwáánu*; opposite: *araar.*

maras: see *kkipwin.*

meriik: pungent taste, e.g., caused by cigarette smoke (*suupwa*).

mwiik: spicy hot taste of pepper, chili and tabasco pepper (Lat. capsicum frutescens); opposites: *patapat, nnepatapat.*

mwoon: sour, taste of vinegar (*finikar*) and lemons (*siitor*).

mwmwán: sour, fermented; taste of yeast (*iis*).

nnekken, nnekeniken: see *kken.*

nnepatapat: insipid, unsalted; literally "of cold taste"; opposites: *pwichikkar, kken* etc.

patapat: see *nnepatapat.*

pwáánu: see *kkipwin, maras.*

pwich, pwichipwich, pwichikkar: hotly spiced or seasoned, pungent taste (literally "hot"); opposites: *patapat, nnepatapat.*

5.13 The Saliva (*chchénún aaw* or *wúú*)

… is considered a "juice" produced by the mouth and throat. If the viscosity is higher it is called *mongomongen aaw*; however, as "spittle" it is *attuf* or *attof*. Its most important function consists in giving food a sliding quality (*mitimit*). It also prevents getting thirsty too quickly. The location of saliva secretion is believed to be mainly under the tongue.

Informants know the two orifices on both sides of the oral cavity at the level of the upper molars, but they do not connect them with the secretion of saliva.

There is no word for mucosa or, generally, for any mucous membrane. For other bodily secretions and fluids classified as *chchénún*, see 5.3.

5.14 The Teeth (*nii*)

The teeth of the upper and lower jaws are divided into two groups each. The incisors together with the canines form the "front row of teeth" *(niin etenimes)*, the remaining form the group of the *niirú*. To the latter belong also the so-called wisdom teeth. The difference between baby teeth and adult teeth has no linguistic designation.

Regarding the "front row of teeth" *(niin etenimes)*: The term contains the morpheme *ten* (row) and *-mes* (eye, frontal, see 5.3). As a rule, the division into *niin etenimes* and *niirú* is also used for the teeth of animals. The clearly distinct canines of dogs, pigs, etc. are called *nipwpwer* (penetrating or protruding teeth).

The gums (*apwaapw*), where the teeth are affixed, are conceptually not counted as "flesh" in the sense of *fituk*. They may also be designated as *wochen nii* ("reefs"). The place in the back of the oral cavity, where upper and lower jaws come together, is called *pwekiikiin aaw* ("corner of the mouth").

Regarding *apwaapw*: this must not be confused with *apwpwaapw* (snapping or gasping mouth movements of fish and the dying). Regarding *wochen nii*: *wooch* are reefs, specifically coral reefs. Regarding *pwekiikiin aaw*: also *neepwekiiki*; *pwekiiki* and *pwokuuku* usually designate corners in the house, in boxes, etc.

Teeth do not have "roots" but, according to the kind of tooth, simply a "beginning" (*neepwopwun*) or a "bifurcation" (*kkeyang*). The upper part (*wúnúún*) in molars shows more or less distinct *pwokur* (depressions). This classification perceives a tooth similarly to a plant: *neepwopwun* designates the stem or stalk between the surface of the ground and the branching (*kkeyang, nekkeyang*); *wúnúún* the treetop or upper part; *wúnúún* may also mean that which stands out, a protuberance, a promontory, etc. Teeth grow (*pwúk*) like plants, and are removed like plants (*wútti*, to weed, to tear out) from their place at the dentist's (*chóón wúttúút nii*, "tooth puller", Goodenough/Sugita 1990:98); *pwokur*, however, does not denote a part of a plant, but depressions in the ground.

Decaying of the teeth as well as a toothache are attributed to invisible animals (*maan*), who eat away the teeth. Such teeth are then said to be *enimaan*, like worm-eaten taro tubers, or wooden posts eaten away by termites.

Several other things are also thought of as teeth. This concerns parts of tools for cutting and piercing, or simply something with a sharp edge, e.g. a knife blade (*niin nááyif*), an axe blade (*niin kkowuk*), a sawtooth (*niin ngerenger*), the teeth of the coconut grater (*niin pweyiker*), the point of a needle (*niin ttikek*), etc. The sharp edges of shells may be called *nii*, even if they are strongly undulated, as with the giant clams (Lat. *tridacna gigas*); *nii* even refers to pearls. With kauri shells (*ngiingi*), made into tools for peeling breadfruit, *nii* refers to the sharpened part (*niin ngiingi*).

5.15 The Chin and the Jaw (*ngáách*)

The description of this area is not quite so simple. Outwardly, *ngáách* refers first of all to the chin and, in a wider sense, the jaw (horizontal branch). Yet here we have an unexpected connection with dentures: false teeth are called *ngáchángách* or *ngáchángáchin nii*.

The reduplicated form *ngáchángách* may also refer to some characteristic or condition. Someone who wears false teeth is said to be *ngácháhngách*. "I will go to the dentist and have him make me a set of dentures," is: "*wúpwe feyinnó reen tenitis pwe wúpwe ngáchángách*" (literally, "… in order to become *ngáchángách*").

The beard, rarely of strong growth among the islanders, is called *énús*. This is the same term as for the antennae of insects and crabs, and for the proboscis of bees, etc.

At this juncture we come to the end of dealing with those body parts that belong to the face. The following parts refer conceptually directly to the head.

5.16 The Ear (*sening*)

Different terms in individual areas are only found in reference to the outer ear. Of its not directly visible parts, only the eardrum (*chechchen nóón sening*) has its own term. It is regarded as the seat of the hearing faculty. This is deduced from the experience that injuries or destruction of the tympanic membrane through loud noises, frequent diving in the ocean, or through pointed objects, result in deafness (*seningépúng, seningapwas*). The phrase *chechchen nóón sening* indicates that the eardrum is perceived as something flat or cloth-like. As a result of injuries it becomes *kkamw* (torn). However, terms for deafness diverge from it: *seningépúng* ("ear closed"), *seningapwas* ("ear dried up").

The Chuukese language differentiates between hearing as perception of noises (*rong, rongorong*) and listening (*éwússening*, "to lift the ear"). For more details concerning the vocabulary for hearing sensations see under voice in 6.2.

The outer ear is divided into two parts. *Seningaas* designates the upper third of the auricle (or pinna) including the depression between head and ear. Blossoms that are occasionally stuck into this space carry a very specific message to other people, depending on the manner in which the blossom is affixed, on which side it is located, and what kind of blossom it is. The second area (*emiin sening*) comprises the greater part of the earlobe and the rim above it. In earlier times, this part was pierced open, parallel to the rim of the auricle, and adorned with ornaments that could be of considerable weight. (For more details see LeBar, 1964:162-164.) The cartilage is called *awaaw* ("leaf vein"), the ear canal (external auditory meatus) is the *pwangen sening* ("ear hole").

Both terms, *chéén sening* for the auricle and *awaaw* for its cartillage, indicate that the external ear is thought of in a similar way to a part of a plant: leaves of plants (*chéén irá*) are *awaaw*, i.e., they have leaf veins. "Ears" are also the pointed ends on the leaves of various kinds of taro. Mushrooms are called "ghost ears" (*seningen énú* or *soope*). Euphemistically, *sening* stands for the external part of the female genitalia (*seningen feefin*).

5.17 The Cranial Roof (*móóng*)

... cannot be delineated exactly. It is understood to be the place on the head where one may carry a load (*owuwomónga*, to carry something on the head).

The reduplicated form *móngómóng* is found in designations for the topmost place of a mountain (*wóón móngómóngun chuuk, winimóngómóng*); a column of numbers for counting people ("headcount") contains this morpheme as a classifier: *emóng, ruwómóng* etc.

5.18 The Fontanel (*móngósópwon*)

… indicates a conceptual connection with the cranial roof. Besides *móngósópwon*, there are also the terms *masakapwon* and *masokopwen*. The fontanel is solely a term used for babies. Adults only have the *móóng*.

The fontanel is closely connected to the concept of the beating of the heart or of breathing; both are thought to be identical, as will be shown later in discussing the activity of the heart and respiration (*mii ngasangas*, "it breathes," pulsates). There is, however, no connection at all between the fontanel and the so-called concept of the soul. Women assert that a baby's fontanel must be kept warm, as otherwise it may become ill.

5.19 The Back of the Head (*kúú, epinikú*)

Some body parts, most of which belong to the head, are subsumed under the generic term of *ennemá* or *neeniyen ennemá, neeniyen mákkáy*. One of the most important of these is the back of the head. Injuries on such areas are seen to be especially life threatening. Of animals intended to be slaughtered it is said that they would already be dead after the first blow, if one could hit one of their *neeniyen ennemá*.

This expression means "place of fatal injury"; a person is *en*, if he or she receives contusions; *má* means unconsciousness and death. Apart from *kúú* and *epinikú*, the following body parts belong to the *neeniyen ennemá*: the forehead (*chaamw*), the place between the eyebrows (*neepwopwun féét*), the place at the end of the nasal bone (*náttipwo*), the temple (*esen mwéngé*), the place behind the auricle (*núkún sening*), and the back of the neck (*núkún wúú*).

Regarding the term *epinikú*: *epin* designates the end of something long, especially when it is a hollow object, an object in a vertical position, or the bulging end of something elongated; *epin fénú* is the (frequently western) end of a stretched out island.

5.20 The Scalp Hair (*meeten mékúr*)

As already mentioned, the hair growth of the body does not form a unified concept. The hair of the head is looked upon as fibre (*meet*), just as one would extract it from plants. Often *mékúr* alone is sufficient as designation for hair. Fibres produced from banana plants are called *meeten wuuch*. Cords made from coconut fibres (*núún*) are twisted together from several *meet*.

Two areas of hair growth have particular terms. The crown is called *fasen nichchok* (nest of the bird *nichchok*, perhaps the Japanese bush warbler [Lat. *cettia diphone*]. A child having two crowns is thought to be lachrymose. The hairy parts between ear and temple are called *péwún arong* (fin of the fish *arong*). The sideburns (of a beard), too, may be called by this term. The connection to the name of the fish is unclear.

Hairs grow (*pwúk*) like plants, and fall out in the way fruit and leaves do (*mwmwor*). Accordingly, a bald head is called *mwmwor* or *paan*. Hair colours: *chón* (black), *par* (red), *ón* (blond, yellow), *pwech* (white, gray, especially in old age). Hair forms: *wenechchar, takkich* (smooth), *rúúrú* (wavy, curly, frizzy). Hair styles: *ffires* (plaited), *tinetin* (parted, "split lengthwise"), *réét* (bun or hair knot, in earlier times common for both men and women).

5.21 The Brain (*tupwu*)

It is not just contained in the cranium (*péépéén mékúr*) but, according to the thinking of the islanders, also fills the spine as marrow. Apart from both halves of the brain (*kinikin*), there is no further division. Its function is unknown. A few of the informants vaguely surmised that a person needs it for thinking (*ekiyek*). But even physical phenomena such as headaches (*metekin mékúr*) and dizziness (*mwáániyen*) are not attributed to the brain. They simply happen "in the head."

As for counting people when allotting food or such, the cranium (*péépéén* or *pésséékún mékúr* is used as well as the already mentioned term for the cranial roof (*móóng*); *péé, péépé,* and *pésséék* mean the empty shell of the coconut, which is also used as a container.

Chapter 6
The Neck

6.1 The Term *wúú*

The neck, *wúú*, is delimited from the back of the head by the hairline, and in the front by the transition to the horizontal section of the chin (*fáán ngáách*). Its transition into the torso cannot be determined exactly. The base of the neck is called *pwopwun* or *neepwopwun wúú* ("stem, stalk, beginning"), as with the stem and stalk of plants.

In another context, the base of the neck is called *neemwakékkéén wúú* or *neeyafanamwakké*. But in this case it refers rather to the place between, and somewhat above, the collarbones. A piece of jewelry worn around the neck is simply *fáán wúú* (under the neck).

The back of the neck (the nape) is thought of as the "above-ness" or "outside-ness" of the neck (*wóón wúú*, *núkún wúú*). These terms are used in speaking of the place on the neck, where the bar or yoke (*waas*) with its two baskets for carrying smaller burdens is put. At the same time, this place, like the temple and the forehead, is thought of as especially vulnerable, and injuries to it as life threatening: it is a *neeniyen ennemá*.

The vertebrae of the neck (*chúún núkún wúú*) are "bones of the back of the neck." Because of their mobility, the neck is thought of as a joint (*neekupukupun wúú*), like the elbow and the knee. Movements possible with the help of this "joint" are: *okunnu* (to turn the neck), *rootiw* (to bow or bend), *chimw*, with the expansions of *chimwátá*, *chimwetiw* (to nod or dip, also said of a boat bobbing up and down on its lateral axis), *afanakkaw*, *afanakkawa* and *ásseenga wúú* (to crane one's neck). Wordless negation is not called shaking one's head but something like "neck shaking" (according to dialect, either *núúmúúti*, *núweti*, or *núwénúweti wúú*).

The throat, located between the two strong sinews (*senin wúú*, "neck rope") at the anterior part of the neck, is delimited by the chin area above (*fáán ngáách*), and is called *tiyor* or *chiyor*. This term denotes (besides *nóón wúú* and *nettiyor*) also the interior of the neck, specifically the pharynx, the esophagus (*tiyoren mwéngé*), and the air passages (*tiyoren ngasangas*). The opening between the oral cavity and the esophagus is called *pwangen tiyor* ("gullet hole"). It is noteworthy that the so-called *foramen magnum*, the large passage in the base of the skull, through which the brain is connected with the spinal cord, is likewise called *pwangen tiyor*.

The larynx (*chúún tiyor*) is classified as a bone (*chúú*), and is, according to the notion of the islanders, essentially involved in crushing food. Initiating the process of swallowing (*woromi*, *wokupa*, to swallow) produces suction in the throat, pulling the larynx upward and drawing the food from inside the mouth downward. While it passes through the larynx, the food is being "mashed" (*pwpwo*). Components that cannot be broken up into small pieces can get stuck in the larynx, causing strong irritation and coughing.

In other dialectal areas (the Hall Islands north of Chuuk) the larynx is called *féwúnúpwpwo*. This term refers to a pestle-like working tool, made of stone or wood, that is used to pound cooked breadfruit or taro tubers on a wooden plank into a homogenous mash (see illustrations by Krämer, 1932:125 and LeBar, 1964:17-18).

There is no term for the thyroid gland. A goitre as a malformation of this organ is called *wúwapwo* ("inflated neck") and is considered a sickness (*samwaaw, semwmwen*).

6.2   The Voice (*neewú*)

The larynx is not considered to be a voice box; any connection between it and the voice is denied. This is contradicted by the ancient practice to preserve the larynx of a deceased "breadfruit magician," since his voice was said to be able to call up the breadfruit spirits and thus favorably influence the ripening of the breadfruit.

The former practice of preserving the larynx, even though a direct connection between it and the voice is denied, may perhaps be due to the fact that the cartilage tissue of the larynx in its dried condition was preservable, unlike the rest of the parts of the neck which decompose easily.

Linguistic findings show clearly that the voice is not perceived to be in an immediate connection with any body organ: *neewú* literally means something like "place in the throat" and thus seems to be considered as a function of the interior of the neck.

The term *neewú* appears only rarely without a relational suffix referring to its possessor, e.g., *neewúwey, neewuwomw* (my, your voice) etc. However, the term *nettiyor*, though formed with the same prefix *nee-*, does not mean the voice but only the inside of the throat.

Only people, animals, and spirit beings (*ngúún, énú*) possess a voice, in the sense of *neewú*.

To express vocal characteristics there are many possible word formations available: *neewúwékis, neewúwékúkkún* and *neewúwéngngin* ("voice small," quiet), *neewúwómmóng* ("voice voluminous," loud), *neewúwékken* ("voice sharp," with a shrill voice), *neewúwan aa ttikikken, nger, mengeringer* (his voice sounds shrill, husky, rough, hoarse), *neewúwééch* ("voice beautiful," sounding pleasant), *neewúwangngaw* ("voice bad," sounding unpleasant).

As well as *neewú*, the islanders use the generally synonymous term *woos* for the voice of humans and animals. The differences between these two terms are hard to define; *woos* seems to refer more to the sound or tone of a voice. In compound words expressing characteristics of the voice, *woos* appears more often than *neewú*, but is otherwise of secondary importance. Its subordinate importance may be recognized by the fact that *wosen neewúwey* (my voice) represents an acceptable context, whereas the reversed order of words does not.

Word compounds with the morpheme *woos* for expressing characteristics of the voice: *wosommóng* ("voice voluminous," loud), *wosengngin* ("voice small," quiet), *wosemengeringer* (husky, rough, hoarse), *woseyééch* (beautiful, pleasant sounding), *wosongngaw* (ugly, unpleasant sounding). *Wosotá* is a transitive verb, meaning "to make louder": *wosotá kkéén* (to sing louder). Instead of *wosen neewúwey* (the sound of my voice), on occasion the combination *kookoon neewúwey* is also used.

There is no comparable term for the breaking of the male voice during puberty. Informants describe the phenomenon by saying that the voice of a boy is starting to sound like a taut sinew or guitar string (*mii pong neewúwen emén áát*), but they cannot explain what causes the change in the pitch of the voice.

If a man has an especially deep voice he, or his voice, is said to be *koos* (*kosokos*). This term generally also means the characteristic of a man's voice in contrast to a woman's voice, which sounds *ttikikken*. Musical terms characterizing the pitch of a voice, like soprano, alto, tenor, and bass, originally did not exist among the islanders.

For expressing the different kinds of vocal expressions, the Chuukese language contains a series of words, whose meanings are difficult to grasp, to isolate from each other, and to describe. This is partially due to the fact that the Chuukese language does not really have the different grammatical categories of verb, adjective, and noun.

The activity of speaking is called *kkapas* or *fóós*, with *kkapas* denoting more the activity of speaking, the language, and the individual word, while *fóós* refers more to the speech itself (*aan fóós*, what he says).

The term *mweniyey* (my speaking) can only be used for people (and spirit beings similar to people), denoting articulate expressions of voice; informants say that *mweniyey* is situated in the mouth.

Méngúúngú refers commonly to the noise generated by a person or a crowd of people. By way of contrast, the term *ngiingi* (and related word forms) denotes homogeneous vocal expressions, sounds that become audible in singing, the humming of flies and motors, but also characteristic properties of the voice of a certain person by which he or she can be recognized. Thus, when cowry and similar shells are called *ngiingi*, this could refer to the noise one can hear when they are held to the ear.

Miiniin describes a vocal utterance that can be heard from far away as, e.g., in telephoning (*nóón tenefoon aa fókkun miiniin*).

Further utterances of the vocal kind: *ngngú* (groan, grunt), *ngúúngú*, *ngúúngúúres* and *wúngúúng* (growling, said of dogs; purring, of cats; lowing, of water buffalos; droning, of motors; whooshing, of the surf; rumbling, of thunder), *ngúnúngún* and *mwéngúnúngún* (whispering, to complain about someone in a mutter), *ttik* (chirping, of birds; to be switched on, of radios or other wireless gadgets; lamenting, nagging someone).

Articulation or pronunciation is called *newenew*. This also refers to the characteristic way of someone's speaking: *kaa newenewen ree Tooyis* (when you talk, one can hear that you are a German; you have a German accent); *mii mwirinné newenewomw* (your pronunciation is good).

Chapter 7
The Torso

7.1 The Term *inis* in the Narrower Sense

As a rule, the term *inis*, as explained earlier, denotes the whole body including the extremities; but, without any addition, it is also used for the torso or trunk in a narrower sense (without head, neck, and extremities). This central part of the body, *inis*, is divided into a fairly large number of subdivisions with separate terms, relating to two dimensions – the surface of the body (*wóón inis*) and its interior (*nóón inis*).

7.2 The Shoulder (*afar*)

... is not considered to be part of the arm but of the torso. Informants indicate that it reaches from the neck to the beginning of the arm (*seni neepwopwun wúú toori neepwopwun paaw*). The term *afar* further denotes the shoulder part of garments, like shirts etc. Bottles, too, have "shoulders" in this sense, but then they do not have a "neck." Animals are usually not seen as having shoulders, nor is a mountain said to have a shoulder.

The shoulder has various terms relating to its role in carrying burdens. A person shoulders (*éwúwafara*) a bar or yoke, which itself is called *éwúwafar* (*éwúwéfar*) or *waas*.

7.3 The Thorax or Chest Area
(*neeyéwúng, wuupw, neewuupw*)

The two main sections dividing the chest area are not strictly separable from each other. A space of six inches, immediately below the base of the neck and going right across the chest, is called *neeyéwúng* (with wasps and insects of similar build *neeyéwúng* denotes the front part of the body). Below it lies the *wuupw* or *neewuupw*, which ought to be the actual term for the thorax as it is found in the term for the breastbone or sternum (*chúún neewuupw*), and it alone can refer to the interior chest cavity. If people feel pain in their chest, they say "*mii metek neewupwey.*" On occasion, *wuupw* may also refer to the abdominal region, which otherwise is called *nuuk*. As a rule, this is the case with fish, dogs, turtles, and animals of similar build: the entire underside of their body is more frequently called *wuupw*. There are, however, informants who insist that *wuupw* and *neewuupw* cannot have the same meaning. According to their opinion *wuupw* can only be used for the outside of the abdomen, i.e., as a synonym for *wóón nuuk* or *wóón saa*.

The transitive verb *wupwuri* refers to the behaviour of two roosters getting at each other with swelled breast for a fight, or to the body posture of a hen defending her brood of chicks.

The chest area designated by *wuupw* or *neewuupw* also includes the mammae (*owupw*). They are called by the same word, whether referring to men, women, or mammals. The nipple or teat is called *mesen owupw* ("eye of the breast"). The areola does not have its own designation. The area around the mammae on the human body has local designations like *fáán* ("below-ness of," under), *wóón* ("aboveness of," above), *asen* ("on-topness of," upon), *núkún* ("beside-ness of," next to). The cleavage is called *neefiinen owupw* ("between-ness of the breasts").

The mammae are not counted as round objects: numerals in connection with them do not appear with the addition of -*féw*, but in their singular form (e.g., *eew owupw*, a breast). Depending on their size, however, women's and animals' breasts are said to be *nangattam* (long), *mwochomwoch* (short), or *féwúmmóng* (sizeable), whereas with men they are *féwúngngin*. Once they start to develop, or when their development is complete, people say *mii féw owupwun*.

With children the breasts are called *tét*, referring in the same way to both girls and boys. Girls, when their breasts start to develop, are called *ttipwúk* (*pwúk* meaning the germinating and sprouting of plants).

The term *owupw* also serves as the term for several things having a form similar to mammae: the cones decorating the *wúsúús* or *pwpwo*, a tool made of stone or wood, used for mashing taro or breadfruit (see figures by Krämer, 1932:125 and LeBar, 1964:17-18); the tenons of boards (*owupwun paap*) or beams when joining pieces of wood; a body part of the *woonón*, a shellfish of the mangrove area, that is only similar in form.

Hill-like elevations are *wupwowupw*. In *Amwachang* this term is found as a plot or place name *(Wóón Wupwowupw)*. Mashed breadfruit (*kkón*) that is piled on a bowl to overflowing is said to be *mii wupwátá* or *mii wupwowupwátá*. The bowl itself, in this case, can be said to be *mii wupwowupw ewe kkama*.

Milk, as secretion of the mammae, is called *chchénún owupw* and is thus classified as "juice," just like the drinkable contents of the coconut (*chchénún núú*). Infants that are nursed are drinking *chchénún owupw*; whereas milk imported in cans, or from cows and water buffaloes, that is drunk from vessels, is called *minik*.

Owupw is conspicuously connected with terms to do with propagation: The verb *owupwu* can mean "to suckle, nurse, breastfeed" as well as "to help someone get a child, to get blessed with children" (also *owupwáátiw*).

A clan with an abundance of children is said to be *mii wupw ewe eyinang*. Starting with this fact, the term for the mamma can be analyzed as a compound of the morpheme *o-* (a variant prefix with causative sense) and *-wupw*. The compound *wupwutiw* means "being born" or "to have been born." Informants admit, however, that this interrelation of terms may be coincidental.

A traditional unit of length is *tinewupw* (*etinewupw* etc.), the distance between the fingertips of the arm stretched out sideways and the middle of the chest.

7.4 The Abdominal Area (*nuuk, saa*)

For the abdominal area there are the terms *nuuk* and *saa*, depending on the dialectal region. Both can refer to either the abdominal wall or the inside of the abdomen. On occasion, *nuuk* may stand for the entire body cavity and, with wasps, spiders, and similar animals, for the hinder part of the body. For a more exact differentiation between the outside and inside there are the additions of *nóón* ("inside-ness") and *wóón* ("above-ness").

The creases in the abdominal wall are called *numunumun nuuk*, or it is said that the abdomen is *ttáránnum*. An abdomen distended by sickness, pregnancy, or overeating is *pwo*.

Closely connected with the expression *nóón nuuk* for the abdominal cavity is the term *neenuuk*, which is, however, clearly differentiated from *nóón nuuk* in its meaning. *Neenuuk* denotes a spot in the upper region of the abdomen, approximately where the sternum ends (*fáán mwáár*). This, according to the islanders' notion, is the place where anger, anxiety, joy, etc., but also thoughts, memories, and intentions have their seat, i.e., where the soul's emotions make themselves felt and intellectual processes take place. This location is not equated with any bodily organ like the heart, the liver, or the stomach. Nor is it regarded as an organ itself. If one opened the abdominal cavity, it would not be visible. Neither does it possess any properties of an independent entity in the sense of a European notion of the soul. At the point of death, it stops all its functions, just like the other body parts, and does not exist any longer after that. A detailed description of this extremely nuanced notional area is found in later chapters (starting with ch. 15).

The term *fáán mwáár* (*fáán mwári* etc.) for the pit of the stomach (the epigastrium) and part of the vaulted ribs below *neeyéwúng* is linguistically hard to analyse; *mwáár* and its reduplicated (more frequent) form *mwárámwár* refer, as a rule, to a wreath of flowers and similar decorations worn around the neck or on the head. There does not seem to be a connection between these two terms. With breadfruit, *fáán mwárin* refers to the concave side that is put on the fire first when grilling; in the case of mountains it refers to overhanging rock ledges, and with curved tree trunks it is likewise the concave side that is meant. The corresponding opposite in each case is *sékúr* (the back) or *núkisékúrún* ("behind-ness of," [at the] back).

When speaking of the surface of the torso, the term *nuuk* (on *Toon* more frequently used than *saa*) means the abdomen (or belly) from the vaulted ribs downwards to the start of the pubic hair (*seni fáán mwáár toori pwaar*).

The morpheme *nuuk*, in another context, points to the "middle or centre," e.g., in compounds like *nuukanap* (waist line, centre of a circle), *nuukanapen mataw* (on the high seas), *nuukenipwin* (midnight), *nuukeyinéw* (the middle child of a couple's three children) etc.

The body part termed *nuuk* comprises mainly the stomach (*chúkúnúkan*), the liver (*émmún*), the intestines (*taar*), the kidneys (*féwún nóón*), and, in the case of women, the uterus (*neeniyen ménúkón*, "place of the child"); these organs will be described later in connection with the inside of the body (7.15 ff.). *Nuuk* is, furthermore, the place where several physical sensations have their seat, e.g., *echik* (hunger), *mét* (feeling of satiation), *ngan(angan)* (feeling of orgasm), and *máánééné* (nausea, seasickness, literally something like "liquid death").

Mahony describes (1970:182-183) a magic ritual, based on a sexual motive, to which he gave the name *nukan*. While its connection to the term *nuuk* is obvious, apparently it is closer to *neenuuk*, the location in the body where emotions have their seat.

7.5   The Navel (*aporonong, ppu, taar*)

It is located in that part of the surface of the trunk, which is designated as (*wóón*) *nuuk*. Apart from the more frequently used term *aporonong* there are the words *ppu* and *taar*. Behind the latter we find an instructive connection of terms.

The word *taar* usually means the intestines and specifically refers to the umbilical cord (*taren ménúkón, senin taar*) of the newborn (including animals). It is not seen as a blood vessel (*waan chcha*), but rather as part of the digestive tract. Informants are unable to give any exact information about the function of the umbilical cord, although they know that it is somehow connected to the placenta (*pey, chiyenen ménúkón*). With the newborn the umbilical cord has to be tied before it is severed because, otherwise, there is a perceived danger that bowel contents might come out.

Immediately after a birth, one also has to be careful that the umbilical cord is not stretched, otherwise the child might die of *ppummey* ("stretched umbilical cord").

If a child is born with the umbilical cord wrapped around it, the expression *mii ámwárámwár ewe ménúkón* is used, the explanation being that its mother, during pregnancy, must have frequently worn wreaths of blossoms (*mwárámwár*) – the customary headdress beloved by men and women alike.

One can tell by the pulsating movement (*pichipich, ngasangas*) around the navel whether a newborn is alive or not. Altogether, the navel plays an important role in diagnosing sicknesses. The strength of the pulse in the area surrounding it is seen as an indication of the general health of the patient, and with pregnant women also as a clue to the correct or incorrect position of the uterus (Mahony, 1970:207, 209).

The compound terms *pwangen taar* ("bowel hole") and *nóón taar* are being used when referring more exactly to the navel depression. Whether *aporonong* points to a connection in this sense, when separated into its morphemic parts, e.g., *-nong* (into something), remains to be seen. Unsolved is also the meaning of the term *imwenungun* (for the remainder of the dried up umbilical cord that later falls off), which A. Fischer (1956:93) discovered on the island of *Romónum*; *imwen ngúún* (sic) means "house of the soul" (cf. 21 and Goodenough/Sugita 1980:81).

7.6 The Back (*sékúr*)

The backside of the body, compared with its front, exhibits only little differentiation of terms. It comprises the back proper (*sékúr*) and the area of the posterior (*kuwoku*).

The back reaches from the neck (*núkún wúú*) down to the posterior (*kuwoku*). The hips are not part of it. As a rule, animals also have a back. Fish are an exception, as their back part is called *iniin* (edge, sharp-edged dorsal fin, back of a blade, flat-board roots of the breadfruit tree). However, with larger fish and turtles one may use *sékúr*, but not metaphorically, as in the back of a hill. The back of a crab is *wóón péér* ("above-ness of the shell"). Colloquially the islanders use the expression *núkún sékúr* ("outside-ness," surface of the back) for the entire back part of the body. In connection with this, there exists the noun *núkisékúrún* (backside), which may also stand for the corresponding local term (at the back of, behind). Thus, *núkisékúrún irá* refers to the convex side of a curved tree trunk, *núkisékúrún maay* to the convex side of a breadfruit, in contrast with their concave side (*fáán mwárin*).

The groove, tracing the path of the spine, has multiple terms. It is called *neewááwáán sékúr*, *pwokuren sékúr*, or *warawaren sékúr*. The flat protrusions on either side are called *iniinin sékúr* ("rim of the back"), just as with the dorsal fin of fish. The compound *neewááwá* indicates a free space, cleared of plants, not covered with growth (*wá*, cleared of growth; *wáási*, to remove growth); *pwokur* are all kinds of depressions in the ground as well as the indentations on a dental crown (5.14); *warawar* means groove, or ditch.

Beyond this, there are terms for the area around the shoulder blade (*péwúkéré*, *núkún péwúkéré*), the section below that to about the middle of the back (*núkún épúng*), and the soft parts on top of the hips (*neepwakakkak*). The latter form the sitting area where little children with their legs spread can be carried comfortably.

This way of carrying is called *efiti*. If a child is carried on the back, it is called *achchékú*, in contrast to *ámwmwa*, which is said of the way a child is carried so that it looks back over the shoulder of the person carrying it.

Informants explain the term *núkún épúng*, for the section below the shoulder blades to about the middle of the back, by the fact that it makes a booming sound (*púng*) when one beats upon it.

The soft parts on top of the hips are designated *neepwakakkak* because they are thought to have the consistency of sodden, swampy soil (*pwakak*).

There is a remarkable expression for a place on the back, which is specified when one wants to indicate pain in the area of the apex of the lungs: *núkún émmún* ("outside-ness" of the liver).

The sides of the body (*neepeek*) from below the armpit (*fáán paaw*) to the hips cannot be unambiguously assigned to either the front or back of the body. Informants are more likely to allocate them to the back. Their sensitivity to touch is called *rúkúfe(e)n* (ticklish).

7.7   The Region of the Buttocks or Posterior (*kuwoku*)

… is comprised of the buttocks proper (*nimmóót*) and the hips (*wiina*). When referring to the hips, one usually uses *wóón wiina* ("above-ness" of the hip). The term *nimmóót* for the posterior indicates the meaning of sitting in the syllable *móót*. In addition, there is the term *féwúpwopw* and the less socially acceptable *féwún niwiit* and *núkiinóng*; the seat of the pants is called *féwúnúpwopw*.

Finally, there are terms for the cleft of the seat (*wáát*, *neewáttin*) and the anus (*niwiit*), which plays a role in humorous idioms. When someone is searching intensively for an object that is obviously visible, the others jokingly say, *mii nónnómw fáán niwitumw* (the sought object is under your seat; you are sitting on it; it is going to bite you, etc.). Further terms for the anus, specifically for its darker coloured area are *fachochchow* and *fóchochchow*.

There is no term for the perineum (the area between the anus and the genitals except for the paraphrase *neefiinen* ... ("in-between-ness of"...).

7.8   The Genital Region (*ekinissow*)

For the islanders, the sexual organs and their functions represent a distinct area of taboo. This is clearly evident in the structure of the vocabulary assigned to the genital region. One can distinguish two extremes. The "actual" designations for the sexual organs and their parts usually also belong to the vocabulary of vulgar and obscene ways of expression. Wherever these are not intended or must be avoided, terms for other body parts are being used whose form is reminiscent of sexual organs (e.g., the ear for the female genitalia), or metaphors are being used, whose sense is difficult to recognize for the uninitiated.

Informants mark the obscenity of such a word by saying that it is *péchékkún* (strong), or by saying that it is *pin neeyin mwáán me feefin* (taboo between men and women).

Because of this characteristic the vocabulary for the genital region supplies the islanders with material for aggressive purposes. Participants in a dispute would thus name persons that are sexually taboo for the opponent – usually his mother or his sisters – in connection with the genital region. Such a *kkapasen óttek* or *kkapasen ámángngaw* (obscene swear word) means a more or less serious insult, which is usually followed by a row that may end in blood.

Indeed, it seemed at first rather strange to *Namiyo* and *Mwékút*, my two informants, that I of all people should be interested in this vocabulary. At the beginning of our joint work of recording their ideas of body, soul, and spirit, they just could not understand why I would want to write all this down. After we were finished with the area of the genitalia and navigated again, so to speak, in waters where we were not constantly confronted by heavy taboos, and after it became clearer to them why I put such importance on exact linguistic material, they explained to me one day that they had again and again discussed the question of what would induce me to record their "filthy" expressions and collect them in a card index (and in alphabetical order to boot!).

Neutral designations for the genital region that may be used by men and women alike, and even in mixed company, are *kúkkún inis* (literally "small body," body part, or member) and *ekinissow*.

Thus, e.g., a physician who needs to diagnose a disease of the genital organs, may ask his patient to *kepwe ékúnaangeniyey ekinissowumw*, i.e. to undress.

As a rule, *ekinissow* does mean nakedness in the sense that the pubic area is uncovered; but one can also say of other body regions that they are *ekinissow* when they are bare: *aa aaya raweses, nge aa ekinissow inisin* (he wore trousers, but his upper body was naked).

Conceptually, there seems to be a connection between the genital area, designated as *ekinissow*, and the sense of shame that can be described with the term *kin* (without the sense of respect contained in *sááw*).

Much less general than *ekinissow* is the term *pwaar*. It denotes the triangle men and women have, which is formed by the pubic hair including the external genitalia. Animals do not have a *pwaar*.

The pubic hair, like other body hair, is called *wúnéwúnen, téréwúnen,* or *méréwúnen pwaar*. Additionally, the term for the underarm hair (*kkor*) may also stand for the pubic hair. Someone with thick pubic hair is said to be *fisikkor*.

The condition of the *pwaar* determines how desirable a person is as sexual partner. A woman with a pronounced mons veneris is said to be *pwarochuuk* (*chuuk*, hill, mountain). It is believed that a *pwaar* of this kind indicates that she will achieve her orgasm faster.

Here, too, there exists a whole series of terms for the genital area. They vary according to groups of islands or dialectal regions. On *Toon*, the terms *ákáAká* and the metonyms *chaamw* (forehead), *fáán maas* (*maas*, eye, face), *fáán mesen mwáán* (male genitalia), *fáán mesen feefin* (female genitalia) are not considered to be obscene for either gender; by contrast, *nifáttá* is counted as obscene.

7.9   The Female Genital Organs (*ekinissowun feefin*)

The work with informants regarding this body region is fairly problematic. The ethnographer really ought to question women in this respect. In normal circumstances, this would be impossible, unless he were married to an islander. On the other hand, men are rather good informants when it comes to female genitalia. Their interest in this topic of discussion is seen in the plethora of terminological knowledge which, in their case, borders on abundance. The preferred location for their discussions on this topic is the meetinghouse (*wuut*). Hence the designation *fóósun neewuut* ("meetinghouse language") for this vocabulary.

It is noticeable that, depending on the informant, very different terms are given for the external genitalia of the woman. Among other things, this difference comes about when one informant uses a term for all of the genitalia, where the other uses it to refer only to one part of them, depending on what village or dialectal region he comes from.

The following three terms for the external female genitalia are not considered offensive language: *chaamw* (forehead), *sening* or *chéén sening* (ear, auricle), and *sáyipé* (braided fan in rhombic form, pictured by LeBar, 1964:37, fig. 28). Also *ssáát* (cleft or crack) is counted as unproblematic, though it seems to be avoided.

Chep and *túú* are regarded as highly offensive but "fitting" terms for the female genitalia. Under certain conditions the terms *fiir*, *foo*, and *raapw* can be used in their stead, though, as a rule, they mean the labia majora. *Wáát* (the pudendal cleft) may also stand for the whole.

The word *fiir* shows especially clearly how dependent its meaning can be on the informant and his background: for my informant *Mwékút* from *Pwene* it is the labia majora, Goodenough/Sugita, 1980:124, in contrast, labia minora. Instead of *foo*, one can at times also hear *aamen foo* (*aam*, rim of a container, also of boats). Apart from signifying the labia, *raapw* also refers to the wattle of a rooster.

The highly offensive term *mwaa* (*mwaan feefin*) signifies either the entire female genitalia or the vagina and the vaginal orifice, depending on the informant. Elbert (1947:331) even gives the meaning as uterus. *Par* (usually the colour red), however, is not offensive and, again depending on the informant, means either the entire female genitalia, the labia majora, or labia minora.

The clitoris is called either *féwútún* (hardly offensive) or *michikken* (very offensive). It is seen as the organ responsible for the female orgasm (*ngan, nganangan*).

For the smell of the female genitalia, produced by uncleanness or soiling through urine, the designations *mwas* (*pwoomwas*) and *eeng* (*pwooyeeng*) are being used. Both are highly offensive.

Totally in contrast to the external sexual organs of a woman, the internal ones have conspicuously few terms. Likewise, there is virtually no word taboo connected with them. Vaginas as birth channel and uterus (*neeniyen ménúkón*) are not differentiated linguistically. The expression for this consists of a word combination that means something like "place of the child (infant, newborn)". The existence of the hymen is indeed known, but there is no word for it, just as little as for the Fallopian tube, the ovaries, etc. The only exception would be the uterine cervix. It is called either *mesan* ("its eye," meaning the pointed end of the uterus), or *énú*.

This term is rather surprising, as it usually stands for everything the islanders consider to mean a spirit being (nature spirits, spirits of the dead, of the ancestors, etc.). However, there do not appear to exist any conceptual connections between these. Detailed information regarding concepts of spirit beings will follow in later chapters (24 ff.).

With animals, the uterus (including the vagina) is called *neeniyen néwún* ("place of the young"); with birds it is *neeniyen sokuun* ("place of the egg"). For the ovaries of fish, the term *rúú* (*rúúwen iik*) is used.

7.10 Menstruation (*semwmwenin feefin*)

It is seen as a woman's sickness, since it has to do with loss of blood, when the woman appears in a state of *semwmwen*, i.e., "not as she actually ought to be."

Besides *semwmwen*, there is the term *samwaaw*. Both words for sickness contain the negational particle *-sapw* in its frequent forms of *se-* and *sa-*. *Semwmwenin maram* ("moonsickness, monthly sickness") is also spoken of.

To say of a woman that she is *chcha* (she is bleeding) is considered a breach of good manners. The use of this term is restricted to menstruating animals (goats, dogs). However, this way of expression would be unproblematic, if one wanted to say that a woman had incurred some injury anywhere on her body.

According to the notions of the islanders, the uterus is constantly filled with blood until menopause sets in, having to be renewed regularly every four weeks. The heart (*féwún ngasangas*) alone is seen as a blood producing organ. There are no words for menarche and menopause.

During her menses a woman cannot become pregnant (*pwoopwo*), because there is not enough blood, or none at all, present in her uterus. Nevertheless men are to abstain from intercourse during this period. Menstruating women are *apwangapwang* (weak, feel unwell), *rochongngaw*, and *nisossoong* (aggressive, suffering from mood swings, depressions). Because of their body odour they are being avoided by good spirit beings, while evil ones feel attracted by it. This is the reason why women are considered to be especially vulnerable during their menses; and this vulnerability would be transferred to men who have had sexual contact with them.

In earlier times, men were not even allowed to eat together with women and girls who had their period. The females had to separate themselves from their group. For this reason the condition of a menstruating woman is also called *nó núkún* (to go outside). During this time they used to live in huts in the bush (*imwen nó núkún*) provided for this purpose; these were also called *imwepwut* (*pwut*, bad?) and, especially for girls in the menarche, *imwerá* ("house of twigs"?, girls' house).

Even to this day, if at all possible, their condition has to be kept secret from their male relatives who, in reference to the women and girls concerned, come under the taboo of incest (fathers, brothers, etc.). At least, one must not speak of it in their presence.

If a woman's symptoms of her period are subsiding, it is said that she is *wúk seni semwmwenin feefin* (*wúk*, at the end).

Irregularities at the start of menstruation are no reason for worry, for its failure to set in does not constitute a clear sign of dysfunction or that the woman is pregnant. In the first place, it is known of quite a number of girls that they became pregnant before their first period; and, secondly, menstruation can fail to occur for other reasons, too; e.g. while a woman is breast-feeding her child. The explanation given for this is that a woman could have lost so much blood from the uterus during childbirth that it would take longer to make up for the loss.

There are very different opinions on the exact onset of the menarche. On its own it occurs at the latest when a girl reaches the age of about sixteen. It is taken for certain that the menarche sets in when a girl has had intercourse. There are therefore girls who, according to general opinion, start to menstruate already at twelve years of age. For this reason, the onset of the menarche is actually an embarrassing situation for any unmarried girl. Since she can hardly hide her condition, she is at once open to suspicion and rumours that she had intercourse with a man.

From the time of the onset of the menarche, a girl no longer belongs to the age group of *nengngin*. She has now become a *féépwún* (young woman).

The beginning of the menopause is considered as a sign that ageing (*chinnap*) has set in. There is no precise explanation for the failure of the period to appear. People are convinced that there are women who have become pregnant even after their menopause.

7.11 Pregnancy (*pwoopwo*)

This condition, in contrast to menstruation, is not looked upon as a sickness. It is rather seen as a purely physical process and is in no way causally connected to the pre-existence of the "soul," i.e., of the spirit-like double (*ngúnúyééch*) of the child that is to be born.

As to the term *pwoopwo*, this is a reduplicated form of the morpheme *pwo* (swollen, bulging, bloated). The form *pwoopwo* stands, without exception, for the concept of pregnancy, also with animals. A swollen leg, e.g., can only be called *pwo*.

Other things that can be *pwo*: fish (*iik*), automobile tires (*táyiya*), balloons (*fúúseng*), pillows (*pinnu*), etc. A goitre is said to be a *wúwapwo* ("bloated throat"); individual symptoms of elephantiasis are *pecheepwo*, *wunupwo*, etc. (swollen legs, testicles, etc.). A chubby-cheeked child is *sapopwo* ("bloat-cheeked"). Things like breadfruit, pumpkins, and stones that may look like balls, but have no elasticity, cannot be *pwo*; rather, they are *féwúmmóng*.

In contrast, the (reduplicated) term *pwoopwo* for the condition of pregnancy points to a marine animal (*pwaaset*) of the shore region, which puffs itself up when it is being touched; and it is contained in the terms for especially high waves (*nóópwoopwo*), for swimming floats and urinary bladders that children use as toys (*nikapwoopwo*).

The causative verbs in this field of terms show the same structure: the simplex form *ópwoow* means "to blow up, to bloat, to fill to a bulge," the reduplicated form *ópwoopwoow*, by way of contrast, means exclusively "to impregnate, to get pregnant."

A woman becomes pregnant when the blood (*chcha*) in her uterus is mixed with sperm (*weet*), even without any orgasmic reaction on her part. This starts a kind of clotting process resulting in a foetus. Blood and sperm must be present in about equal amounts. Normally, the amount of sperm from a single time of intercourse is less than the amount of blood contained in the uterus. For a pregnancy to start it is therefore necessary to have intercourse several times. The gender of the child cannot be influenced.

As to the clotting process: The blood in the uterus is said to be *mii wúkúnó* or *mii ppet*.

The following physical changes are seen as indications for a woman to be pregnant: Her period fails to come in, her breast nipples get darker and become erect, she suffers alternately from a lack of appetite and a craving for food, she vomits often (*mwmwus, eningngaw*), and loses weight (*kichúúchú*), her face gets spotty, her eyebrows fall out, she suffers from mood swings, and develops a craving for food that smells and tastes very strong or sometimes is even unappetizing.

From the colouration of the breast nipples one can supposedly deduce the gender of the child: if the areola is noticeably dark (*chón*, black), the woman will bring a girl into the world.

Strong tasting foods, craved by pregnant women, are unripe fruit (*féwún irá mii méngúch*), vegetables, and raw produce (*mwéngéén tánnipi*, "food from the garden, the plantation"). There are women who break open cigarettes in order to eat the tabacco they contain. Even such revolting things as faeces from cockroaches are said to have been ingested by women during their pregnancy.

On the other hand, there are those foods, especially among the strong tasting ones, that are absolutely taboo (*pin*) for pregnant women, because their odour and taste are detested by benevolent spirit beings. If, e.g., a pregnant woman ate *épwét* (fermented mashed breadfruit), she would be defenceless against attacks of evil spirit beings, because benevolent spirit beings, who ususally protect a pregnant woman, would avoid being near her if she smelled of fermented breadfruit.

Moreover, pregnant women should never eat while walking. People are of the opinion that this would extend the coming birth process in an unpleasant manner. Also, they should not quench their thirst with water, but with coconuts. Water is cooler and, therefore, the embryo prefers it as a drink to the contents of coconuts. It would then grow more quickly and be bigger at birth, thus complicating it.

When it is clear that a woman does not have her period anymore because she is pregnant, people say that she is *nu* or *kkonu*. If she has pregnancy complications, she is *nungngaw* or *kkonungngaw*, which specifically also refers to morning sickness. If she has no complications, she is *nuuyééch* or *kkonuuyééch*. Another possible way of expressing the condition of a woman after her period fails to set in, is *nuuseni ewe maram* (*maram*, moon, month).

As a rule, a pregnancy lasts nine months, though, according to the opinion of the islanders (men!), it may be extended to eleven months. After that, there is no longer any possibility of bringing the child into the world since, by then, it will have become too big. Mother and child will have to die.

Some know from miscarriages that, in about the third month, the embryo looks something like a mudskipper (*nusupaat*, periophthalmus). The comparison is based on the bulging eyes of this fish, located at the top of its head. As a rule, the notion is widespread that, though the embryo is small, it does possess all the proportions of an infant already shortly after the beginning of the pregnancy; it is merely getting bigger until the time of birth.

7.12 Birth (*faamw*)

The foetus is viable approximately from the sixth month of gestation. The birth process starts when the contractions set in (*cheewuchen*, *metekin* or *ngiiyówun faamw*, "birthing pains"). The periodic change between painful contractions and painfree phases during birth is explained as follows. The birth canal is divided into sections (*seeng*) and knots (*pwásuk*, knees or "knots," as in bamboo and grass blades). If, during its passage through the birth canal, a child comes to a knot, the woman giving birth will sense labour pains, which will last until the child has passed that location. The narrower the knot is formed, the more unpleasant will be the sensation of the particular labour pain. The following section, until the next knot, will then be pain free.

According to this notion, a long drawn out birth is called *seengettam* ("long-sectioned"), a short one correspondingly *seengemwoch* ("short-sectioned").

The vocabulary of the Chuukese language for the term "birth" and its conceptual domain shows a cognitive structure, which clearly deviates from the corresponding European term "birth." The term *faamw* only means birth in the biological sense (in the case of an animal one would say *eten, eteni*, to cast its young, or actually "to align in a row"). Of a child and its birth, by way of contrast, one would use the term *wupwutiw* (*wupwutiuwan*, its birth; *aa wupwutiw*, it is born; *wupwun neeroch*, "born in the dark," i.e., father unknown). This is based on the morpheme *wupw* (fruitful, having many children or descendants), which also occurs in the word form *owupw* (breast, udder) and *owupwu* (to suckle; cf. 7.3).

Another sub-area of the term "birth" is denoted by the morpheme *nnéw* and its compounds. The basic meaning is "having born children" (*néwúnéw*) and "possessing children" (*néwúni*). A woman is *nnéw* when she easily gets pregnant or has given birth to many children. The inflected forms of the word *naaw* (child) denote a very close proprietary relationship of a personal kind, usually related to something living (*ney, nowumw, néwún feefin* etc., my, your, his daughter etc.), but also to personal material possession (*ney waas*, my watch). And lastly, we find the morpheme *nnéw* in the term for the local midwife (*fin énnéw, fin énéwúnéw*), who is sometimes also called *chóón afaamw*.

When a woman cannot have children, she is *riit* (infertile, barren). Causes for infertility can either be found in physical defects of the woman, or the sperm is lacking the necessary mana (*manaman*), so that it remains ineffective. As an explanation for female infertility, A. Fischer was told (1956:91) that it was due to *pwichikkar* (heat; here it means some kind of sickness on the part of the woman or man).

The functions of the amniotic fluid (*chchénú, chchénún nóón neeniyen ménúkón*) and the slimy secretions (*mongomong*), covering the skin of the newborn, are unknown. There is, however, an assumption that the child drinks the fluid. If the child is conspicuously covered in slime, it is said that the woman must have had intercourse shortly before giving birth. To prevent the start of such rumours it is suggested that only close relatives should attend a birth.

For islanders of older generations, the crying of a newborn was reason for concern. It could perchance be that an evil spirit being (*soope*) has crept up to the child in order to torture it. This all the more so if, possibly, its benevolent spirit double (*ngúnúyééch*) is not yet present und thus cannot exert its protective function against attacks of malevolent spirit beings on the body (cf. 25.3.5 and 25.3.8). On the other hand, crying could also indicate that, e.g., the umbilical cord has not been taken care of properly, etc. If a newborn should not exhibit any expression of life, it will be gently caressed (*pisipisiri*) and petted (*tóófi*), in order to activate the blood circulation and the breathing.

Twins (*nipwpwe*) only attract attention among the islanders because of their rare occurrence. There does not appear to be any assumption of a special connection between a twin birth and the supernatural, in contrast to several other ethnic groups. At most, a woman giving birth to twins repeatedly raises the assumption that she may possibly have two uteri.

Deformed newborns, however, give rise to the concern that the deformity (*fokun*) was caused by evil spirit beings. Even such harmless appearances as birthmarks or nevi that disappear with time, raise the suspicion that the woman in question had brought an evil spirit being into the world (*ewe feefin aa néwúni soope*). This means either that a malevolent spirit being (*énúngngaw, soope*) caused the deformity of the child that had otherwise been normal before its birth, or that such a spirit being is indeed its biological father. Premature infants, too, are frequently considered to be *soope* and then neglected accordingly (cf. 24.10 ff.).

There appears to be no term for "miscarriage," although terms meaning "premature birth" (*waamerip, wammék*) do exist. The meaning of both word forms (something like "vessel destroyed") suggests the conclusion that the essence of the term is to be seen in the strong loss of blood occurring during a miscarriage. The foetus is said to be *nus* or *mwmwet, mwetenó* (drop off, lose its attachment). Heavy physical work and accidents, but also psychological causes like fear, a shock etc. are seen as likely to trigger a miscarriage.

Likewise unknown is the real function of the placenta (*pey*). It is assumed that the unborn child sucks on it (*tumwuri*) and drinks its "juice" (*aa wúnúmi chchénún*). The umbilical cord is classified as an intestine (*taar*; cf. 7.5).

The placenta, which is rejected as afterbirth, is also called *chiyenen ménúkón* (companion, friend, attendant of the child); something that is closely related to another thing, or is constantly around it, is called *chiyenan*. As a rule, the afterbirth is buried in the ground (*ireey, ireenó*, to bury). According to A. Fischer (1956:92), women reckon with complications during later births if this is not done carefully.

As soon as the afterbirth appears, the actual process of birth is considered to be finished. Now the woman who gave birth is said to be *sapan* ("bent over"). This seems to be a similar metaphor to speaking of the "confinement" of a woman. Presumably there is a connection to the body posture usually assumed by women about to give birth.

From the start of its existence to the point in time when the newborn starts to crawl or walk, it is called *ménúkón* ("reclining being"). For subsequent developmental phases there are the terms *nooyiroch, nooyis, tipáte, setipeen*, and *semiriit* as generic terms. (For the meaning of the last three, cf. 15.4 and 20.5)

7.13 The Male Sexual Organs (*ekinissowun mwáán*)

The term for penis (*see, tááng*) is subdivided into its root (*neepwopwun*), the shaft (*fóchun*), the foreskin (*sinin, kinin*), the glans (*kooch, ruumw*), and the orifice of the urethra (*pwangan*). Neither of the terms for the penis should be used in mixed company, *see* being more strongly taboo than *tááng*. Humorous sounding expressions like *éwút* (finger), *éwútúnap* (thumb), *éwúnúfóchun pecheen* (his third leg), *éwútún pecheen áát* (a boy's toe) or, generally, *kúkkún inis* ("small body," body part, member) serve as substitutes. Designations for the scrotum (*suun, wuun*) may, in certain circumstances, be used instead of the terms for the penis.

The root of the penis (*neepwopwun*) is called by the same term as the part of a tree trunk above ground or as the start of an activity. The word for the shaft (*fóchun*) refers to the form of elongated things in distinction to round or flat things, e.g., *fóchun pinawa* (loaf of bread), *fóchun mangaak* (bolt of fabric), *fóchun chúúfén* (nail shaft), etc.

The foreskin is denoted by expressions that generally refer to the skin; *siin* and *kiin* are the corresponding basic forms without any relational suffix. This is similarly true of the orifice of the urethra: the basic form *pwaang* means "hole."

Of the two terms for the glans, *ruumw* is especially interesting. It means "barbed hook," such as fishing rods and spears are equipped with. The point of the glans is called *mesen kooch* or *mesen ruumw* ("eye"), the groove of the glans either *mwirin kooch, mwirin ruumw* ("behind-ness"), or *fáán kapakap*, which also refers to the grooving of a coral reef, the overhang of a mountain side or a rocky cliff. The smegma is called *tipap*. Its function is unknown.

Conceptually, scrotum and testicles form one unit (*suun* or *wuun*, in West Chuuk also *épwpwék*), whereby the testicles are part of the whole (*féwún suun* etc., stone, round thing). The seam dividing the scrotum in two halves, running along the underside of the penis and ending in the frenal band, is called *óó* (fishing line). Men are afraid to injure it, let alone "rip it off" as this, in their opinion, would lead to death. For this reason it is sometimes also called *óón manaw* ("thread of life"). Informants indicate that such injuries could come about during intercourse through uncontrolled movements by the female partner. This fear is apparently an expression of subconscious sexual conflicts and anxieties evidenced by men in psychological testing procedures (Rohrschach and Thematic Apperception Test). (Detailed information on this may be found in Gladwin and Sarason, 1953.)

Ailments or pain in the area of the male genitalia are designated by the term *fingngaw*. For the characteristic pain caused by a blow on the testicles, there are the designations *ffiyó* and *ngiiyówun mwáán* ("men's pain").

The testicles are viewed as causing the urge to copulate, i.e., they effect erections (*ppech*). This is based on the observation that animals, e.g. pigs, evidently no longer have an erection after their gonads are removed. To castrate is called either *reyi*, *reyiiy* (to cut) or *wuneey* (to lacerate).

The fact that sperm (*weet*) is produced in the testicles, is not known. This, according to the opinion of the men, is generated in the spine. The consistency of the spinal marrow, for which (apart from *tupwu*, brain) there exists no specific term, is taken as evidence for this. Excessive sexual intercourse, therefore, leads to phenomena of "dehydration" in the spine. One of my informants saw confirmation of this in the backache he regularly experienced after indulging in intercourse without long enough intervals.

The term *weet* for sperm, again, is under a strong taboo. There are multiple substitutions: *chcha* (blood), *chénúfaak* (body secretion of thin liquid, e.g. perspiration), *moong* (viscous body secretion, e.g. the secretion from the nasal mucosa), *mongomongen ekinissow* (secretion from the prostata), *minik* (canned milk), *appach* (sticky substances, e.g., resin of the breadfruit tree). The consistency of the sperm is designated by the adjective *ppúnús*.

7.14 Sexual Intercourse (*fe*)

It is based on a need (*mwechen*), a physical disposition, called *nifeefe* (something like the urge to copulate). The term *nifeefe* contains the morpheme *fe* (transitive *feey*), both of which are extremely taboo. One substitute for *fe* is *kkóón reen* (to lie with). *Nifeefe* also means wanton lust in the sense of an inordinate interest in sex. There is apparently no word for animals in heat. An insect resembling a dragonfly, which can be found on Chuuk, is called *nifeefeechón*, obviously because of its bodily form and the manner in which it gets nectar from blossoms.

The phase of sexual arousal is accompanied by a sensation denoted by the word *rúkúfeen*. At the onset of erection, the penis is *manaw* (alive, fully functional); after its subsidence it is *má* (dead, extinguished, non-functioning) or *ménéngúnéng* (flaccid).

The orgasm (*ngan, nganangan*) is conceptually perceived, not as a process, but as orgasmic sensation accompanying the ejaculation (*kkus*) of the sperm. As to the term *kkus*: This must clearly be distinguished from the word form *kus*, though both are closely related in their meaning. *Kus* (with phonemically short *k* in the initial sound) refers to the spurting out of liquids through narrow openings, pipes, etc. *Kkus* (with phonemically long *k* in the initial sound) pertains, in relation to men, exclusively to the process of ejaculating sperm. Of a nocturnal ejaculation (a so-called "wet dream") a man would say *úwa kkusiitiyey reen ááy ttan, reen ttanen feefin*.

The way in which the terminology for the area of the sexual organs is connected with the culturally conditioned concept of maleness and femaleness has been demonstrated by Moral Ledesma (1996).

7.15   The Inner Organs (*pisekin nóón inis*)

The medicine of the islanders knows no surgical procedures. For this reason, their knowledge of the inner organs is not so much based on their own observations but on inferences gained from slaughtering animals and transferring these conclusions to humans.

Inner organs are regarded conceptually as things (of value) in one's possession (*pisek*): home fixtures, furniture (*pisekin iimw*), tools (*pisekin angaang*), etc. *Pisek* can also refer to parts of a motor (*pisekin mwesiin*). The reduplication *pisekisek* means wealthy, rich.

For the interior of the body, ususally denoted by the term *nóón inis* ("inside-ness" of the body), there is a second expression: *neewut*. This is also used to refer to the interior of the earth (*neewutun fénúúfaan*), the interior of fruit, of gadgets like clocks etc. In the case of human beings it would refer to anything located underneath the skin (sometimes also *neechú*).

Notions about the function of inner organs are rather sketchy and simplistic. They are essentially limited to two areas: the processing of food in the body and the activity of heart and blood vessels.

7.16   Food Processing

Solid food particles, ground up by chewing, leave the oral cavity via the pharynx (or gullet), are being minced some more by the larynx, and end up via the esophagus in the stomach. (Oral cavity, pharynx, and larynx have been described in 5.10-14 and 6.1.)

In the process of swallowing, it is necessary to distinguish clearly between swallowing solid food (*wokupa, wokupóónó*) and liquids (*woromi, woromóónó*). Medicine (*sáfey*) is hereby considered to be liquid, even if it is in the form of pills. To swallow something unchewed is called *woropwúnnúúw*, hiccup is *ssúk*. To choke on something (*áchátá*) actually means coughing in reaction to choking.

Digestion is exclusively the task of the stomach (*chúkúnúkan*). The intestinal tract (*taa, taar, aaf*), by contrast, only serves the purpose of eliminating digested food, without being part of the digestive process.

The stomach contents consist of matter the body can utilize (*iyoréchchún, ngúnúyéchchún*), and other material that is hardly or not at all useable (*iyorongngawan, ngúnúngngawan*). The process of digestion is, therefore, understood as separation of good components from bad ones, and that in a manner of wringing something out (*wunguung, wunguti*) from the contents of the stomach. The notion of wringing something out appears to be obvious. When preparing certain foods, the islanders use a procedure by which solid nutrients can be separated from liquid ones in a simple manner: by wringing something out. Most often they are after the liquid. Islanders thus separate, e.g., *arúng*, the white, oily juice of *taka*, grated coconut, by wrapping the flakes in a cloth or in the cloth-like covering of the coconut sheath and wringing it out. The unwanted pressed-out components, called *kitan* (wrung-out matter) are thrown away. Hence this word is used to denote human and animal excrements (*kiten mwéngé*).

As to the terms *iyoréchchún* and *iyorongngawan* (here with the suffix of the 3rd pers. sg.): a liquid exhibiting cloudiness is *iyor*, e.g. lemon juice, dirty water, etc. As to the terms *ngúnúyéchchún, ngúnúngngawan* and their connection to islanders' concept of the soul, cf. 21.3.

The word *chúkúnúkan* for the stomach is apparently composed of the words for basket (*chúúk*) and eating (e.g. *anan*, with suffix for 3rd pers. sg.). Besides this, there are the terms *niinan, niinanen* (*neeniyen anan*, "place of food"?) and *kopwur*; in rare cases, *nuuk* and *saa* (abdomen, abdominal cavity) can be used for it. Apart from its function as digestive organ, the stomach is the seat of the sensation of hunger (*echik, fiyon, móór*), which arises when it is empty.

To have an appetite for some special food (*mwóón*) is something different; like thirst, (*kaaka*), it is located in the mouth.

A hungry stomach may make itself heard. For this, the Chuukese language contains the onomatopoeic word *tórókókkók*. When an islander says "*mii tórókókkók nóón nuukey*," his or her stomach is growling. Indigestion and nausea are called *eningngaw* ("to have eaten badly"). The other mean-ing of *eningngaw* (something like: unfavourable wind conditions) is a homophone and quite accidental. To vomit is called *mwmwus*.

The fact that the Chuukese language possesses several words to refer to the intestinal tract, even though only very limited functions are attributed to it (eliminating excrements), may be due to its conspicuousness among the remaining bowels when slaughtering animals: *taanap, taranap, affanap* (big intestine); *taakúkkún, taangin, tarekis, affakis* (small intestine); *tarerúúrú, afférúúrú* (wrinkled intestine). Other meanings of the word *taar*: the sticky, spaghetti-like shapes extruded by sea cucumbers (*penichón, penipen*) when sensing danger; with newborn it is the umbilical cord, and finally the navel itself (in expressions like *nóón tarey* etc.; cf. 7.5).

The intestinal contents are called (besides *kiten mwéngé*) *páá, fenin*, and *chchefenin* (the latter two with 3rd pers. sg. suffix), less appetizing *pwise, omwu* or *ómwu; chche, peepeetiw*, and *fenifenitiw* mean to defecate. Diar-rhea: *feyisseni, chopwunó*. Flatulence: *sin, pwpwir*.

All the remaining organs with digestive and eliminatory functions are not connected to this by the islanders. When asked what purpose these or-gans could serve, informants react by shrugging it off and saying "*raa ánisi inisich*" (they help our body). Apparently they have their own designations because they are so noticeable in slaughtered animals on account of their size and shape:

The liver (*émmún*), the function of which is unclear.

The gallbladder (*etin, pwáánu, maras*); *etin* refers to its shape. With corn and bananas it means the set fruit that is still covered with husks or the leaf sheath; *pwáánu* and *maras*: bitter taste. By means of the gallblad-der contents evil spirit beings (*énúngngaw, soope*) can be kept at bay.

The pancreas (*epinget*); the word refers to the leaf sheath of the coconut in fruit (*etin núú*) that is used for fuel in its dried-up state. Other word forms: *epenget, epénget*, and *epúnget*.

The kidneys; the word for them is kept especially generic: *féwún* (or more exact: *féwún nóón inis*) means countless round things like fruit, seed etc. Sometimes the kidneys are called *féwún rúpwúng*, like the fruit of the Caroline ivory-nut palm (Coelococcus amicarum), whose seed is kidney-shaped.

The term for the urinary bladder is also rather generic: *neeniyen chuuchu* ("place of urine"), which also refers to the fly (of pants) at the corresponding body part. Urine (*chuuchu*), accumulated from unusable liq-uids (*chchénún* or *chchénúngngawen nóón inis*) that have been ingested with the food, are collected in the bladder. Any connection to the kidneys is obviously unknown. In addition, the following terms are used for urine: *siisi* (used with children); *nippiis* (with a stronger word taboo than *chuuchu*); *achchénún* (strong word taboo); *siir* (again a strong word taboo, on *Toon* a *kkapasen óttek, kkapasen neewuut* (cf. 7.9).

The bladder of slaughtered animals that is inflated for playing ball, is called *nikachopwuchopw* ("thing that makes a bursting noise"). The same is true of the air bladder of fish and of a marine creature that could not be identified.

7.17 Breathing, Heart and Circulatory System (*ngasangas*)

In scientific medicine it is, to say the least, uncommon to deal with breathing and the system of blood vessels in one and the same chapter, since breathing and the system of blood vessels are considered to be inde- pendent processes, each clearly allocated to only one bodily organ – the lungs or the heart. On the other hand, there is a rather close connection functionally between these two, because the lungs are quite an essential part of the blood vessel system and blood circulation. Not so, however, in the thinking of the islanders.

When the question is asked, where the breath of air is going when we inhale, the answer, without exception, is: into the heart, where it is said to get the blood moving. By way of contrast, no function at all is assigned to the lungs within the process of breathing.

This is all the more surprising when many islanders, while slaughtering pigs, discover that the respiratory tract (*tiyoren ngasangas*, "breath gul- let"), via the bronchial tubes, ends in the lobes of the lungs. The explana- tion for these peculiar notions about the nature of breathing is found in the meanings of the word designating the respiratory process (*ngasangas*).

Most often, *ngasangas* is used to describe the breathing of humans and animals. The terms for air and breathable air are not differentiated (*ásápwáán*). Breath itself is called *eniyenin ngasangas* ("the wafting of the breath"). The word *ásápwáán* is also the generic term for different kinds of wind: *mor* (light air movement); *echinifú* (strong wind); *ménúmén* (storm); *ewiniyár* (cyclone); etc.

There are terms for various kinds of breathing: *apwpwaapw*: the gasp- ing for breath by the dying; the same is said of the breathing movements of fish; *kkinó*: when someone has been diving for a long time and is now totally exhausted and panting for air, he or she is *kkinó*; the same goes for intense laughter, crying, or when someone drinks greedily and gulps for air in between; *mwi*: panting after strenuous running; *mwiyemi*: asthmatic breathing or wheezing due to a cold, perhaps accompanied by a rattling noise. This noise is called *ngáángá*. It also occurs when paper or fabric is being torn. *Ppeyis*, *eppeyis* means to stop breathing; in the figurative sense it refers to enduring pain or frustration, to grit one's teeth; *wusi* means blowing, e.g., to extinguish a flame or remove dust from some object.

For smoking cigarettes there is the peculiar linguistic form of *wún* or *wúnúmi suupwa* ("to drink tobacco"). Perhaps the islanders at first had come to know tobacco from earlier visitors to the islands as chewing tobacco. Everything that is liquified before it is swallowed (sugar, ice cream etc.) belongs conceptually to foods that are beverages. In this way, *wúnúmi suupwa* could originally have meant to chew ("drink") tobacco, which was then ultimately transferred to smoking tobacco. However, I regard this explanation as problematic, since it is also possible to say "inhaling tobacco (smoke)" (*ngaseri*).

The word *ngasangas* is expressed in a series of compound terms referring to kinds of breathing: *ngaseri* (to breathe something, e.g., *ngaseri suupwa*, to inhale tobacco smoke); *ngasaraanong* (to inhale something); *ngasaraawu* (to exhale something); *ngasanap* (to breathe deeply, to sigh); *ngasepwpwich* ("to breathe hotly," to fume with rage, to lie dying); *mwiyengas* (to breathe heavily, to wheeze).

The term *ngasangas* further describes the breathing of fish. They are said to breathe sea water (*iik raa ngaseri sáát*). It is generally believed that with them, too, the flow of the inhaled water goes into the heart. The function of the gills (*or, oren iik*) is not known.

Besides this, though, *ngasangas* denotes the motions, e.g. of jellyfish, by which they propel themselves in swimming, the lifting and lowering of the rib cage, and – here especially important – the movements of the beating heart. So then, the central semantic characteristic of the word form *ngasangas* is not really the inhaling and exhaling of air or water, but the rhythmic movements connected with it.

In certain situations the pulsating movement of the heart can also be called *pichipich*. More frequently, though, it has to do with smaller movements like the pulse beat that can be felt in the navel (*pichipichin* or *ngasangasen aporonong*) and on the fontanel of a baby (*pichipichin* or *ngasangasen móngósópwon*). It is, moreover, known that pulse and fontanel exactly follow the heart in their movements. Nevertheless, people do not feel for the pulse in order to determine whether a person is still alive, but they feel and listen around the cardiac region.

The characteristic of rhythmic motion is fundamental to the thought pattern which causes the islanders to make the assumption and the statement that breath goes into the heart. The rhythmic movements of the rib cage and the heart are both called *ngasangas*. In addition, the heart itself is given the analytical term *féwún ngasangas* ("round thing of breathing"). On the other hand, the lungs, because of their consistency, are called, like sponges (*farawa, ammat, sopwusopw*), by terms that show no liguistic or conceptual connection with the process of breathing. Besides, informants express their doubts whether a person really possesses them. This is only known for sure from slaughtered animals.

Likewise, no breathing significance is attributed to the diaphragm. It is simply called *refiref* (dividing wall). The fact that the abdominal wall bulges out when a person breathes in is caused by the heart being inflated by the inhaled air. To the question why, then, the heart keeps on beating even though a person stops breathing, and why the heart is beating faster (*púngúchechchech*) at a sudden fright, informants have no satisfactory answer.

Apart from the reduplicated word *ngasangas*, which essentially denotes the breathing process, there is the simple form *ngas* (free). A person is *ngas*, when coming out of unconsciousness, released from prison, finished with one's work, when a woman has accomplished giving birth to a child, when one has a feeling of relief after some psychological strain, etc. Similarly, this is ultimately true of the compound term *ngasónó*, meaning (in a figurative sense) to defecate or urinate (*imwen ngasónó*, lavatory, formerly also the brothels of the Japanese occupational forces).

7.18 Coughing (*faafa*)

Completely analogous to the islanders' notions of the breathing process, the heart is thought to contract jerkily and expel the inhaled air upwards. In doing so, the abdominal wall retracts.

There are the following designations for various kinds of coughing: *faafa*, general cough and generic term; *áchátá*, cough caused by choking on food or drink; in serious cases, parts of the food may have lodged in the heart; *moor*, a cough due to a cold; the slime-like secretion *rúngérúng* (sputum), expelled with this kind of cough, ultimately comes from the heart; *naaw, nnaaw*, cough caused particularly by a fishbone stuck in the throat.

7.19 The Blood (*chcha*) and Blood Vessels (*waan chcha*)

Blood is the property of all living beings, classifiable as *ménúmanaw* by the islanders. But there are a few exceptions, e.g. crabs, of whom it is said that they do not have any blood.

Blood (*chcha*) is generated by the heart, loss of blood replaced by it (including blood lost in the menstruation period). There is no concept of any blood circulation system, though it is known that blood does not flow freely in the body, but in blood vessels (*waan chcha*). The fact that blood is moving in the body is due to the "breathing motions" of the heart.

The European/Western concept of the blood vessel is rather close to that of the islanders. It is a *waa* (means of transport), which includes things like vehicles of all kinds, boats, cars, but also airplanes, toy kites, water skis, and especially larger vessels and pipes used for transporting liquids.

Larger and notably conspicuous blood vessels (*waanap*) and smaller ones (*waakis*) are differentiated. Arteries are called *waa pichipich* (pulsating vein) or *waa meefi* (touchable vein, artery).

This term is to some degree problematic. Elbert (1947:225, *wa mefi*) understands it to denote a nerve. Goodenough/Sugita, likewise contains a corresponding entry (1980:360, *waan meefi*). In the course of discussion about Elbert's *wa mefi* with my informants, I came to the conclusion that they possess no concept of nerves whatsoever. On the contrary, in slaughtered animals clearly noticeable, thicker strands of nerves are taken to be blood vessels because they are hollow. Moreover, sinews and tendons are also referred to as *waa*.

Life itself is considered to reside in the blood (*manaw aa nómw nóón chcha*), since loss of blood quickly leads to the death of a body. In case of injury to a larger vein it is said to be *ta* (broken) or *ssúk* (it flows, bleeds). Coagulated blood is *periper* (*periperin chcha*, scab, crusted blood). Other terms in this connection: *wúwa chcha*, I am bleeding ("I am blood"); *mii chcha pey*, my hand is bleeding; etc.

Chapter 8
The Extremities

8.1   The Concepts *paaw* and *peche*

The terms for the parts of arms (*paaw*) and legs (*peche*) contains quite a series of parallels, indicating that both are conceptually organized in the same manner. Both are subdivided in *seeng*, i.e. in segments similar to two nodes each on blades of bamboo and grasses. Knee and elbow are called correspondingly like these nodes (*pwásuk*), i.e. the extremities are organized conceptually like parts of plants. In using the term *seeng* it needs to be kept in mind that it possesses a kind of focus: If the compounds *seengen paaw* or *peche* are being used, the islanders primarily understand them to mean forearm or lower leg respectively.

It is striking how the Chuukese language deals with terms for hand and foot. Their functions are described linguistically as if they were activated by the arm or leg as an entity. Thus, nets are mended with the "arms," likewise washing, writing, waving, scratching, pointing, and even plucking a guitar string is done in this way, while one drinks, so to speak, out of the "hollow arm." The range of possibilities of expressing physical concepts differently is indicated by the expression *emén aa ochopwu péwún* (someone is clicking with his or her fingers). And even fingernails and toenails (*kkún paaw* or *peche*) are linguistically parts of arms and legs.

8.2   The Arm and Its Parts (*paaw*)

It starts at the shoulder (*afar*), which itself is not counted as part of the arm. It is subdivided by the joints (*neekupukup*) in the above mentioned *seeng* (upper arm, forearm) and the hand (*kumwuch*) with the fingers (*éwút*). The armpit (*fáán paaw*) is conceived as part of the arm. (Regarding the hair-growth here, cf. 7.8.).

For the upper arm there is also the expression *neewoon paaw*; *neewo* meaning origin, beginning, the thickest part of a tree trunk above the root, but also a person's ancestors and stories about them. Sometimes, *neepwopwun paaw* stands for the top part of the upper arm.

The muscular system of the arm, just as the musculature of the body as a whole, is less marked conceptually. The flexor muscle of the upper arm (*féwúwiichoon paaw*) and the calf muscle (*féwúwiichoon peche*) are the only ones bearing any designation as such. The rest of the bodily musculature is simply called flesh (*fituk*).

The term *féwúwiicho* is composed of the term for round things (*féwún* etc.) and *cho*, the term for the physical strength of humans and animals (water buffalo etc.).

The tendons (*sáán*, rope, cord), likewise, are terminologically hardly differentiated: On the arm and hand they are called *senin paaw*, on leg and foot *senin peche*, if they are not simply seen as *waa* (vessels; cf. 7.19).

The elbow (*pwásukun paaw*), in striking contrast, is linguistically different. First of all, it forms a joint (*neekupukupun paaw*), has a "heel," i.e. the point of the elbow (*epippinin paaw, epinipinin paaw*, more rarely also *kipwinin* or *neepwúkúwen paaw*). On the inside, it exhibits a fold (*nekkóónun* or *neemwanúún paaw*) and ultimately forms the crook of the arm (*neemóónun paaw*), a place that is especially important for carrying items.

All these terms are also found in other places: The terms for the point of the elbow are also used for the seeds (*kipwin*) of breadfruit and parts of plants (e.g., *pwúkúwen iich*, node of a bamboo); the crook of the arm can describe a valley (*neemóónun chuuk*) and similar depressions in the ground.

The arm (and the leg) is bent (*nnum, nnumaanong*, to put something in pleats or folds, to crease), and stretched (*áwenaawu, eyitiyewu*). With the term for the crease directly in the elbow (*neemwanú*), it must be noted that its actual conceptual focus is the hollow of the knee, and that the morpheme -*mwanú* may mean the linear measure of an "ell" (*emwanú*, one ell, etc.), even though this is measured with the outside of the forearm, whereas the location itself is on its inside. The linear measure *féchchuk* is the distance between the elbow of one of the bent arms (with the hand in front of the chest) and the outermost fingertip of the horizontally stretched out other arm.

The term "joint" has decidedly different nuances of meaning for the islanders than for Europeans. Joints, in the sense of *neekupukup* ("fracture sites"), are all those connections in the body that allow movement of both connected parts, i.e. the knee joint, joints of the hand, finger, foot, and toe, as well as the flexible locations in the neck and hips; but not the jaw, shoulder, and actual hip joints. These are not considered to be "fracture sites" (*neekupukup*), but "connector points" or "interstices" (*nekkamas, nekkochuun*), just like the sutures between individual skull bones, or the place where bivalvular shells are hinged together. Exactly formulated, this fact must be expressed as follows: Every place on the body, where two parts come together, may be called *nekkamas* or *nekkochuun*; however, *neekupukup* are only those that can be moved against each other. Misunderstandings may, of course, arise because, e.g., *neekupukupun paaw* can mean the elbow joint as well as wrist or carpal joint. Clarity is gained either by the context or by pointing out the appropriate joint referred to.

The actual hand is called *kumwuch*, i.e. everything situated between wrist and fingertips. This, however, does not at all correspond to what Europeans understand the term to mean. Activities of the hand are, as has been mentioned already, always activities of the entire arm. The designation *kumwuch* is being used in a much more limited way. It only refers to the bulge at the end of a body part described by *paaw*: the hoof of cattle and horses, distinctive paws, but also the hand clenched into a fist.

To clench one's hand into a fist is called *kumwuchuuw* or *kumwuchuffengenniiy paaw* (thus, actually, "to clench the arm into a fist"!).

For this reason, birds cannot possess any body parts which can be termed *kumwuch*. Their wings are called *paaw* (arms); the same goes for the pectoral and ventral fins of fish and the front legs of four-legged animals. In specific cases, bird wings used as means of transportation are called *péwúkáás*, *péwúkássin* (*áás*, to fly). With pieces of clothing, *paaw* or *péwún* means sleeve. It should be mentioned in this connection that there is a large bat species, the fruitbat or flying fox (*péwúte*), whose name derives from the fact that, in its resting position, it wraps its wings around its body.

In contrast, *kumwuch* is used as a measure of capacity: *ekumwuch rayis* (a handful of rice), etc.

There are no terms for the side and ball of the hand. The palm of the hand is called *nóón paaw* ("inside-ness of the arm"!), the back of the hand, *núkún paaw* ("outside-ness"); *wóón paaw* ("above-ness"), by contrast, is associated with the arm and means, among other things, the place where one wears a watch.

The creases and skin lines of the palm of the hand and on the fingers (*nikakkaanen nóón paaw*) conceptually form a connection with tracks left by animals: *nikakkaanen pwáápwá nóón ppi* (crawling tracks of a turtle in the sand). From this, *neeniyen enikakkaan* (ruler [for measuring]) and *iyé aa enikakkaana nóón neyi pwpwuk* (Who has scribbled [doodled] in my book?) have apparently been carried over.

It remains to be mentioned that the word *paaw* can also refer to food items taken along as provisions on sea voyages. The agreement is purely incidental.

8.3   The Fingers (*éwút*)

… are composed of segments (*seeng*) and nodes (*pwásuk*) just like arms and legs, in the same way bamboo and grass blades are described. However, these segments (of fingers and toes), partly have their own designation.

The first segment of a finger, counted from the root, has no proper term; the second one is called *móónap* (large segment); the third, *móósich* or *móóngin* (small segment). For the thumb, the *móónap* segment is missing.

The finger root bone and the first segment can indeed be called *neepwopwun*, like the start of the upper arm and thigh, but not *neewo*. The fingertip is called *mesan, mesen éwút* ("eye").

The fork between two fingers (or toes) is called *kkeyang, nekkeyang, nekkeyaang* or *nekkaang*, like branches and similar objects. In connection with this, there is the distance between thumb and little finger, the distance measure *eyang, rúwéyang* (one span, two spans, etc.).

The fingernail (and toenail) is called *kkú* or *wúúk*, often with the addition of the corresponding body part (most frequently with fingers, e.g., *kkún* or *wúkkún pey*, my fingernail). The lunula, the crescent-shaped, paler area at the root of the nail is called *maram* (moon). Here we have a parallel with the English derivation from Latin (little moon). Furthermore, *kkú* and *wúúk* refer to the claws of cats, dogs, and birds, and occasionally also to the hooves of cattle. Some verbs for activities executed with the aid of fingernails and claws are: *epwerika* (to scratch oneself), *nómwuti* (to scratch with the fingernails, scratching of a cat), *sinini* (pawing the ground).

By reason of their various properties and functions, the fingers are called by the following names: *éwútúnap*, ("big finger") thumb; used also for the claws of crabs, crayfish, and scorpions, the hindlegs of grasshoppers (*nifichimas*), and the spur on the legs of chickens etc.; *éwútúttiit*, index finger; contains one of numerous morphemes for the concept of "direction"; *éwútúnuuk*, middle finger; *nuuk* means middle (and abdomen); *éwútúsápwáák*, (the useless, clumsy finger); ring finger; *pwáák* means dexterous, useful; *éwútúkis, éwútúngin, éwútúsich*, little finger.

Conceptually, the fingers are afforded special significance. That is to say that the term *éwút* can be used to designate quite a number of things, which elsewhere cannot be classified as fingers: Toes of humans and animals, also of birds; the legs of insects, crayfish, crabs, and spiders; the legs of starfish, tentacles of jellyfish, rays of light sources, and the hands of time pieces and measuring instruments like a compass etc.

Of light sources with clearly visible rays, people say that they are *nikéwútút*. Tentacles are only called *éwút* when the animals in question are small. On larger animals, like an octopus (*nippach*), the tentacles are called *paaw* or *péwún* (arms).

8.4   Right- and Left-handedness

The Chuukese language contains numerous terms for spatial orientation (Caughey, 1977:13-15, et al.); so also with left and right. Here, the right side appears as the male side (*peniyemwáán, penimwáán*), the left as the female side (*peniyefeefin, penifeefin*). Moreover, there are the terms *peniyefich* (right; actually "the useful, dexterous side"), and *peniyemééng* (left; though the ending -*mééng* does not mean the opposite of -*fich*); *méng* (with short phonemic *é*) means soft (connection?).

Consequently, there are the terms *péwúmwáán* (male hand or arm) for the right hand or arm, and *péwúfeefin* (female hand or arm) for the left. Beyond this, and logically consistent, there are the terms *péwiifich* (right, useful, hand or arm) and *péwiimééng* (left hand or arm).

In designating right- and left-handedness, the Chuukese language goes a step further: Right-handedness presents itself as a positive characteristic, whereas left-handedness is linguistically identified as negative. When people acknowledge themselves to be right-handed, they say that they are *iifich* ("direction adept"), *iiwen* ("direction straight") or *iiyééch* ("direction good"). Left-handers, correspondingly, call themselves *iimééng* and *iingngaw* (*ngngaw*, bad).

In addition, there is always the possibility to say that one is right or left adept or inept (*tameyééch* or, respectively, *tamangngaw reen péwúmwáán*, or *péwúfeefin*). For the corresponding predisposition regarding the legs, there are no such terms.

8.5   The Leg (*peche, taang*) and Its Parts

Since the extremities display both in their terms and concepts multiple parallels, much of what refers to the leg has already been dealt with in the description of the arm and its parts. For this reason, it is often superfluous to enlarge on a term because it can be compared with the corresponding position on the arm.

Alongside the frequently used *peche* there is the synonym *taang* for the leg, which is also the term for the shaft of the outboard engine (*tangen mwesiin*) of a boat.

The upper thigh, in contrast to the upper arm, has its own term (*aféé*). It may, however, also be called *neewoon peche*; though *neepwopwun* is only its beginning in the groin region. It is not endued with a muscle: The musculature of the thigh is called *fituk* (flesh). While sitting, the top, where, e.g., a child may sit, is called *wóón aféén*, and underneath *fáán aféén*.

The femur or thighbone (*chúún aféé*) contains marrow (*fituken nóón chúú*, "flesh inside the bone"). Its porous inside is *aropwangapwang* or *fichepwangapwang*.

The knee and the elbow share the same term (*pwásuk*). Conceptually, though, the knee is afforded greater significance, i.e., to the hearer, *pwásuk* always brings to mind the image of the knee first. In the narrower sense, *pwásuk* only refers to the front part (also *neepwúkúwen pwásuk*) that is important for kneeling (*fótopwásuk, fótopwúkú*). The term *neepwásuk* is therefore also used for the knee as a whole.

The kneecap is called *kirupw* or *kirupwun pwásuk* (term for the coconut in its first stage of maturity) or *péér* (shell of the coconut).

Regarding the hollow of the knee (*neemwanúún pwásuk*), cf. the corresponding position at the elbow (8.2). The tendons in the hollow of the knee are called *senin neemwanú*, in contrast to *senin peche*, which primarily means the hamstring or Achilles tendon.

The lower leg (*seengen peche*) possesses the only designated muscle on the leg generally (*féwúwiichoon peche*, calf muscle), and is called *wuwóór* on the front segment between knee and ankle, corresponding to the tibia or shin, providing the bone belonging to it with its name (*chúún wuwóór*, lower leg bone).

The foot, like the hand, is conceptually rather insignificant. Everything done with it happens, as with the arm, in conjunction with the whole, i.e. with the leg. There is, however, the term *pachapach* for the foot, which can also refer to the hooves of cattle and horses. In linguistic terms, however, the parts of the foot are parts of the leg; thus, the sole of a foot (*fáán peche*, "below-ness" of the foot); the toes (*éwútún peche*, "foot fingers"); the toenails (*kkún* or *wúkkún peche*); and the ankle (*kipwinin* or *kirupwun peche*). There are no terms for the indentations around the ankle and bulges on the sole of the foot.

The term *iipw*, difficult to describe but needing to be mentioned here, does not refer to any body part; rather, it is used as a possessive classifier and numeral for everything belonging to the foot. Several expressions: *ipwan suus* (his shoes); *rasen iipw* (footprint); etc.

Some expressions for activities performed with the legs or feet: *fátán* (to walk [on foot]); with vehicles: to be in motion); *ssá* (race, run); *chchep* (to tread or kick with the foot), and *chepetek* (stumble); *pwu, pwuuri* (to stomp, to scrunch, to run over with a car, to infringe a law); *pwuuri núkún peche* (to twist or sprain one's foot); etc.

Chapter 9
The Skin

9.1 The Terms *siin* and *wúnúúch*

These two terms are obviously totally exchangeable. They refer to the skin of humans and animals, even in the processed form of leather (*sinin kkow*, cowhide). In the case of plants with a pronounced surface layer or bark, *siin* (*sinin*) would likewise be the term used.

9.2 Properties and Conditions of the Skin

It serves to envelop the body (*aa túkúmi inis*). The Chuukese language contains a whole series of terms for describing properties and conditions of the skin. In order to understand the following list it should be observed that, grammatically speaking, properties and things do not actually appear as separate categories of adjectives and nouns. The terms listed here in alphabetical order are, therefore, only inconsequential in their translations. For the islanders it is in principle irrelevant that, in English, "sweat" (*moonoon*) becomes something concrete by being also a noun, whereas "wrinkly" (*nnum*) is an adjective. For them, it is a matter of both, things and properties or conditions.

Properties and conditions of the skin in detail:

sór, sóór: mole or birthmark.

karakar: dry, chapped, depleted; flaps of skin that become detached after a sunburn.

kiin: irregularities on the skin, skin disease.

kinas: wound, injury, injured.

kúng: brown, skin color of the islanders.

mátáttár: rough, giving a sickly impression.

moonoon: sweat; it comes from inside the body, because the skin is *pwangapwang*, i.e., it has openings; sweat tastes salty (*kken*); *moonoon* refers also to the steaming up of glasses and bottles containing cold liquids; synonyms: *faak, chchénúfaak*.

móó, mómmóó: scar, scarred, pitted; *móón* or *neemóón iimw* also means the place where a house once stood; an adage (*mwiitun*) says: *aa mómmóó kinasen núkún, nge ese mómmóó kinaseyinón* (something like: exterior wounds heal, but injuries of the mind do not).

mwúúr: wart, verrucous.

nekenek: a (purposely) self-inflicted scar; an ornamental scar; islanders also do this to themselves as a sign of affection, e.g., touching one's arm with a burning cigarette (Gladwin/Sarason, 1953:11-12); synonyms: *pwét*.

nnót: puss, festering.

nnum: wrinkly, crinkly, withered; a frown line; *ttáránnumun nuuk* are fat folds ("spare tires" or "love handles") on the stomach; synonyms: *pwpwach*.

pwech, pwechepwech: white, skin color of most foreigners (*ree wóón*).

pwét: synonymous with *nekenek*; *niképwét* means ornamental or burn scar, but refers also to the suckers on the tentacles of an octopus.

pwónó: liver spot; the reduplication *pwónópwón* means crusty, scab, e.g., on a wound.

pwpwach: synonymous with *nnum*.

pwpwoy: blister on the skin, blistered; *pwpwoyichén* is a skin blister filled with liquid.

rawaraw: pimple, acne; sometimes also wart, verrucous.

ruupw: frambesia (yaws), leprosy, tinea.

chón: black, skin of islanders further darkened by the sun.

chchékún: callus, callous; horny layer of skin; crust, crusty; bread can be *chchékún*; synonym: *sinichchékún*.

téréwún: hair on the skin, hairy (though not referring to scalp or pubic hair; cf. 5.20); with birds: feather, feathered, plumage; with fish: scale, scaly; with sheep: wool; synonyms: *méréwún, wúnéwún; étéréwúna, éméréwúna* to pluck (chickens), to scale (fish).

ttir: pustules, slight swellings on the skin through insect bites, working with some kind of taro (*kká*); after sunburn, blisters filling with sweat under the peeling skin; *ttirifféw*: goose pimples, caused by cold, sudden fright, or excitement.

Chapter 10
Physical Sensations

10.1 The Term *meefiyen inis*

Islanders basically differentiate between feelings or emotions having their seat in the chest cavity (*meefiyen neenuuk* or *neetip*), and sensations of a purely physical nature (*meefiyen inis*). For the terms *neenuuk, neetip* and their corresponding sensations they have comprehensive and differing notions that are dealt with from chapter 15 on.

Since there does not exist any concept of a nervous system, it is assumed that bodily sensations are experienced at the locations where they arise. Thus, the feeling of hunger (*echik, fiyon*) has its seat in the stomach; thirst (*kaaka*) in the mouth and throat; and pain (*metek, ngiiyów, cheewuch*) at the indicated aching area of the body. In this connection, no function is ascribed to the brain (*tupwu*; cf. 5.21).

10.2 Bodily Sensations in Detail

The following list of sensations, thought to be physical by the islanders, contains quite a number not considered applicable by Europeans and, for that reason, they are difficult to explain. That *chika*, e.g. (see below), should be a bodily sensation is, at first sight, a bit unconvincing, and yet local informants describe it emphatically as *meefiyen inis*.

Bodily sensations not exclusively registered through the skin (in alphabetical order and not arranged according to pleasant, neutral, and unpleasant) are:

awaaw: the feeling of being in an uncomfortable position while sleeping, because of some annoying object under the sleeping mat (*kiyeki*); *awaaw* also means leaf-veins or the thicker cartilage of the outer ear.
áchikichik: the feeling of being able to stretch while squinting and tired, but with pleasure.
ef: the feeling of having a stiff neck.
eyiyemáámá, eyiyeménú, eyiyessumw, eyiyengngaw: the feeling of physical weakness, fatigue, listlessness.
eyiyonoon describes the condition of plants letting their leaves hang down for lack of water.
éwúmanaw: the opposite of *éwúmáámá*.
éwúmáámá: feeling of weakness, similar to *eyiyemáámá, eyiyessumw* etc.; opposite: *éwúmanaw, maamaaw* (see below).

sáchúng: feeling after physical over-exertion, backache.

fingngaw: feeling of having pulled a muscle, with men especially also in the genital area; synonym: *mwááng*.

fféw: feeling a chill; "cold" as an attribute of things, in contrast, is *patapat*; *ttirifféw*: goose pimples, hence also a sensation of the skin.

kkak: synonym for *chika* (see below).

maamaaw: feeling of well-being, of health.

máánééné: feeling of nausea or being seasick (literally liquid death).

ménú, ménúúnú: feeling of sleepiness; the opposite: *mwasenes* (see below), *sáfeen éménúúnú* ("falling-asleep medication") a narcotic or anesthetic.

mét: feeling of satiation.

mopw: feeling of suffocation.

mwasenes: feeling of being wide awake; the opposite: *ménú*.

mwáániyen: feeling of dizziness.

mwááng: synonym for *fingngaw* (see above).

mwet: feeling of having a cramp.

mwosset: appetite for some seafood, fish.

mwóón, mwóón mwéngé: appetite for something particular, even when one has already had sufficient to eat.

nikéchéwúnúún: a numb feeling in the feet, e.g., after sitting for a long time; the feeling one has after an injection of a local anesthetic, e.g. at the dentist's.

ngan, nganangan: feeling of orgasm.

ngnger: strong craving for something to eat, gluttony.

chika: the feeling one gets from a fishbone stuck in one's throat; synonym: *kkak*.

chikar: the feeling of being well again after some illness.

wun: a feeling of revulsion towards certain foods, e.g., if they are too greasy.

Body sensations that are essentially felt via the skin are:

áretong: searing pain; sunburn; pain caused by salt in a wound; *nim-maatong* is a kind of jellyfish whose touch produces this stinging pain; synonym: *wusuus*.

kéét: itchiness (pruritus); synonym: *pwerik*.

kkar: searing pain caused by touching a hot object.

pwerik: itchiness; *epwerika* to scratch oneself; synonym *kéét*.

rúkúfeen: feeling of being tickled; in addition also feelings of sexual arousal.

wusuus: synonym for *áretong* (see above).

Chapter 11
The Bones

11.1 The Term *chúú*

There is no word for "skeleton". The expression used is *chúún aramas* (human bones), *chúún iik* (fish bones) etc. The term *chúú* is also used for parts of the body made of cartilage, e.g. the larynx (*chúún tiyor*).

11.2 The Terms for Individual Bones

... are almost always compounds consisting of the term *chúú* or *chúún* and the word for the relevant part of the body, e.g. *chúún paaw* (arm bone), *chúún féét* (bone above the eye socket). The following bones or bone compounds are exceptions:

chúún kuwoku: sacrum.
chúún neemwakékké, chúún neeyafanamwakké: collar bone.
chúúnap: ("big bone") backbone; the vertebrae are called *seeng* or *kinikin* (sections) as with grass stalks, bamboo or millipedes; a tall person is *chúúnapattam*; with boats *chúúnap* refers to the keel.
chúún sepiyen wumwuné: the two shovel-like bones of the pelvis with the sockets for the hip joints; also *chúún wiina*; it is not clear how the expression *sepiyen wumwuné* (literally "bowl of the fish" *wumwuné*) is arrived at.
chúúráárá: (roughly: "bone with branches"): rib cage; rib, when classified as a long object, e.g. *efóch chúúráárá*.
In addition there are a number of compounds with the term *chúú* which to some extent are used figuratively:
kichúúchú: thin.
neechú: general term for the inside of a person; his character, his disposition.
chúúchú: bony; characteristic of a fish containing more bones than meat; *chúúchúúmwáán* and *chúúchúúfeefin* are the poles on the sail of an outrigger canoe.
chúúfén: ("bone with point or thorn") nail; *chúúfénúúw* to nail.
There are the following expressions for particular bone formations:
kirupw, kurupw, neekirupw, neekurupw: ball joints of the arms and legs; *kirupw* and *kurupw* refer to the first ripening stage of the coconut
neeyafféwún, neekinikin, nekkamas, nekkochuun, nekkóónun: seams between the skull bones; bone joints; places where the bone sockets are located; cf. also the section on the arm and its parts (8.2).

Chapter 12
Sleep

12.1 The Terms *annut* and *méwúr*

Sleep is purely a physical matter. It happens when the body has become tired (*ménú, ménúúnú*), not because the benevolent spirit double (*ngúnúyééch*, "soul") intends to leave the body. Nor is waking up evidence that it has returned to the body.

A dream (*ttan*) is first and foremost a physical event but is linked in special measure with the concepts of the person's spirit double. This is explained in detail in Part 3.

Chapter 13
Death

13.1 The Terms *má* and *máánó*

The extinguishing of physical life can have a great variety of causes. If someone dies before reaching old age, this is either because malevolent spirit beings have brought about his death, or because (under normal circumstances) benevolent spirit beings (ancestral spirits) had to punish him for some evil act, or because the mana of a spell had a fatal effect on him, or because his benevolent spirit double (*ngúnúyééch*) had abandoned him for an immoderately long time (cf. 26). If death does not occur for any of these reasons, then it is down to the weakness of old age.

A person is considered to be "for ever dead" (*máánó*), if no sign of breathing or activity of the heart can be perceived. His death is purely a physical phenomenon, for his benevolent spirit double is still with him even after the moment of death and will not abandon him straightaway.

The Chuukese language has two synonyms for the concept of "death": the more frequent *má* and the crude *pe*. The term *má* not only describes living beings whose breath and heartbeat has stopped, but also those who are unconscious through a blow on the head. It is completely probable that they will continue to live after this kind of "death". *Má* also refers to plants whose leaves droop, engines which stall under too great a load, flat batteries, burnt out light bulbs, lame or numb arms and legs, an impotent penis etc., i.e. anything which has lost its normally present efficiency of movement or function. If it is clear that a living being can no longer be brought back to life, then such a one is said to be *máánó* ("died away").

Chapter 14
Conclusions

14.1 The Place of the Body as a Concept in the Thinking of the Islanders

Speakers of the Chuukese language have about 1250 words at their disposal for exchanging a vast variety of information about the term body (*inis*), its anatomy and physiology. From the linguistic structure of this material, from its practical usage, and from the statements of indigenous informants about physiological processes, it was possible to acquire a variety of understandings about the conceptual basis of their notions of the body, insight into the cognitive fundamentals of those notions, and impressive examples of the relationship between language and reality.

The body, its limbs and other parts, are conceived as forming a hierarchical structure. They behave as parts of a whole, i.e. several limbs or parts of the body together form a larger limb or larger area over and above the smaller units, and several of these superordinate units form the next larger one etc. up to the body as a complete overall concept.

The vocabulary for the parts of the human body are carried over to those of animals in the same sense. Many parts of the human body are conceived as being organised in the same way as parts of plants (extremities, teeth, hair etc.)

There is a much greater variety of terms for the exterior of the body than for the interior. Notions of physiological processes (breathing, metabolism, pregnancy etc.) are correspondingly less distinct and in part deviate considerably from the biological reality.

14.2 Excursus: Language and Reality

While investigating the term *ngasangas* for both breathing and heartbeat my field research uncovered an unexpected and interesting aspect of the notions of the body. What struck me particularly was the fact that all the people I asked affirmed without exception that the breath went into the heart, and that, even when I clearly pointed out their own observations of the air passages of slaughtered pigs, this produced no doubt in their minds that their assertion was correct.

The record of the conversation with my informant Namiyo about this was particularly revealing. At first, like all the others who were asked, he affirmed that the breath went into the heart. When I asked him if, when slaughtering pigs, he had not noticed that the airways didn't go into the heart but into the lungs he interrupted me spontaneously, saying that he had often been puzzled by that. Perhaps it was different with pigs, he added, but he maintained that anyway, normally the breath goes into the heart.

This assertion is significant in a number of respects. Namiyo had discovered that the airways behaved differently from what he and everybody generally had accepted and thought to be correct. He is puzzled about it, but is also able to recognise and express the inherent contradiction. But what is noteworthy is the fact that he is clearly unable totally to accept the reality of something he has often observed, because the notions (the "theory") owned by him and all the others who were asked is at odds with the observed state of affairs.

The practical situation surely demands that many other islanders must have come across this contradiction before Namiyo did. What has enabled the "theory" to hold despite the clear contradiction with reality? It is very apparent that the language used has always obstructed any correction of the theory and is still obstructing it. The process of breathing and the beating of the heart are denoted by the same term *ngasangas*, and the heart is called *féwún ngasangas*. This connection induces the notion that the breath goes into the heart.

Of course a semantic constellation of this kind does not necessarily have to lead to such misunderstandings. The German word "Messe" can mean an industrial trade fair, a Roman Catholic service, and the dining room on a ship, but that does not have to result in problems of understanding. The Chuukese language also has plenty of words whereby very "diverse" objects can be denoted by one and the same term on the basis of a single common feature, without leading to confusion. However, the semantic properties of the word *ngasangas* do indeed lead to wrong conclusions which persistently defy correction, even in the face of the clearest of experiences of reality. Namiyo may well be puzzled that reality does not correspond to the "theory", but this does not lead him seriously to doubt the latter.

This results in a further problem. The way this (incorrect) "theory" has come about and is supported leads to distorted notions of other aspects of the process of breathing. If an islander is asked what sort of ailment (*semwmwen, samwaaw*) coughing (*faafa*) is, the prompt reply is always that it has to do with a disease of the heart (*semwmwenin féwún ngasangas*).

The linguistic properties of the word *ngasangas* provide impressive evidence for the truth of a (only occasionally challenged) principle of language relativity known as the Sapir-Whorf-hypothesis (Sapir-Whorf-thesis by now), which is of great significance both for linguistic and ethnological studies. It claims:

"that all observers are not led by the same physical evidence to the same picture of the universe unless their linguistic backgrounds are similar, or can in some way be calibrated" (Whorf in Carrol 2000:214), and "that users of markedly different grammars are pointed by their grammars toward different types of observations and different evaluations of externally similar acts of observation, and hence are not equivalent as observers but must arrive at somewhat different views of the world" (Whorf in Carroll 2000:221).

The way the linguistic properties associated with the term *ngasangas* make "different" processes appear "the same" or at least "similar" is illustrated in the following experiment: The two situations

   a) a jellyfish **swims**, and
   b) a person **breathes**
are rendered in Chuukese as
   a') *mii ngasangas emén nimmaatong*, and
   b') *mii ngasangas emén aramas*.

If the two sentences a) and b) are shown to ordinary unbiased speakers of English and they are asked if the two actions (in bold print) are in principle the same or different they answer as a rule that they are basically different. By contrast Chuuk Islanders assert that they are basically the same (a' and b').

That which the two events reveal to the naked eye must be the same to both an English observer and an islander. Nevertheless their understandings of the concept are very different. A speaker of English has learned to describe the two events with different terms. One might also say, in English it is (among other things) the observable differences between the two events which are retained in the language and are conceptually placed in the foreground. This is why (to an English person) they are viewed as basically different. By contrast an islander has learned to portray the two events using identical language terms. His language has made the observable commonalities between the two events the essential conceptual feature, i.e. the rhythmic movement characteristic of both. Hence he regards the two as basically similar concepts.

The consequences of the semantic properties of the word *ngasangas* are also noteworthy on account of an immediate connection with each other. It is true that using the same term for both breathing and heartbeat because of the common feature of rhythmic movement is in itself logical and coherent. But the theories it gives rise to (the breath going into the heart and coughing as a "disease of the heart") are conclusions which cannot be explained simply by the feature of rhythmic movement.

The following is also worth noting about this example: in investigations involving the relationship between language and reality it is always emphasised that the influence of linguistic structures on the speaker's perception of reality should be taken little account of, because first and foremost it is reality which has given form to human languages, because historically reality existed before language structures arose.

This argument does not hold here. On the contrary, the example of *ngasangas* clearly shows that it has led to ways of thinking which contradict reality and that it still maintains those ways. It is these ways of thinking which make the islanders reluctant to recognise the observed reality in this area of their perception.

As has already been pointed out, this only applies when speaking without much reflection. No one is so governed by the structures of his language that he is unable to learn consciously to grasp the realities of things, even when the structures of his language are against it. It has been obvious for centuries that the rhythm of day and night is due to the rotation of the earth. Nevertheless, in many European languages the event is expressed in terms of the rising and setting of the sun. This in no way prevents anyone from recognising what is really happening. This is also true for the islanders on Chuuk.

Despite this, the linguistic structure of *ngasangas* programmes the perception of reality in advance, resulting in false notions. A child surrounded by the language of his environment adopts its ways of thinking without the option of any alternative. In the case of *ngasangas* the child is governed first and foremost by these structures and so acquires a false interpretation of the reality to which this term is assigned. In this instance language is clearly the primary influence, the filter through which reality has necessarily to be perceived.

Part 3
The Concepts of Soul, Mind and Spirit

Chapter 15
Foundational Patterns of Meaning and Terms

15.1 Basic Assumptions

When a member of European or Western society observes islanders' moods and feelings being projected outwards for all to see, he is at first unable to discern any fundamental differences between their inner world and his own: it seems to be full of physical well-being, of unreserved joy and enthusiasm, spontaneity and exuberance. Anger and hatred on the other hand are subject to an effective psychological restraint mechanism; they are therefore not so quickly apparent (Gladwin/Sarason 1953:226-228, passim). Expressions of physical and inner pain are considered signs of immaturity and thus bring shame. A man wanting to save face needs to bear such feelings with outer calm. Only women and children are permitted to express them openly.

Behind the evident similarity which the Westerner reckons to note as he compares the various expressions of feelings among islanders and members of his society back home there are in fact enormous differences. Before long he realizes that islanders express their feelings in speech and writing more often and more spontaneously than he would. From the way that they speak about them much can be learned about the way they understand these responses. Language, grammar and vocabulary form a tapestry of patterns and categories in which, alongside all the other areas of their culture, their emotional world is organised by notions and terms; what emerges is akin to a chart.

Correspondence is a particularly rich source for understanding their realm of emotions. There is hardly a letter where the writer does not report in detail what sort of a mood (mostly an unpleasant experience) he is in at the time, and what has caused it. I have taken the majority of the following details of terminology from letters like these.

The Chuukese language and its structures are what indicate to any foreign visitor where the differences lie in the respective emotional worlds of the islanders and visitors; a completely different structure of terms and notions lies beneath the external similarities; for the islanders various notions belong to the category of the emotions which would not belong there to the Western way of thinking.

15.2 The Term *meefi*

Chuuk Islanders group physical and "emotional" feelings under the general heading *meefi*. By this term they mean all sentiments which they note change their physical and emotional make-up. However, there are a number of features distinguishing physical *meefi* from emotional.

Informants, when allotting these feelings to one group or the other, sometimes use the term *meefi* linked with *inis* and *neetip*. Physical ones are then *meefiyen inis*, „emotional" ones *meefiyen neetip*. These phrases do not generally feature in common use.

Apart from hunger (*echik*) and thirst (*kaaka*), physical *meefi* sensations include only those perceived by touch, pain and heat; this excludes sensations aroused by hearing, sight, smell and taste.

The workings of the sense organs are called respectively *rong, rongorong* (hearing), *kúna* (seeing), *tini* (smell) und *nneni* (taste). To describe the characteristics of things and their impact on the sense organs the islanders use a wide-ranging vocabulary allied to their concept of the body, which was treated in chapter 5 on the various organs (ear, eye, nose and mouth). A concept such as "the five senses" is quite alien to the islanders. The role of the nerve system and the brain in the arousal and perception of what they understand as physical and "emotional" feelings is equally unknown to them. The same is true for perceptions of hearing, eyesight, taste and smell. There is no term for nerves. The terms for brain and the spinal marrow (both called *tupwu*) are used only in relation to the production of sperm (especially the latter; see 5.21).

The significant difference between both types of feelings is that physical *meefi* arise at any part of the body and are sensed there; "emotional" *meefi*, on the other hand, are only sensed in one place.

15.3 The Place in the Body where "Emotional" *meefi* are Detected

If an islander is mentioning his feelings he occasionally gestures to a place around his upper abdomen roughly where the sternum ends. This is the place where the emotions of anger, anxiety and joy reside, i.e. where in the Western understanding emotional stirrings (*meefi*) are felt.

This place in the abdomen is not associated with a body organ like the heart, the liver or the stomach. Nor is it considered an organ. If one opened up the space, no organ would be visible. Like the Westerner's notion of soul, it has no features of an autonomous substantial nature. When death occurs it ceases to function just like the other body parts; from that moment it no longer exists. (For the functions of the heart, liver and stomach see chapter 7.15-19).

According to the circumstance and context, the place in the body where emotional *meefi* are detected is called *neenuuk*, *neetip* or *tipey* (here and subsequently always with 1st person sing. suffix). But it is not just the seat of emotions such as anger, anxiety and joy; islanders always point to this place when they refer to thinking and considering, remembering, intending, expressing the will and personal qualities. For a foreigner these notions and processes (apart from the will and personal qualities) fall into the realm of the "mental", the intellectual, and are reckoned to reside in the head. For the Chuuk Islanders these notions and processes are reckoned to be functions and conditions of that place in the body where the emotional *meefi* are instrinsically manifested.

It must be acknowledged that in some way the head (*mékúr*) is involved in these matters, too. Some informants suppose that thinking occurs in the head and not in the abdomen. Also, there are reliable idiomatic contexts where the head and thinking are equated directly (*iyeey mékúrey* = *iyeey ááy ekiyek*, this is my head = this is what I am thinking or intending). Sometimes even characteristics like self-control and its opposite occur linked with the head (*mékúréchchow* or *mékúráppán*). In such instances however there are almost always completely matching terms which establish a direct connection between the relevant concept and the abdomen (*mékúréchchow* = *tipeppós*, serene, calm, consistent). The fact that the terms linked linguistically with the head can only deal with those of minor significance is demonstrated by the following remarks: 1. The same informants for whom thinking takes place in the head deny the question of a link between thinking and the brain; 2. when the term for the head is mentioned in connection with thinking or character traits, simultaneously the term *neenuuk* or *neetip* appears; 3. the collection of contexts which form the basis for this study contains such a small number of statements with the term *mékúr* that this scarcely comes into the reckoning in comparison with the contexts with the term *neenuuk* or *neetip*.

At this point a terminological matter arises that must be resolved if we wish to avoid any confusion over terms and seek to conduct our argument clearly. From this point on in my study it is too impractical to repeat the words *neenuuk*, *neetip* and *tipey* with the explanation "place in the upper abdomen where emotional responses and intellectual processes are evident". The feasible options each have their particular drawback and are thus only partly satisfactory. Of the three designations from the islanders' usage one is possible. The perspectives driving this choice allow for no clear distinction between the possibilities. The term "soul" is too closely linked with the person and his substantiality, a link which is unfamiliar to the islanders. Even the use of inverted commas would not suffice to indicate the unwarranted differences from the connotations of "soul". To express *neenuuk* or *neetip* as the seat of the emotions, intellect and character the least bad translation seems to be the acronym **s.e.i.c.** or SEIC.

In what follows my intention is that SEIC should mean what the Chuuk Islanders understand by *neenuuk, neetip* and *tipey*, i.e. a place in the upper abdomen where processes in the non-physical realm of feelings and emotions, of the various expressions of will and the workings of the intellect are active and are recognised; a place where their make-up reveals traits, among others, of character and personality.

Defining SEIC thus results directly from the material forming the basis of my research. The islanders themselves are not in the position to give an explicit definition.

A person's SEIC in this sense contains all that flows from self-induced impetus relating to one's own will-power whether as animal, human being or spirit being. Plants and inanimate things do not possess a SEIC in the terms of *neenuuk, neetip* and *tipey*.

The islanders name the components of reality *mettóóch* or *meen,* and they group them conceptually into the following categories: inanimate things and plants (*irá*) are things in the narrowest sense: animals (*maan*) and people (*aramas*) make up the category of the *ménúmanaw* (living beings); spirit beings (*ngúún, énú*) are not *ménúmanaw,* although they are considered (like plants) living entities (*raa manaw* = they live).

Much that according to scientific criteria pertains to the animal kingdom is reckoned by islanders as plant life, especially regarding marine fauna. The islanders consider, for example, sea sponges (*farawa, ammat*) as plants because they are not capable of autonomous movement, and cannot therefore belong to the animal world.

As a criterion for the distinction between man and animal the SEIC is particularly significant. People are different from animals by their greater intelligence (*tipáchchem*), through having a spiritual-emotional-intellectual quality considered as among the attributes of the SEIC.

15.4 The Terms *neenuuk, neetip* and *tipey*, and Their Meanings

These three names that the islanders give to the SEIC in various language contexts mean the same despite their formal distinctiveness, but are each unique in having a particular semantic feature emphasising one aspect of the SEIC more than the others. Among my collection of language samples the word form *neetip* is the most frequent. In most contexts the three terms are interchangeable without the phrase losing its meaning. Where they cannot be swapped the issue is generally one of linguistic convention, rather than semantics.

The term *neenuuk* labels the SEIC as "a place in the abdomen, in the middle"; this raises the question of its belonging to the physical realm. The initial syllable *nee-* is a prefix with a host of uses. It alters the names of things such that they appear to be places in time and space. *Nuuk* means the stomach from the ribs down. When preceded by *nóón* its meaning refers to the lower intestines, and sometimes the whole stomach cavity (*nóón nuuk*). The word "middle" is apparent in compounds such as *nuukanap* (waistline; centre of a circle), *nuukanapen mataw* (in mid-ocean) and *nuukenipwin* (midnight).

The word *neetip* denotes that the SEIC is the seat of all emotional and mental phenomena embraced by the word *tiip* (meaning roughly: psychological make-up, that which constitutes the SEIC). Furthermore the word *neetip* emphasises more strongly that the SEIC is the starting point for intentions of the will and of ambition.

The morpheme *-tip* is a variant of *tiip*, which is the umbrella-term for all processes and qualities of the SEIC, a phenomenon that we shall investigate; *neetip* means roughly "location of SEIC dispositions".

Within the designation *tipey* (*tipomw* etc.) for the SEIC the most prominent place is taken by the SEIC's intentional aspect, of the will and of ambition. The word is often heard in conversation, even when reference is to character traits or to somebody's nature or behaviour. This meaning is not so pronounced in the words *neenuuk* and *neetip*.

In rare circumstances the term for the upper abdomen (*fáán mwári*) can refer to the SEIC itself. *Fáán mwári* is the word for the place at the front of the body under which the SEIC is reckoned to be housed. This term is used when people talk about unpleasant emotions (*meefi*): *nupwen emén aa ngeniyey óóch kkapas ámáyirú ika weyires, e chop* (*nnúch*) *me fáán mwári ewe kkapas* (if somebody says something surprising or unpleasant to me the message causes a twitch in my upper abdomen, it is an unpleasant nagging feeling).

The fact that the islanders don't make any fundamental distinction between an "emotional" (in the Western sense) realm as the hub of their feelings and a "mental" one as the centre of intellect had been evident in the description of notions of the subordinate or unknown role of the head and the brain in the act of thinking, remembering, etc. (cf. 5.21). The equating of "mind-intellect" and "heart-emotions" is highlighted by the fact that *neenuuk, neetip* and *tipey* (abbreviated artificially to SEIC, as I have said already) can embrace the European and Western concepts such as heart, state of mind, personality, nature, character, ego, self, attitude, mindset, intention, will, opinion, thought, conscience and many other notions blending into one another. The most significant contextual examples are as follows:

SEIC means heart and state of mind, in so far as these imply the seat of a person's will and emotions: *aa fééri reen wunusen neenuukan* (he does it wholeheartedly); *aa fesir neenuukan* (he has a gentle SEIC, he is gentle and kind by nature).

Descriptions of personality traits, of personal manner and character occur when it is said of somebody that he has the SEIC of a specific age group or of a spirit being: *aa tipen semiriit* (he has the SEIC of a child, is childlike, is somewhat wayward); *aa tipen énúwén* (he has the SEIC of an adolescent, he is easily distracted, is not yet reliable); *aa tipen mwáán* (he has the SEIC of a grown man, is courageous, decisive, is a strong personality). Striking by their descriptions are qualities such as deviousness, meanness and negligence in the phrase applied to a woman *aa tipen soope* (she has the SEIC of an evil spirit being, is a callous mother).

The three terms for the SEIC can stand for a person's ego or self: *wúwaa pwaapwa = neetipey aa pwaapwa* (I am cheerful); *sipwe raweey tipan* (let us trick him, deceive him); *wúpwe amonnáátá neetipey ngeni ena ráán* (I shall prepare myself for that day); *aa neenuukeni neenuuken saman* (he is like his father).

Rather similarly, SEIC stands for a person's attitude and mentality *iiy emén sowufénúúfaan me neenuukan* (he has the SEIC of a secular person, thinks like a worldly person and has a secular frame of mind).

There are numerous examples where SEIC as a term stands for intentions and concepts allied to the realm of the will and its expression. Examples for intention, plan, wish: *aa mwechen sineey neetipey* (he wants to know my SEIC, wants to find out my intentions, what I have in mind); *aa móónó neetipan* (his SEIC has come to nothing, he has given up his plan); *wúwaa tipen feyinnó* (I am emotionally inclined to go, I intend going); *tipeni mooni* (out to get the money); *epwe ánneta nóón tipan* (he ought to demonstrate the inner workings of his SEIC, ought to declare what he is intending); *aa wor tipan ngeni* (he has a SEIC against him/her, has something against him/her); *wúpwe pwááráátá tipey* (I wish to disclose my SEIC, want to express my wish). Examples of resolving and deciding: *aa apasa pwúngún neetipan* (he speaks out the resolve of his SEIC, says what he has decided); *wúwaa finááátá neetipey* (I have chosen my SEIC, I have decided). An example of will, intention and striving for: *aa fééri, aa épwénúwátá neetipey* (he does/accomplishes my SEIC, does what I intend, carries out my will). An example for spontaneousness and openness: *wúwaa wúrenikemi fáán neetipey* (I tell you honestly, openly, freely). An example of approval, approbation: *aa fééri fáán tipen saman* (he is doing it under his father's SEIC, with his approval).

Less numerous are the contexts where SEIC represents items from the realm of the intellect. Examples of opinion and thought: *tittipey pwe kepwe feyitto ikánááy* (I have been thinking the whole time that you are coming today); *aa siwiniiy neetipan* (he has altered his SEIC, his opinion).

SEIC signals to somebody whether he is acting in accordance with ethical norms or against them. It is his conscience. When somebody has a bad conscience the phrase is *aa weyires neetipan* (his SEIC is unpleasant, difficult to tolerate).

In special circumstances the islanders use the form *neetip* as a euphemism for parts of the body which are under sexual taboo and must not be called by their proper name. So pains caused by indigestion and constipation are called *máán neetip* (death or paralysis…) which need treating by *ráwáán neetip* (massage) (Mahony 1970:208); furthermore *neetip* euphemistically refers to the uterus and to the female sex organs in general.

15.5. The Inside and Outside of the Seat of the Emotions, Intellect and Character

The SEIC does not have a prescribed form. Some processes, however, at work within its realm are linked with locational conceptions of what is internal and external (*nóón, núkún neetip*). Thoughts and feelings, i.e. *meefi*, arise "in" the SEIC. Memories, everything that is heart-warming, as well as resentments towards a person are "brought in" (*emwmweni nóón*) and "stored in it" (*isóni, ónómwu nóón neetip)* either over the long term or to be duly sifted and settled. Thoughts can preoccupy one so totally that they "cannot emerge from one's SEIC, in other words, they never intend going out of mind (*resapw toowu me neetipan*).

The grammatical structure of the language of Chuuk is such that the terms for the inside (*nóón*) and the outside (*núkún*) (including all the various terms denoting place in these contexts) appear not only as prepositions and adverbs, but as nouns too. The substantives *nóón* and *núkún* in this respect relate the concepts of inside and outside to tangible characteristics of SEIC.

Chapter 16
Characteristics of the Seat of the Emotions, Intellect and Character (SEIC)

16.1 Assumptions

In the previous chapter the SEIC was defined as a place in the upper abdominal cavity where the processes of the immaterial world of feelings, emotions, expressions of intention, and intellectual activity occur and impinge on the consciousness; their defining features emerge as character and personality traits.

Summarized like this, the characteristics of the SEIC comprise a host of individual notions from the realms of the emotion, intellect and character coming together to form a mosaic.

What the Chuuk Islanders understand as SEIC characteristics needs to be seen as allied to the basic notions they have of the nature of things. Plenty of evidence indicates that a specific quality of a thing means not its attribute but an overall condition of whatever it is, manifesting one of the various ways of its being. An example: the word *chcha* signifies blood. If it is said of somebody that his hand is *chcha*, that means that it is bleeding or bloody. The same word stands for an actual autonomous term (blood), as well as the quality of something (bloody), such that the thing and its characteristic are one and the same (the hand is *chcha*). The characteristic occurs here not as an attribute but as an overall condition of that defined object's being.

The same is true for the SEIC. The word *soong* means anger. If a person feels anger one can either say *aa wor aan soong* (he possesses anger) *neetipan aa soong* (his SEIC is angry), or *aa soong* (he is angry). The same term *soong* means by itself the term anger, the characteristic of a person's SEIC when he is in such a mood, and finally the nature of the person himself. This is the case also with personality traits such as courage (*pwara*), mental capacities like intelligence (*tipáchchem*), etc.

There is no doubt that the SEIC also resembles just such a phenomenon like this, with its permanent features and its changing ones. Understood in these terms, the processes and capabilities from the emotional, intellectual and character realm exhibit the overall conditions of what the islanders mean by the SEIC. These all belong to an overarching concept, which they term *tiip*.

16.2 The Term *tiip*

The fact that all the processes and capabilities are brought under one umbrella term in the realm of the emotional, the intellectual and of the character leads to the conclusion that for the islanders there is not much fundamental difference in concept between emotions such as joy and fear, mental phenomena such as thoughts and memories, and eventually also characteristics such as self-control and patience. **Joy (*pwaapwa*), fear (*niwokkus*), a thought (*ekiyek*), reason (*miriit*) or humility (*mósónósón*) are all defined as types of *tiip*.**

For the foreigner from a European and Western society it is unusual and difficult to comprehend when terms such as joy and reason co-exist under one heading. Because he classifies these terms under the distinct headings "soul" and "mind", there is (for example in German) no word embracing both with the same brevity and clarity as the term *tiip*. Yet to avoid overloading the import of the meaning with words from the Chuukese language I am using as a substitute for the term *tiip* the expression "disposition of the seat of the emotions, of the intellect and of character" abbreviated to **disposition of the SEIC**, and I mean by this term all the processes and aptitudes from the realm of the emotional, the intellect and the character which the islanders term *tiip* and which include the components of the SEIC.

This word *tiip* is the so-called "independent form" of *tipey, tipomw* etc. (Dyen 1965:11, §70), of word forms therefore which are used in describing SEIC; *tiip* itself can never mean the SEIC, only its component qualities.

16.3 The Terminology for Dispositions of the SEIC and Their Structure

The overriding term for all the types of SEIC dispositions, *tiip,* heads a rich word field containing the lexical items for dispositions arranged conceptually. From their relationships a number of important conclusions can be drawn relating to the corresponding general term"seat of the emotions, of the intellect and character".

Collecting the lexical items for the emotional and mental dispositions highlights the important role of the term *tiip*. When identifying an unfamiliar term, a researcher can use *tiip* to decide easily whether he is dealing with a SEIC disposition or not. The lexical item is a member of the word field if his informant answers the following question in the affirmative: is the item a kind of (*eew sókkun*) *tiip*?

Dispositions within the SEIC belong to two distinct categories. The islanders distinguish *tipeyééch* (good dispositions), neutral (no name) and *tipangngaw* (bad dispositions). Following this, *pwaapwa* (joy), *tipáchchem* (intelligence) and *tipemecheres* (benevolence) count as good, but *niwokkus* (fear), *tiparoch* (stupidity) and *tipeweyires* (obstinacy) as bad SEIC dispositions. The remaining ones that are neutral are processes of the mind such as *ekiyek* (thinking), *chchemeni* (remembering), *weewe* (understanding) and some others. This model results in three concept groups, which subdivide into two or three levels of SEIC dispositions:

tiip		
tipeyééch		*tipangngaw*
good SEIC dispositions	neutral value SEIC dispositions	bad SEIC dispositions

Table 2

The structuring of these terms in Table 2 which give the three dispositions results in rather insignificant perspectives as regards clarifying the SEIC terminology as the islanders understand it. The second way of classifying the SEIC dispositions is of quite a different kind.

In addition to the above-mentioned categories good, neutral and bad, each disposition has a further feature, the fact that its occurrence is either linked with a SEIC movement (*mwékútúkút*) or not. Those which are linked with a SEIC movement are only occasionally present, and they are called *meefi* (*meefiyen neetip*), the others are reckoned to be largely available continuously and are unmarked on this level; they are therefore directly categorized under the generic term *tiip*.

According to this principle characteristics and intellectual aptitudes are considered for the most part long-term SEIC dispositions; emotions and mental processes are by contrast only occasionally evidently linked with a movement of the SEIC (*meefi*).

The second far more complex model, shown in Table 3, groups the dispositions of the SEIC into two rather large concept groups, in contrast to the first; but they are split into five or six levels, demonstrating for the term *meefi* a notably hierarchical structuring. This second structure of the *tiip* word field is the more important one for the Chuuk Islanders; perspectives emerge here that allow useful conclusions to be drawn for their concept of SEIC.

It is worth noting that neither of the two models results in any way to groupings reflecting the European and Western distinction of aptitudes and processes of the intellect, character traits and emotions.

"Character traits", i.e. dispositions of the SEIC which are not a type of meefi and, apart from being divided into good, value-neutral and bad, display no particular structure."

tiip							
mecheres				**meefi**			
pwaapwa					**weyires**		
				chchow	**mwechen**	**neetipeta**	**niwokkus**
chchengen	achoocho	áreere	achaanú	aapaap	ánáán	chéééné	éwüirek
meseyik	chá	(che)chchemeni	chipwang	fén	mááyicha	chchúng	kker
mwânek	chip	eküyek	chchimw	fitikopwut	mwecheniya	énúükü	máyirú
	chchen	eneefiina	chchopwa	kkowumw	mwecheyisow	mangiringir	nisiin
	efich	éwüchcheyáani	ekütekit	mángngaw	mwóón	mitingngaw	niweniw
	epinükünük	fini	engnginó	ningeringer	nóchcheey	mü	piireyir
	ing	ffén	ku	nónówó	nómwunaawit	mwún	rúng
	kinammwe	memmeef	mennin	opwut	sóssót	nameni	rúúké
	kinissow	ménnüükü	mokunón	soong	ssiyé	nichippúng	
	kirises	méngüüw	mwaramwar		tawaat	niyamaam	
	menemen	namanam tekiya	nikééké			nóniinen	
	mwaar	nenneyiruk	nuukeni			pwpwos	
	ngon	nónnón	nükürar			ósoonapa	
	pwara	nükünük	ósópwiisek			siit	
		óóroora	riyafféw				
		piit	ruk				
		ppiiy	rüwérü				
		sinneni	sáaw				
		weewe	tipemwaramwar				
			ttong				
			wosukosuk				
			wosupwpwang				

Table 3: The structure of the terminology for dispositions of the seat of emotions, of the intellect and character (SEIC)

Chapter 17
Dispositions of the SEIC Which are not Types of *meefi* (Capacities of the Intellect and Characteristics)

17.1 Presuppositions

What is typical for this sub-group of the SEIC dispositions is the fact that as a rule they are continuously available or at least available over longish periods; this is true irrespective of whether the SEIC is in motion or not. Overwhelmingly the dispositions relate to intellectual aptitude and to character traits for which indeed the characteristic applies of being constantly present and involved.

The dispositions of this sub-group have predominantly metaphorical designations, whose concrete basic meanings are the features of material things, such as shape, size, hardness, etc. The manifold aspects of the emotional, of the intellect and character (by nature abstract and not easily made graphic) are made concrete and vivid in these metaphorical depictions.

As I have said, SEIC dispositions can be arranged into categories: good (*tipeyééch*), value neutral and bad (*tipangngaw*). This arrangement is clearly evident in the structure of this sub-group (and the value neutral carries hardly any weight because instances of it are rare. The vocabulary for the dispositions of SEIC mostly occurs as contrasting pairs. The SEIC is, for example sharp (*kken*) and blunt (*kkopw*), bright (*saram*) and dark (*roch*), straight (*wenechchar*) and crooked *(tipepwpwór)*.

Here a number of peculiarities come to light. Qualities which in their concrete meaning form genuine opposites do not necessarily have in their metaphorical meaning these counterpart equivalent contrasting dispositions of SEIC. Furthermore, it often occurs that two contrasting pairs of terms both mean something in the concrete realm, but in the emotional/mental realm only one of them does. In the contrasting pair short/long only the "short SEIC" has a metaphorical sense, namely a lack of persistence (*tipemwoch)*, but there is no "long SEIC". Some attributes such as high and low tolerance of frustration can be expressed metaphorically in many ways. The disposition "serenity" sometimes rests on a tall (*wátte*), and sometimes on a deep (*ónónnón*) SEIC.

17.2 The Metaphorical Labels Attaching to the Dispositions of This Group in Detail

The following grouping of SEIC dispositions of this kind into five groups – metaphors of shape, quality, rest, movement, the human body and others – is not common among the islanders and serves only to make the portrayal clear. Even the sequencing is more or less arbitrary, because it is without significance. In the contrasting pairs good SEIC disposition is placed first.

1. Metaphors of Shape:

The SEIC is large (*wátte, pérémmóng, tipemmóng, nuukómmóng*): one of the commonest paraphrases for positive human characteristics and intellectual competencies such as a high degree of tolerance of frustration, patience, self-control, stamina, reason, understanding, insight and lucidity in thinking. Adults have a large SEIC.

A rather different meaning pertains to the term *tipemmóng*. A SEIC like this is beyond measure in its wishes, full of craving and (sexual) lust (*tipemmóng wóón feefin*). *Nuukómmóng* on the other hand connotes positive qualities such as acute consideration for something, interest and involvement in the fortune of people closest to one, especially the feeling of responsibility a father has for the good of his family.

The SEIC is small (*kúkkún, tipekúkkún, móósich, péréngngaw*): the smallness of the SEIC is evident in all the negative characteristics and intellectual competencies being expressed as small: minimal degree of tolerance of frustration, impatience, insufficient degree of self-control, cowardice, a lack of stamina, a lack of reason, lack of wisdom, and much else. Children and adults are *tipekúkkún*. As persons get older their SEIC increases in size and the negative qualities turn into good qualities (see 20.5).

The SEIC is deep (*ónónnón*): *ónónnón* is the word for when water is very deep. Similar to a large SEIC, a deep SEIC is characterised by a high degree of tolerance of frustration. The person concerned shows emotional stability, self-control, patience, a lack of fear and panic, and a pronounced calm about losing face (see the metaphors relating to calm and passivity, *tipeppós*).

The SEIC is shallow (*petepeet*): this is the term describing the nature of shallow reef water of near the shore. A shallow SEIC is the exact contrast in all respects of a deep SEIC, describing a person with a low tolerance threshold, of unstable emotions. Somebody with a flat SEIC easily bursts into tears, gets angry easily and doesn't enjoy fun.

These two metaphors (*ónónnón* and *petepeet*) link the SEIC with how the sea behaves. In a storm the ocean deep is much less turbulent and less dangerous for boats than the reef shallows. The greater and lesser depths of the SEIC – like its large and small size – equate to an important distinction between adults and children.

In other parlance the SEIC is flat and even (*chééché*): the broadness of the SEIC akin to an expanse of cloth or to a featureless landscape betokens openness and wholehearted truthfulness. A person with a SEIC like this is happy to disclose his intentions and is transparent about how he is feeling (*achééchéé ngeni emén tipan*). People always know "where they stand with him".

The SEIC is high (*tipetekiya*), and pointing upwards (*tipetá*): both expressions refer to a presumptuous person's intentions, expectations and attitudes which do not match reality, namely false ambition and the attempt to create a reputation for oneself. In this meaning the phrase *namanam tekiya* must be used. It includes personality traits such as pride, presumption, arrogance and insolence. It will be mentioned later in the context of feelings of scorn; its opposites are *tipefesir, tipetekisón, mósónósón*.

A SEIC turned upwards (*tipátáwiniyaas*) is used in contexts of false opinions of self, and a lack of modesty with regard to one's own prospects. The usage of this metaphor is evidently restricted to cases where an ugly young man is wooing a particularly pretty girl where the likelihood of winning her as his bride is slight.

The SEIC is low (*tipetekisón*): *tekisón* means the opposite of *tekiya* (the height of trees, houses and mountains). A person who is *tipetekisón* behaves modestly; does not have overreaching expectations nor a false opinion of self; is the epitome of what ideally the Chuuk Islanders understand by a humble person.

The SEIC is short (*tipemwoch*): someone with a short SEIC does not have much staying power and avoids implementing decisions. As mentioned before, there is no corresponding long SEIC. Instead there are other comparisons. Tenacity requires a sharp SEIC (*tipekken*). The word *nikiitú* for tenacity is not metaphorical.

The SEIC is straight (*wenechchar*): honesty, candour; similar in meaning to the previous *chééché*; a person with a straight SEIC, speaking his mind without deceit, and above all telling the truth. The motives underlying his actions are clear and when he promotes a cause he sees it through.

The SEIC is crooked (*tipepwpwór*): marked by dishonesty, deceit, deviousness and doublespeak; in every way the opposite of the previous *wenechchar*. Similar psychic dispositions arise when the SEIC is *rikirik*, not moving in its right course (see below on metaphors of movement).

The SEIC is open (*ssuuk*): attentiveness, involvement, passionate involvement in a person or cause; the concept even embraces feelings of attraction (see below on metaphors of the human body and 20.5)

The SEIC is closed: expressions of locking (*épúngóónó*) und blocking (*pineey*), together with words evoking lack of attention and interest, even uninvolvement and aversion.

Linked with notions of openness and exclusion are occasional references to the door and window of the SEIC (*asamen neenuuk*). Closure and openness mark important stages of the SEIC's development (20.5).

The SEIC is able to identify (*weewe*): this notion is especially hard to understand and explain; the person is in full possession of his faculties of understanding and appreciating. With new-born babies the SEIC is not yet *weewe* but grows into this disposition. The following is seemingly fundamental: understanding and realising are only possible for a person if his or her SEIC is able to identify with whatever needs grasping and realising (*aa weewe reen eey mettóóch*, it becomes identical through this = understands this). We shall return to closer scrutiny of *weewe* in relation to a SEIC when its dispositions of feelings and emotions are not always evident (see 20.5: *weewe*, language acquisition and education).

The SEIC is united (*tipeyeew*): agreement and harmony; a person espousing a cause and giving approval to it declares he is *tipeyeew* (*ngeni*); people who have achieved an agreement have united their SEIC (*aa chu neetipeer*).

The SEIC is divided: the above term *tipeyeew* has several opposites. Where people hold a variety of opinions, they are *tipefeseen*. The meaning includes everything from their holding a range of views to declaring dissent.

A further opposite to *tipeyeew* is *tipeyáyey*, meaning a SEIC tuned to a different wave-length than other people's and insistent on opposing their wave-length.

The SEIC is divided (*kinikin, tipekinikin*): someone is biased, in that he supports one view and refuses to countenance another, even though it would be appropriate to consider each in turn; sometimes *tipekinikin* refers to a person trying to "serve two masters".

The SEIC is distant (*toowaaw*): also somewhat of a contrast to *tipeyeew*; a person whose SEIC is *toowaaw* does not agree with a decision, or is quarrelsome.

The SEIC is contrary (*sókkofeseen*): possessing a different kind of SEIC, namely holding variant and contrary opinions (*aa sókkofeseen tipey me tipan*).

The SEIC is confused (*fitikooko, nikoppin*): a person in a muddle, not knowing how to help themselves when something unforeseen occurs or where speed is of the essence; panic; specifically *fitikooko* means strife, violent disagreement. More rarely, the SEIC's disposition is likened to fishing lines being in a hopeless tangle (*nikoppin*).

2. Metaphors of Quality:

The SEIC is good or fine (*tipeyééch, neenuukééch, neetipééch*): with its opposite one of the most all-purpose terms in the storehouse of SEIC dispositions. It means firstly all the intellect's positive qualities and competences, all pleasant emotions and states of comfort. In a specific case *tipeyééch* (the other two terms are rarer) refers to a friendly attitude towards others: benevolence, insight, attentiveness and an understanding nature.

This positive sense is however only conveyed if *-ééch* is added as a suffix. Placed as a prefix to a substantive it means Schadenfreude, delight at somebody's misfortune (*échchún, fichin tipei pwe aa feyiyangngaw*, serves him right that he has come to grief).

The word *tipeyééch* can be used of the quality that makes certain types of wood easy to work with (*kurukur aa tipeyééch*). There is no certain link with contexts involving emotions (*tiperi maay*, to cut pieces of breadfruit).

The SEIC is bad or ugly (*tipangngaw, neetipangngaw*): The opposite of *tipeyééch*: all negative characteristics and aspects of the intellect: all unpleasant feelings and dispositions of mind and spirit; in particular an unfriendly attitude towards one's fellows, such as hostile intentions, constant peevishness and irritability; akin to a child's inconsolable nature.

With age people become more *tipangngaw*. The deterioration of the SEIC is evident in that older people think less quickly, are unable to learn new things, find it harder to tolerate mental and emotional pressures, and they get angrier and easily lose their poise (20.5).

Neetipangngaw on the other hand signifies as a rule sorrow, disappointment, depression. Only seldom does the word imply that the SEIC has a reduced level of tolerance of frustration and a tendency towards acts of aggression.

The suffixes *-ééch* and *-ngngaw* are much more wide-ranging in their meaning than good and bad or fine and ugly. They embrace the quite general concept of high or low quality, of usefulness or uselessness. They are not restricted to the realm of aesthetics.

The SEIC is light (*tipeppán, pwpwas*): *ppán* are objects which do not sink in water. Having a SEIC like this means – especially in arguments – having a low tolerance of frustration, e.g. the person cannot help voicing his opinion where caution would be necessary, or he is short-tempered. As a rule children are *tipeppán*. Similar SEIC dispositions occur if it is small or lacking depth.

In this connection the metaphor involves the head: *mékúráppán* means the same as *tipeppán* (*mékúr*, head).

Feelings such as relief following reconciliation, or of being consoled after a painful loss are combined with a further image of lightness and ease: the SEIC is *pwpwas* (dry, wispy, light).

The SEIC is sharp, (*kken, tipekken, tinikken*): involvement, especially in carrying out a plan; commitment to a cause, being motivated, care, endeavour and perseverance (*tinikken*), based on a personal interest; not, however, astuteness (*tipáchchem*); workhorses and the like, and spiders, have similar kinds of SEIC.

The SEIC is blunt (*kkopw, tipekkopw, tinikkopw*): conveys a lack of involvement, a short attention-span, a lack of enthusiasm, and laziness; but not stupidity or slow-wittedness (*tiparoch*).

In non-metaphorical terms, *kken* and *kkopw* are features of sharp-edged tools and blunt ones respectively; *kken* has the additional meaning of tasting of salt or containing salt.

The SEIC is hard (*péchékkún, tipepéchékkún*): *péchékkún* is associated with a variety of notions such as hardness, strength, physical energy, health, corpulence, plumpness, stiffness, erection, intensity, strictness and moral offensiveness. In view of this range of meanings *péchékkún* applies to the most diverse dispositions of the SEIC, according to the situation. To the metaphors of quality belong only those where the SEIC is compared with things having little or no plasticity; (for the additional meanings of *péchékkún* see under the metaphors of the human body).

Tipepéchékkún is an inflexible, stubborn person who cannot be spoken to and who treats others to his brand of harshness, and merciless rejection. The rigidity of the SEIC can reach such a degree that the islanders speak about the SEIC turning to stone (*éféwúwóónó neetip*). A rare synonym for *tipepéchékkún* is *efingngaw*.

The SEIC is soft (*tipepweteete, nuuk pweteete, tipepwakakkak*): allied to this term first and foremost are qualities such as politeness, approachability, flexibility, a spirit of reconciliation and a readiness to help, goodwill and gentleness; less common also insight, understanding and patience. By dint of careful persuasion one can sometimes make a hardened SEIC soft (*epweteeteey neetip*).

In a child the SEIC is soft at first. Increasing solidity is an important feature of a child's development into adulthood and old age (20.5).

The SEIC is tenacious (*woreef*): a similar meaning as *péchékkún*; implacable by nature, deficient, obtuse; tenaciousness in the SEIC can imply avarice, where a person can only be separated from something that belongs to him under duress. The comparison is as follows: the object from which he needs separating is just as difficult to disengage from the SEIC, (*aa woreef seni neetip*), like filleting fish.

The SEIC is tame (*mwotuk, tipemwotuk, fesir, tipefesir*): animals and pets that are harmless and tame are *mwotuk* or *fesir*. In humans this means a specific type of harmlessness, namely honesty in regard to material possessions, not however general meekness. A person spotting something valuable or money lying on the ground and not taking advantage of the opportunity is an *átámwotuk*, a meek soul (applying to a woman: *niyemwotuk*). In rare cases the terms for tameness in the SEIC equate to humility.

The SEIC is fierce (*mwacho, tipemwacho*): dishonesty as the opposite of a tame SEIC; somebody considered as *tipemwacho* will be met with suspicion especially in relation to valuables and money.

The SEIC is warm or hot (*pwich, pwichikkar*): being interested in something, motivated to defend a cause, but not love or other feelings of affection; the hotter the stronger. Heat in a person's SEIC is never linked to notions of aggressive tendencies; (cf. the metaphors of movement below: *pwuropwur*).

The SEIC is clear (*ffat*): a feature of liquids containing no suspended matter; on the one hand meaning a clear train of thought, acuity; on the other hand decisiveness: people whose SEIC is *ffat* know what they want.

The SEIC is bright (*saram*): together with its opposite this is one of the most significant items from the range of SEIC dispositions; in physical terms *saram* (brightness, lighting, illumination), the impact of illumination (*ttin*) through a source of light; when the sun shines the world becomes *saram*.

A SEIC that is *saram* is highly capable – the person is intelligent, witty, quick on the uptake, with a good memory, plenty of insights and ideas; he thinks clearly and concentrates well. He possesses all those characteristics prized by islanders as virtues: self-control, meekness and modesty, friendliness, with winsome behaviour, etc. Virtues pertaining to a bright SEIC include those relating to *miriit* (reason, amenable behaviour, and sound common sense).

The SEIC is dark (*roch, rochopwaak, kkiroch, tiparoch, rochongngaw*): the opposite of a SEIC which is *saram*; the general term darkness (*roch, rochopwaak, kkiroch*), which comprises the notion of an inferior intellect and character, has two further sub-categories.

A person who is *tiparoch* is of low ability, stupid and slow, having a poor memory and poor understanding; showing a dearth of ideas and insights coupled with a lack of clear thinking, etc.

Incorporated in the word *rochongngaw* (meaning roughly: dark/bad) is a strand of SEIC tending to irritability, violent temper and aggression. Animals are *rochongngaw* when protecting their young.

The SEIC terms brightness and darkness include intellectual aptitude and character traits in a way that typifies the Chuuk Islanders' thinking. Brightness and darkness of SEIC also play a crucial role in conceiving how SEIC dispositions arise through the impact of spirit beings and magic and medical potions (20.2. and 20.3).

3. Metaphors of Rest:

The SEIC is calm (*sé, núwa*): An unpleasant (*weyires*) stirring of the emotions has abated: the person has regained an inner peace, but the memory of the difficulties now overcome is still fresh in the mind.

Similar dispositions are given graphic profile when compared with still weather, no wind and a calm (*núwa*) sea.

The SEIC is motionless (*tipeppós*): boulders and bollards and similar immovable objects are *ppós*; to be *tipeppós* means a high tolerance of frustration in every context, and self-control even when very anxious and in acute pain; tranquillity of nature, infallibility, patience; these are characteristics shared by a SEIC that is big (*wátte, pérémmóng*) and deep (*ónónnón*).

The SEIC can get stuck (*mwéch*); in which case, thinking processes lead to no practical results.

4. Metaphors of Movement:

Relating these to the ever-present SEIC dispositions is problematic. On the one hand the movements indicated here are not actual movements of the SEIC. Rather they are comparisons from the realm of concrete types of movement revealed in their range as genuine metaphors. On the other hand these movements partly signify feelings and emotions (e.g. *pwuropwur*, delight and anger), to the extent that they cannot be understood simply as ever-present SEIC dispositions. The judgments made by my informant Namiyo were crucial for classifying movements within this range; he identified them as *tiip*, but not as *meefi*.

The SEIC is able to move freely (*ngas, ngasónó*): a person has managed to free himself from mental and emotional burdens; or else deliberations and efforts that have borne little fruit over time have now resulted in a worthwhile outcome; similar in meaning to *pwpwas*; the reduplication *ngasangas* is used for real physical movements such as breathing, beating of the heart and the thrusting movement of jellyfish.

The SEIC turns (*kun*): a person's interest focuses on something specific by virtue of the SEIC orienting itself. When somebody does not understand something it may be because their SEIC is pointing in the wrong direction. Conversely, a person can be prevented from understanding by another person deliberately turning his SEIC away (*okunnu neetipan*). It is as if somebody were to direct a person on to the right path or off to a side-path.

The SEIC bubbles (*pwuropwur*): water is *pwuropwur* when simmering, or when foaming in a stormy sea; the SEIC experiences elation, the joy of getting involved, or enthusiasm for an idea or for a particular thing; in a different context this image can be linked with feelings of aggression; pleasant sensations such as joy, etc. are frequently associated here.

The SEIC has momentum (*ngngúpwir*): the property of a pebble thrown sky-high and falling to earth a great distance away; motivation; enthusiasm for pursuing a goal; similar to the preceding *pwuropwur*.

The SEIC falls flat, has fallen down (*ttur*): all feelings of disappointment, reluctance and hopelessness; low spirits, but not anxieties, nor a lack of courage.

The SEIC shakes (*chchúng*): the feeling of having been unjustly treated; vibrating strings are *chchúng*; (*échchúngúchúng*, to cause to tremble).

The SEIC is off-course (*rikirik*): a boat veering off course is *rikirik*; it describes the SEIC in terms of dishonesty, insincerity, deviousness and speaking with forked tongue; similar in meaning to the SEIC being crooked (*tipepwpwór*).

The SEIC has veered off course (*ttók*): somebody is pursuing a wrong target, having misguided role-models and values (*óttóka*, to lure somebody from their proper path).

The SEIC has lost its way (*mwánechenó*): somebody has been misled and is on the wrong track; similar in meaning to the previous *ttók* (*ámwánechóónó*, to lead someone astray).

The SEIC is exchanged, altered (*siiwin*): somebody has altered his opinion and stance on an issue, such that his intentions may have also changed (*emén aa siwiniiy neetipan*, somebody has changed his SEIC, has rethought the issue).

In a more general context *siiwin* (or *wún*) may mean any significant change, even one of mood.

The SEIC is in constant flux or change (*winiwinikkis, tipepaat*): its attitude is wavering; no decision is long-lasting, the person's opinion is easily changed, or he may not have an opinion; this last meaning is also conveyed by *tipepaat*.

The SEIC is slow to change (*winimmang*): a person is not easily convinced, and is not easily dissuaded, and for that reason doesn't just abandon decisions; to be *winimmang* can thus count as a positive or negative characteristic and mean consistency as well as stubbornness.

5. Metaphors of the human body:

The SEIC is strong (*péchékkún, tipemaaw*): having a SEIC like this means a person is able to withstand mental and moral pressure, does not buckle, does not lose his poise, can put his point across consistently and does not easily lose heart. The SEIC of a person can be reinforced (*épéchékkúna*), by encouragement or by siding with him. These are the positive meanings of *péchékkún* (stability, strength, energy, physical well-being and health) which give it context. The less common word *tipemaaw* means the same thing, namely dynamism and willpower.

The SEIC is weak (*apwangapwang*): indecisiveness, a lack of will and drive, little spirit of enterprise; in a combatant this tendency used to be attributed to his having had sexual intercourse on the eve of warlike encounters (which therefore in the past was strictly taboo, *ónówut*, but which nowadays to some extent is recommended before sporting competitions). Specifically *apwangapwang* means a poor tolerance of stress, a lack of stability, physical weakness, ill-health, and little intensity.

The SEIC is lifelesss (*tipemáámá*): Chuuk Islanders mean by *má* not just death but any circumstance where a creature or object shows no sign of life, such as unconsciousness; it refers to a car engine stalling, a run-down battery; *tipemáámá* means indecisiveness and apathy, an absence of energy and drive and will.

The SEIC is alert (*pwpwék*): adventurous, with the spirit of endeavour, drive; but not intelligent nor similar.

The SEIC is tired (*ménúúmú*): lack of enthusiasm and similar contrasts to the previous *pwpwék*.

The SEIC is hungry (*fiyon, echik*): in a concrete sense this is just a physical feeling; in the context of SEIC it means undefined feelings of being dissatisfied and unfulfilled.

The SEIC is thirsty (*kaaka*): attaching to feelings, the term is synonymous with *fiyon, echik* above.

The SEIC is satisfied (*mét*): feelings of satisfaction and of being fulfilled.

The SEIC is surfeited, overfull (*ku*): aversion towards people, hostile weariness towards people, things and activities; in concrete terms *ku* is the experience of having overeaten food that one otherwise enjoys eating.

The SEIC has a bruise (*en*): the feeling of being targeted and got at, i.e. after somebody has pricked one's conscience.

The SEIC has a strained muscle (*fingngaw*): any unpleasant feeling, especially soulful feelings of sadness, and even aggression; somebody who is generally not good to have around and who is bad tempered. Physical strains are treated by massage routines (*ráwááni, seneti*). Both terms can be used also for the removal of SEIC strains; then they describe reconciliation, softening and mood-enhancing through encouraging talk.

The SEIC is hurt (*kinas*): an injury to the SEIC (in the sense of an open wound) occurs when one has been insulted or unjustly dealt with: feelings of being neglected; bearing hurt, disappointment, and rejection; sometimes feelings such as bereavement (*neetipeta*) are involved.

The SEIC is in pain (*metek*): every kind of unpleasant feelings, especially those that are brought on by bruising, hurt and strain to the SEIC (see above).

The SEIC is bitten or stung (*óóch aa kkúúw neetip*): when people learn that their misdemeanour has been made public, or when they themselves have just become aware of it, then the effect on the SEIC is likened to being stung. Feelings such as remorse and self-accusation prevail. In another context irritation and anger are the result, for example after the "sting" of having been unjustly criticised or gossiped about. Concretely *kkúúw* is used not just for being stung, but of being deliberately targeted and hit (by a spear or a stone).

The SEIC is scarred (*mómmó*): the nasty effects occurring after a wound to the SEIC has abated: one is able to cope with an emotional battering. The difficulty of getting over a humiliation, a slight or unjust treatment is the message of the following saying: *aa mómmó kinasen núkún, nge ese mómmó kinaseyinón* (an external wound heals over, but an inner one doesn't).

The SEIC has eyes and can see (*aa wor mesen neenuuk*): when its eyes are open (*nnenó*) the SEIC shows an alertness and an attentiveness and concentration: these are akin to the SEIC's state of openness and awakeness (*ssuuk, pwpwék*).

The SEIC is blind (*chuun, mesechuun*): not precisely the opposite of the above, but a lack of understanding and an inability to recognise what constitutes correct and incorrect behaviour.

The SEIC has ears and can hear (*aa wor seningen neenuuk*): so that the SEIC can especially absorb everything that a person takes to heart, warnings, encouragements, consolation, etc. Notions of the SEIC being deaf are not known.

The SEIC has a voice: the SEIC can speak as a kind of voice of conscience (*mweniyen, méngúúngú*); when a person suffers, his SEIC utters plaintive moans.

The SEIC tastes bitter (*maras, kkipwin*): all feelings of aggression; disappointment, exasperation; bereavement.

6. Metaphors of a different kind:

The SEIC is linked to something (*riiri*): become familiar with something, so that one is loath to give it up; being bound to the island of one's birth, to the customs of those around one; even a thing can be bound to the SEIC (*riiringeni*) or separated from it (*mwúúseni*).

The SEIC as a garden plot: if one wishes to entrust something to somebody, one plants it in that person's SEIC (*fótuki nóón*), and anything that one finds difficult to part with and that needs removing from one's heart is pulled out like a weed (*wiyátá*).

17.3 List of Non-metaphorical Terms for Dispositions of This Group

The following listing is the least complete of all. There is enough evidence that there must be more lexical items extant. Even my informants often had specific difficulty in classifying a term under the various categories of SEIC dispositions (*tiip*) or of excluding a term with any certainty.

ánneyaasoochik, ánneyaasoosich, rongosoosich: obedience.

ánneyaasoonap, rongosoonap: disobedience (see also *núkúmmach*).

The formations *rongosoosich* and *rongosoonap* illustrate a conceptual link between (dis)obedience and hearing (*rong, rongorong*).

fáchewén: cheekiness; proof of the fact that a person is *namanam tekiya*.

kichiyééch: generosity; *kisááseew* synonym.

kichingngaw: avarice, stinginess.

kirikirééch: loving-kindness, goodness.

kirikiringngaw: heartlessness, roughness, meanness, grubby-mindedness and behaviour; characteristic of all spirit beings having evil intentions towards humans (*énúngngaw*); synonyms *chúwangngaw, chúngngaw, sóróngngaw*.

kkémwéchúféw: meanness, small-mindedness ; (*émwéchú* to grasp).

miriit: an emotional disposition of crucial importance; *miriit* is reason, ability to make good judgments, accountability, reasoned behaviour and healthy understanding. By reasoned behaviour is meant behaviour which is correct in the terms of Chuuk culture. Anybody acting against this cannot be *miriit*. Every abuse of Chuuk Islanders' norms, tradition and customs is proof of the fact that a person is not *miriit*, not responsible, not at least at the moment of acting incorrectly. In this sense anybody is acting incorrectly and thus unreasonably who, for instance, arranges a bonfire like a

European does, or who roasts breadfruit on a spit or – if he is a man – thinks of fishing using a rod and line (which is reckoned to be women's work!).

Somebody doing this runs the risk of being considered crazy (*wumwes*), even if he is known to be intelligent (A. Fischer 1956:85 "The Japanese are frequently referred to as 'crazy' because they were not Christians"). Rational thinking in the Chuuk islander's sense of the word is ethnocentric thinking.

Intelligence (*tipáchchem*) doesn't inevitably imply that the person concerned is bound to be *miriit*. Yet it is supposed that an intelligent person is more likely to act in a *miriit* manner than a less intelligent person.

This mental and emotional disposition is esteemed more than intelligence. The reason for this is that *miriit* epitomises all that the islanders reckon as virtues, namely a respectful attitude to one's seniors (*mósónósón*), good characteristics such as courtesy and a willingness to help; in short, any type of good behaviour. A woman displays *miriit*, if she calls out for help if she is being sexually pestered by a man.

Especially *miriit* are people who have naturally high tolerance when frustrated and display self-control. It is said that men have this tendency more than women because in difficult situations they keep a cool, clear mind. Conversely, girls are *miriit* at an earlier age than boys.

To qualify as *miriit* you only often need to live unassumingly, behave sensibly and fit into the community without showing off. This applies even to animals, e.g. dogs or water buffalos when they act sensibly by doing what is expected, and fulfil their purpose by barking if needed and by not biting if unnecessary, and responding to commands.

Feelings of aggression like anger and hatred prevent people and animals from displaying *miriit* subsequently.

This term plays a very significant role within kinships. Chuuk Islanders consider that first of all proper behaviour consists in bringing advantage to one's social group. The high form and notion of *miriit* is evident by the fact that when a person is recognized as a relation or as belonging to a group this in itself is called *miriitiitiiy* (Goodenough/Sugita *miriitiiy)*, and applies even to animals that recognise their owners.

A new-born baby does not have a developed SEIC, so cannot be *miriit*. This fact is so obviously a characteristic of children that a child of 0-14 years old is called *semiriit* (in a broad sense unreasonable). An adolescent remains *semiriit* in a court of law until his majority 18th birthday.

Development of the SEIC requires an increase of *miriit*; this reaches its peak as an adult (*mwáán* or *feefin*). As a rule even the elderly reach a degree of *miriit* that younger people cannot manage. Yet in extreme old age there is very often a dropping-off of the SEIC and an absence once again of this characteristic.

In the course of their physical and emotional development everybody tends to increase in *miriit* as a consequence of their intellectual aptitudes unfolding. With children and adolescents frequent help must be available. To educate somebody (*emiriiti*) means for the Chuuk Islanders making him *miriit*, i.e. bringing him to appreciate appropriate behaviour within the culture's meaning of the word. This happens by shaming (*ásááwa*), threats (*eniwokkusu*), corporal punishment (*wichiiy*), linked with pointing out that spirit beings may possibly punish, and that one must address the person's conscience using words that give rise to *miriit* (*kkapas emiriit*), and which are still common as an appeal to reason among adults. *Miriit* is the goal of SEIC development and the goal of all efforts at upbringing in the Chuuk island community.

A person attaining a high degree of *miriit* disposition is a wise person indeed (*átámiriit* or *niyemiriit*). This confers high status upon a Chuuk islander, one that is not usually obtainable before adulthood. Hence this term comprises everything to do with leading a mature life.

And finally all those spirit beings that show themselves powerful and thus to be feared and honoured (*énúúsór*) are characterised by a high degree of *miriit*.

wumwes: Apart from a few exceptions the opposite of *miriit*; a lack of reason, mental incapacity, dishonourable actions, crazy behaviour, madness. A person who is consistently unpleasant, refuses to comply with his community and goes against what Chuuk Islanders expect from their fellows is termed *wumwes*. He lacks normal healthy common sense.

In addition *wumwes* describes the SEIC dispositions which give rise to extreme acts. To this belong all aggressive feelings (*chchow*) tending to smouldering hatred, mayhem and destructiveness, but also love and obsessiveness driven by an idea which blinds the person to everything else. One can make a person w*umwes* by goading him and getting on his nerves (*owumwesi*).

Wumwes applies also to all those folk who have abnormal speech, and to those with handicaps and those who are deaf. People with physical abnormalities (such as Down's syndrome and those born crippled) are not in fact *wumwes*, but evil spirit beings (*énúngngaw, soope*).

Such spirit beings (including *ngúnúngngaw*, a human's evil spirit double) are – together with more usual causes for angry responses – fully involved in the birth of these SEIC dispositions. Their presence around a person, and particularly their physical contact with them and their bite cause *wumwes*. Epilepsy and symptoms like those of a heart-attack are manifestations of *wumwes*.

mósónósón: modesty, reticence, (respectful) silence; includes everything that Chuuk Islanders understand by good manners and unassuming social behaviour; highly prized and an important goal of upbringing (A. Fischer 1956:101,103); proof of *miriit*.

nikiitú: endurance, tenacity; constancy and readiness to acquiesce to one's lot in life; unwavering when tempted; faithfulness and reliability; keeping one's promise (*nikiitú wóón pwpwon*); *tupwpwén* has a similar meaning; its opposite is *winiwinikkis* and other words.

núkúmmach: a more general expression for disobedience, but it also means the fact that somebody has not followed advice or doesn't react when addressed; obstinacy, stubbornness.

sine: yet another disposition which the SEIC reveals in greater measure as it develops. This disposition arises on the one hand independently through the process of emotional and intellectual development, but on the other hand *sine* is just the result of all learning processes which a person goes through with experience of life. *Sine* is thus also the knowledge that grows by experience and by learning. The SEIC is *sine* in as much as it has access to this knowledge.

These SEIC dispositions are not so much about the ability just to understand (*weewe*), that is the potential for linking passively acquired facts in a logical manner and understanding them. *Sine* by contrast is the ability to link previously known facts actively and to use them according to the situation for a particular purpose. *Sine* is the term for being skilled at something, one's ability, mastery of facts and competences. The ability to understand (*weewe*) is thus of course the essential prerequisite for this.

It is noteworthy that the emphasis is placed on the learning process which causes *sine* and not so much on the natural development of the SEIC which produces *weewe*. A person who has learned to sing has become *sine kkéén*, and the person who has become a master of a particular trade or profession such as a builder is reckoned as (*chóón*) *sineenap* (a great man of talent, a specialist).

The verbs *sineey* (to know about something, to be familiar with it) and *sinneni* (to realise) are conceptually linked with *sine*.

sáchááfi: obedience, compliance; a character trait demonstrating one's *miriit*.

sooná: falseness, dishonesty, deceitfulness and trickery; the transitive verb *soonááni* means to embezzle, to steal; *sooná* forms many compounds even with elements which otherwise would seem neutral or positive, and which therefore appear inappropriate or misused, for example *tipáchchem sooná* (devious intelligence = guile; *sóróngngaw* has a similar meaning; its opposite is *wenechchar*, among others).

tichchik: diligence; fastidiousness; a person who has regard for the smallest details; its opposite is *tórónap*.

tipáchchem: cunning, intelligence; can also mean knowledge and know-how; the form of the word indicates that this disposition of the SEIC is primarily a matter of memory (*chchemeni, chechchemeni*, to remember, keep in mind); *tipáchchem* is the one quality which distinguishes animals from humans; even spirit beings that prove themselves powerful (*énúúsór*), are reckoned to be especially *tipáchchem*; its opposite is *tiparoch*.

tipemecheres: benevolence, care, insight, gentleness, affability; and credulity; *mecheres* means easy (not hard) and is the term for pleasant feelings; its opposite is *tipeweyires*.

tipeweyires: lack of insight, sternness, stubbornness, unyielding nature; obtuseness; not easy to please; as a transitive verb *tipeweyiresiiti* sometimes has a quite different meaning (to long for); *weyires* means difficult and is the term for all unpleasant feelings; its opposite is *tipemecheres*.

tórónap: indiscipline, untidiness; opposite is *tichchik*.

wúméwúmééch: friendliness, readiness to help, goodness, kindness; *kirikirééch* has a similar meaning and seems to emphasise the outward behaviour rather than the character trait.

Chapter 18
Dispositions of the SEIC Which are Types of *meefi*

18.1 Presuppositions

A feature of the second sub-category of SEIC dispositions is the fact that they are linked with a movement of the SEIC (*mwékútúkútún neetip*); consequently they only exist from time to time. For the most part we are dealing with things such as intellectual processes, and with feelings and impulses of the will that match the feature of only being present from time to time.

Since these dispositions occur similarly in all humans and are yet only occasionally present, we cannot consider them as personality traits serving to distinguish one person from another. However, this group of SEIC dispositions does have one distinguishing feature. When one of them is evident in a cumulative or continuous way then it is treated by the Chuuk Islanders as an ever-present disposition, i.e. a conceptual term from the first group mentioned in chapter 17. People who are known to be of continuous cheer in company possess a SEIC which is always *pwaapwa* (joy, cheerful). This state is expressed as optimism or as calmness (*tipepwaapwa*), hence as a characteristic and thus as a constant SEIC disposition of the person concerned.

Many of the terms grouped here for the occasional dispositions of the SEIC can be given the prefix *tipe-;* they then refer to continuous SEIC dispositions. One more example: *soong* (anger), *tipesoong* (aggressiveness). Even this demonstrates a close link between intellectual processes and aptitudes, qualities and feelings. This is yet another indication that the Chuuk Islanders don't when all is said and done make a great distinction between the two concepts, but reckon them as aspects of a single concept and as characteristics of the SEIC (*tiip*).

It explains also why my informants in many cases found great difficulty in classifying terms clearly under this group, even when the characteristic of SEIC movement was obvious. This was especially evident with *weewe*, a SEIC disposition which on the one hand applies to the ability to understanding, on the other hand applies to the process of comprehension itself. In this latter *weewe* is linked with a movement of the SEIC, but not in the former case. This means that it must be present in both sub-groups of the word field *tiip*.

18.2   The Term Movement of the SEIC (*meefi*)

All dispositions of the SEIC which are linked to the notion of a movement are called *meefi* (see 15.2). Finding a good translation of this term is problematic. For the Chuuk Islanders a thought (*ekiyek*) is just as equally linked with a movement of the SEIC as, for example, the feeling of anger (*soong*). Consequently both are considered *meefi*. However, for the European the term has two distinct meanings. Translating *meefi* by the expression "feeling of the soul / stirring of the heart" or "emotion" would capture only a part of the meaning and would fail to take account of all the intellectual processes contained in the term *meefi*. This is why I use the expression "movement of the SEIC". I mean by this all the feelings and intellectual processes which the Chuuk Islanders understand as occasional conditions (movements) of the SEIC.

These movements include only those *meefi* which are simultaneously SEIC dispositions. In 15.2 above I ascertained that *meefi* could also include physical feelings. These, of course, are not *tiip*. The term *meefi* by itself is an overarching term in a word field comprising the contrasting physical perceptions (*meefiyen inis*) and mental and emotional ones (*meefiyen neetip*). Only these last *meefi* (*meefiyen neetip*) are included in the word-field of SEIC dispositions; the physical *meefi* are not.

The translation "SEIC movements" is a rather inadequate reflection of the wealth of meaning of *meefi*. From the contexts where *meefi* occurs we can glimpse an unusually heterogeneous cluster of its feasible meanings. Providing well-documented statements requires the researcher to investigate the role of morphology and syntax in the Chuuk Islanders' language.

As a transitive verb *meefi* denotes in the majority of occurrences becoming aware of physical sensations (*meefi metek*, to experience pain), but not, however of sense impressions (see 15.2). Terms from the realm of the emotions, such as anxiety or sympathy are not "felt" in the sense of the verb *meefi*; they are "possessed" (*ááni ttong*, to own or possess sympathy).

Meefi as a noun occurs more often in mental and emotional contexts. With a relational suffix, it almost always refers to processes running in the intellect: notions, growth of awareness, consciousness, insights and impressions, ideas, considered judgements and logical conclusions, suppositions and opinions, views and anything one has aired or brought to mind (*meefiyey*, my opinion).

Used with classifiers of general possession, *meefi* functions as a substantive and refers overwhelmingly to the emotional realm: feelings, and sentiments (*ááy meefi*, my pangs of conscience). Clearcut divisions between the emotional and the intellectual realm do not come to the fore.

Chuuk Islanders categorise SEIC movements as pleasant (*mecheres*) or value-neutral (no specific term) or unpleasant (*weyires*).

18.3 SEIC Movements in Detail

1. Pleasant SEIC movements (*mecheres*):

Beside its role as an overarching term for pleasant SEIC movements, there are contexts where *mecheres* refers to notions of ease and comfort, as well as relief, and freedom from physical distress and pain; well-being and the feeling of doing something pleasurable (*mecheres ne fang*, to enjoy giving); and even a person's gullibility.

Specifically, *mecheres* means easy to do, something that is not difficult to undertake. Yet not in the sense of a trivial task. Its opposite is *weyires*.

The pleasant SEIC movements consist of the word cluster joy (*pwaapwa*) and an unnamed word group.

By *pwaapwa* the Chuuk Islanders mean joy, the joy of anticipation, joy shared with others; also gloating, pleasure and notions of being smitten or motivated by something (*pwaapwaa ngeni*). Used with a classifier relating to general notions of ownership the term relates to a gift intended to bring joy (*ááy pwaapwa*). Using various affixes the word accrues a number of semantic extensions *pwaapwammóng* (great joy) *pwaapwakkáy* (easy to delight), *tipepwaapwa* (optimism). Types of *pwaapwa* are as follows:

chchengen: bliss, proud joy, rejoicing, joy of victory.

meseyik: spontaneous joy of surprise; merriment, pleasure, fun; the joy of tension being released.

mwánek: joy linked to physical movement (jumping for joy); exuberance; enthusiasm; (*nek, nekenek, nekitá* to hop).

The other manifestations of pleasant SEIC movements are:

achoocho: keenness and motivation for work; effort, overcoming one's reluctance; despite this last phrase *achoocho* is a pleasant SEIC movement; its opposite is *chipwang*; a synonym is *chófó*.

chá: A feeling of reconciliation, the absence of aggression; it occurs in the wake of *soong* (anger) and similar strong emotions; frequent compounds are *chámmang* (slow grudging process of reconciliation) and *chá-kkáy* (swift reconciliation). Used with classifiers indicating ownership (*ááy chá me reen emén*) and as *pisekin ácháácha* it means a gift to effect reconciliation; opposites are all kinds of *chchow*.

chip: feeling of having been consoled; opposites are all kinds of *neetipeta*.

chchen: sympathy, appreciation, devotion, favour. *Chchen* can also mean love (free of any sexual component). As such it is distinct from *ttong*.

Chchen is a comparatively superficial love feeling. With the classifier of general ownership it can also mean a present motivated by love (*ááy chchen*); opposites are all kinds of *chchow*.

efich: to enjoy something, or enjoy doing something; often linked to particular foods or activities (rarely linked to people); weaker in meaning than *chchen*; *efich* has something spontaneous about it, like its synonym *saani*; opposites are *opwut* and *núkúrar*.

epinúkúnúk: hope, assurance, confidence, lack of worry (especially with regard to the future, or to misfortune and illness); there is a phrase that rich people are *epinúkúnúk*; opposites are *epinúkúnúkúngngaw* and *éwúrek*, but not *nóniinen* (see also *núkúnúk)*.

ing: admiration, amazement, astonishment, considering something impossible; often linked with a feeling of joy, and thus largely synonymous with *mwaar*; not infrequently spelt *ingemwaar*; *ing* however often means being astounded at something disgraceful or act of disobedience; important compounds are *eyingeying* (trying to arouse admiration, boasting, showing off) and *tuneyeyingeying* (to pretend, to boast, bluster); opposite *opwut*.

kinamwmwe: a particularly important SEIC movement; utter happiness, contentment, complete satisfaction (even physical), pleasure (incl. sexual), positive mood, fulfilment, security; every SEIC movement which is a type of *mecheres* is a *kinamwmwe* if it is especially marked; a person having fallen into deep sleep is said to be *kinamwmwe*; also applies to a journey which has been free of incident (*áámi sááy kinamwmwe*); opposite is *riyáfféw*.

In another context, the contrast between *kinamwmwe* (peace) and *fitikooko* (conflict) and *móówun* (war).

kinissow: gratitude, feeling of obligation; *kinissow* is closely allied to the context of exchanging gifts (see Goodenough 1951); when Chuuk Islanders wish to make a request (*tingór*) to somebody, they quite often try to ingratiate themselves with a gift (*niffang*) to achieve their ends more easily; as a term *kinissow* is an expression of thanks and apology; a significant compound is the antonym *kinissowummang* (ingratitude).

kirises: feeling of satisfaction; to have got one's money's worth; almost exclusively following satisfaction of physical (sexual) needs; one is *kirises* when one has eaten a copious favourite meal and still has room for more.

menemen(ééch): contentment in the sense of being content with what one has, being satisfied with a modest amount; weaker than the previous *kirises*; the expanded form *menemenééch* is more common than the simple form; opposites are *tipemmóng* and *mwecheniyá*.

mwaar: admiration, affirming surprise; feeling of being impressed; enamoured by something; interest and involvement; there are no negative overtones with *mwaar*, unlike those, occasionally, for *ing*; a person admiring an impressive achievement expresses words of *mwaar* (*mwaareyiti* to praise); a further key compound is *amwaaraar* (causing a response of wonder and fascination).

ngon: yearning mixed with curiosity, naïve astonishment, marvelling; unlike *mwaar*, the word is not a response to seeing a performance; with *ngon* the response to this feeling is of wide opened eyes; an important compound is *angon* (to try to arouse wonder; to put on a display, to puff oneself up, to pretend; similar to *eyingeying*).

pwara: brazenness, cheekiness (cf. *namanam tekiya*); both are personal characteristics; the form *tipepwara* means boldness, resilience; a less common synonym is *maat* (*átámaat*, hero); faced with a child crying in pain one says *ópwóróók* (cheer up, be brave); opposites are *niw*(*okkus*), *kker* and *mwaramwar*.

2. Value-neutral SEIC movements:

There is no label for these, no over-arching term. They are directly classified under the heading *meefi*, as a single group. The group contains all SEIC movements that broadly belong to the processes of the intellect.

áreere: supposition, conjecture, suspicion (*áreere wóón*, to assume something); *áreere* is thus a direct opposite of *sineey* (to know something for sure, to be aware).

(*che*)*chchemeni*: memory – phenomenon and faculty; to remember something (trans. vb.); in other dialect areas the term *chechchem* occurs; important compounds are: *chchemeto* (to occur to s.o.), *féwún áchchem* (memorial, monument), *pisekin áchchem* (keepsake, souvenir); other words similar in meaning to (*che*)*chchemeni* are *chiwiri*, *émwéchú* (to memorize), *kkémwéchúkkáy* (the SEIC capacity of somebody with a good memory) and *apasa núkún* (to recite from memory); its opposite is *ménnúúki*.

Intelligence and knowledge (*tipáchchem*) are SEIC dispositions which, in the islanders' view, are basically dependent on a good memory.

ekiyek: thought, idea, conception, consideration; final thought, plan, project, aspiration; belief in the sense of supposition; to devise something; *ekiyek* means the actual core within the SEIC devoted to intellectual activity; in some respects it is synonymous with its generic term *meefi*; a number of suffixes make for a variety of nuances of meaning within the thought process, e.g. *ekiyekiyátá* (to devise, discover), *ekimmóngeey* (to think hard about something), etc.

eneefiina: to distinguish; to recognise the distinctiveness of two things; the term has a clear metaphorical dimension (*fééri neefiinan* to create a gap between things; to separate things); *eneefiina* is a transitive verb.

éwúchcheyááni: to hold people and things in esteem, to know the value; opposite is *éwúchcheyangngawa* (to denigrate, to lack esteem for something); both are transitive verbs.

(e)fini: to decide on something, to choose; often as *fináátá* (*neetipan*); the compound *nifinifin* means choosy, biased (also *aapaap*) and is considered a bad SEIC disposition.

ffén: feeling of being taught, or warned, about good things and bad things; the term is difficult to define and understand; the transitive form *fénééw* (advise, warn, instruct) gives rise to the extensions *fénépéchékkún* (to firmly instruct) and *fénépweteete* (to instruct in a kindly positive way); in an intensive form *ffén* results in the feeling of *siit* (being reprimanded etc.); *ffén* should not be confused with *fén* (an insult, affront).

memmeef: notion, opinion; pre-conscious thinking (*wúwa memmeef*, it is dawning on me); the word is not the transitive reduplicated version of *meefi*; *ámeefi* is included in this connection (to convey something without words, to hint at). The word plays a significant role in Chuuk Islanders' notions about dreams (25.3.7).

ménnúúki: forgotten (*ménnúúk, ménnúúk seni*, to be forgotten); transitive verb.

méngúúw: approval; to be in agreement with what somebody says; sometimes synonymous with *ingeyiti* and *mwaareyiti* (to admire); transitive verb.

namanam tekiya: feeling of disdain, pride, arrogance and presumption; cheekiness; opposites are *mennin* and *suufén* (deep respect); *namanam tekiya* can also be understood as a character trait; it is not then a *meefi*.

nenneyiruk: feeling of being surprised; amazement at something completely unexpected, whether something nice or nasty, for example meeting a friend whom one doesn't at first recognise, or the sudden realisation that one has made a mistake; Chuuk Islanders accompany this realisation with the exclamation *ek* (*ek fóósun nenneyiruk*).

nónnón: burning ambition; feeling of wanting to, or being able to, own what somebody else has; *nónnón* is a SEIC movement attributed particularly to children; informants explain *nónnón* as *nónówó* (envy), without any feeling of hostility or ill will.

núkúnúk(*ééch*): belief, trust; to accept as certain, to suppose; the basis of this word and of *epinúkúnúk*(*ééch*) (hope) is the word *nnúk* (firm); both transitive words *áchiyééwú* and *áchíféwúwa* are regional synonymous alternatives; the opposite *núkúnúkúmmang* (mistrust) is formed with the suffix *mmang* (slow, late); a further opposite is *tipemwaramwar* (doubt).

óóroora: deliberation, process of thinking something through, making a plan to reach a solution; in many respects similar in meaning to *ekiyek*; *óóroora* is transitive.

piit: a feeling of waning interest; the feeling of wanting to abandon a plan or a decision, of bringing little enthusiasm to a project; *piit* is the consequence of doubt (*tipemwaramwar*) and general frustration (*weyires*); a stone thrown into the air is *piit* towards the end of its trajectory, and a rocket is *piit* when losing height and thrust; opposites are *ngngúpwir* and *achoocho*.

ppiiy: to consider, review, reflect upon; to proceed with caution; to want to bide one's time; *wúpwe ppiiy* (I will think about it) means that the mind is not yet made up, or that one needs a polite phrase to say when not wanting to grant a request. A transitive verb.

sinneni: to realise, to come to a logical conclusion; *sinneni* as a rule relates to external things, and thus basically refers to the sense organs; the words for exclusively intellectual processes are *meefi*, *weewe* and *weeweyiti*; important compounds are: *sineey* (to know about, to be familiar with), *esinna* (identify, guess), *esissin* sign, puzzle and activity of guesswork), *esissinna* to mark with a sign); the processes of realising and identifying presuppose that the SEIC is *sine*.

weewe: understanding, comprehending, recognizing; the process, so it seems, involves the SEIC at the moment of awareness becoming identical to what needs understanding; *weewe* in a different context refers to the meaning of a word, i.e. its content (*weeween eew kkapas*), the intention behind an action (*meet weeween ewe angaang?*), and the notion of identity (*weewe chék*); I have already dealt with *weewe* as an ever-present SEIC disposition and the presupposition for every act of comprehension (17.2 and 17.3); important compounds: *weewekkáy* (quick on the uptake, intelligent) *weewemmang* (slow to understand, intellectually challenged), *weeweyiti* (realise as transitive verb), *áweeweey* (to explain something), *kkapas áweewe* (explanation), *áweeweengeni* (to explain something to s.o.).

3. The unpleasant SEIC movements (*weyires*):

Besides its function as the generic over-arching term for unpleasant SEIC movements *weyires* occurs in contexts with the following meanings: discomfort, uneasiness, oppression, pain, problem, harsh fate, hardship, suffering, wretchedness, physical and mental anguish, reluctance, and feelings ranging over guilt, inhibition and frustration. Specifically *weyires* also means difficult to do, something which feels burdensome and involves complexities. Its opposite is *mecheres*.

Male Chuuk Islanders show a marked tendency (almost unknown among women and girls) to daub their name prefixed by *weyires* (or *riyáfféw*) on prominent spots along a path, on fences, trees, boulders and even on the back of their shirts. This behaviour arises from a particular kind of *weyires*, namely (culturally induced) sexual frustration (Gladwin und Sarason 1953: 233 „... the Trukese (i.e. Chuukese) male ... devotes much thought and effort to trying to figure out how he can maintain the woman's attention"), and to be *weyires* evokes sympathy (*ttong*).

The pleasant SEIC movements only fall into two groups, whereas the unpleasant groups number five: an undesignated one directly subordinate to the term *weyires*; the group of aggressive feelings (*chchow*); feelings of ambition (*mwechen*), of sorrow (*neetipeta*) and of anxiety (*niwokkus*).

The (undesignated) unpleasant SEIC movements directly subordinate to the term *weyires* are as follows:

achaanú: feeling of reluctance stemming from a lack of success or from failure; resignation; to give up; opposites are *nikiitú, achoocho, ekitekit*.

chipwang: feeling of reluctance stemming from a lack of motivation; weariness concerning an activity one dislikes or tires of; sluggishness, laziness; *echipwang* (causing *chipwang*) is the name for somebody always suggesting a further task when everybody else has hopes of going home (synonyms are *ékkúnéngngin, ékkúnékkis*); opposites are *achoocho, chófó*.

chchimw: compulsion; the feeling of not being able to act freely; should not be confused with *chimw* (to nod); similar in meaning to *ósópwiisek*.

chchopwa: the sensation of being ill at ease; inner disquiet about an unwanted development of events, born of the fear that the time available to complete an assignment is running out; agitation and nervousness when the outboard motor doesn't start, when it is unclear why somebody hasn't arrived for a meeting, when one can't help feeling that something untoward has occurred, that one has lost one's job or that a shameful thing has come to light; the feeling that one is unable to extract oneself from an awkward situation.

chchopwa is also one's response on seeing somebody struggling to cope with carrying an impossibly heavy and difficult load. The unpleasant feeling of *chchopwa* compels one to get involved and help. From this results a specific kind of courteous behaviour. In these sorts of situations courteous folk are *chchopwakkáy* (quickly bothered / unsettled); the opposite is *chchopwammang* (not easily bothered / unsettled).

chchopwa is not a type of *niwokkus*, although it is accompanied by a certain dread.

ekitekit: a determination to achieve; a feeling that induces one to make great efforts; readiness to toil away, to exert onself, to gain victory, even to attempt what seems impossible; *ekitekit* applies to sportsmen bent on victory, to prisoners planning an escape, to a love-sick man wooing a woman, to a field-researcher requiring all his PhD data before his grant money runs out; *ekitekit* is the motivation behind a task force needing to lift a heavy tree trunk (*ekitekit ngeni*); the word evokes the extraction of juice from grated coconut in a piece of fibrous fabric (*ekita taka*) (*kiten taka* is what remains of the coconut after the process); if somebody has no energy left the phrase is *aa kit péchékkúnan* (his energy has been squeezed out of him); *ekitekit* is stronger than *achoocho*.

engnginó: the feeling that gives rise to self-control, to enduring the frustrations and the pain; gritting one's teeth, not batting an eyelid; *eppeyis* (holding one's breath) can be substituted; the ability to feel *engnginó* is an important hallmark of a well-developed SEIC and thus is considered an adult disposition.

ku: excess, weariness, aversion; when one has eaten too much rich food or the same food repeatedly, or one has to repeat the same task or be with the same people; synonyms are *nnotá* (*aa nnotá wóóy*) and *nnú*.

mennin: respect of those in higher positions, and especially respect of what is taboo (*pin*); a sign that a person has the disposition of *miriit* (reason, etc.); opposite is *namanam tekiya*; although an element of dread is present, *mennin* is not a kind of *niwokkus* (fear).

mokunón: feeling of being constrained by the fear of making a fool of oneself.

mwaramwar: feeling of indecision and timidity in a risky situation; feeling of being torn, showing a decisive face to the world but still biding one's time deep down; opposite is *pwara*.

nikééké: feeling of strong attachment to one's spouse; this feeling is always noticeable when jealousy is also involved; *nikééké* itself only refers to relationships between a man and a woman, and essentially only in marriage; actual jealousy as Chuuk Islanders understand it is the same as anger or hatred (*soong* or *opwut*) toward the mischief-maker; jealousy is not therefore a unified concept, but has various components (*nikééké*, *nuukómmóng* and *aapaap, soong, opwut*).

nuukeni: the ever-present tender-hearted thoughts one has towards another; the notion of where in the body the SEIC is located plays a part here (*nuuk*).

núkúrar: disgust and loathing felt on facing something unpleasant (food or unpleasant tasks); transitive *nóów*; opposites *efich, mwóón* and *saani*.

ósópwiisek: feeling of being in a bind, having to bow to the inevitable and accept it; *ósópwiisek* is one's reaction to being told by a superior and needing to be obedient.

riyá(fféw): frustration, and particularly of a sexual kind; plight, anguish of desperation; the exact opposite of *kinamwmwe* and an equally important SEIC movement; each SEIC movement which is a kind of weyires becomes a *riyá(fféw)* when it is deeply felt; both terms contribute to the same context (*weyires me riyáfféw*); the word *riyá* is used less often than the compound *riyáfféw*; yet another important compound is *eriyá(fféw)* (gruesome, frightful situation).

ruk(oruk): a term relating to the intellect; mistake in thought process, confusion, muddled thinking, making a mistake, make a wrong choice; slip of the tongue; the usual reaction to this SEIC movement is the exclamation *ek* as in *nenneyiruk*, with which it is related linguistically and conceptually; compound is a *móówun orukoruk* (a war causing *ruk*, a guerrilla war).

(tipe)rúwérú: indecision when faced with a number of options; one can be *tipemwaramwar* when just one issue is at stake.

sááw: embarrassment, feeling awkward, inferiority complex; compound *ássááw* (giving rise to shame, disgraceful, disgrace); the synonym *kin* is less common; the opposite is *mesemaaw*; (unlike its German translation Scham, the word *sááw* does not also relate to female genitalia).

Sááw is a key term in the Chuuk Islanders' concept of personalilty. Situations where a person can become *sááw* are a source of embarrassment and are avoided at all costs. The options and methods that are available to an individual member of Chuuk society to avoid becoming *sááw* are clearly part of the culture framework where *sááw* acts as a crucial principle of upbringing. Several American anthropologists have studied Chuukese shame orientation (Gladwin/Sarason 1953; A. Fischer 1956; Swartz 1965). Their work has been rather more concerned with the issues of culture and personality research than with the intention of understanding the related cognitive categories used by the islanders themselves.

tipemwaramwar: doubt, indecision, related with *mwaramwar*; opposite is *núkúnúkééch*.

ttong: love, compassion, commiseration; mercy; unlike *chchen*, the word has a clear sexual element. Apart from love between marriage partners, it can in certain contexts mean prostitution (*ttongen re wóón*, love of foreigners); *ttongen enimuuw*, love on Friday, or pay day); important is the strong emotional involvement, the personal commitment which *ttong* involves, but which is absent in *chchen*; *ttong* is one of the strongest feelings maintaining a relationship; Chuuk Islanders long for *ttong* where they feel any kind of frustration (*weyires*); the habit mentioned above of introducing one's name in public with the indication that one is *weyires* or *riyáfféw*, is nothing more than a request to feel *ttong* for the person concerned; compounds *ttongen énú* or *pwáápwá* (love that a spirit being or a tortoise can muster, a bad mother's love); *attong* (evoking sympathy, making a forlorn impression), *iráttong* (Bougainvillea, because it comprises two or more intertwining stems).

wosukosuk: agitation at not knowing what to do, or what to prioritize; feeling when too many demands are placed at once, when something expected has not happened, when overburdened by work and lack of time.

wosupwpwang: helplessness, dilemma; feeling in everyday situations when one cannot do what one wants.

The next group of unpleasant SEIC movements are the feelings of hostility under the general heading *chchow*. In specific terms *chchow* means weight. The difference between its non-abstract meaning and feelings of hostility is signalled in the following way: with the relational suffix (*chchowun*) it means weight, with the classifier of general ownership (*aan chchow*) it means resentment, etc. This term exemplifies how dispositions are conceptualised differently across various languages. Literally *chchow* means something like "heavy heart". By this phrase the Chuuk Islanders don't mean sorrow, remorse or homesickness; they mean anger, irritation, hatred and envy.

As well as its use as a generic term, *chchow* occurs in contexts such as rage, thirst for revenge, involving feelings of anger that are hidden, simmering and lingering. It is often used with *soong* (anger) and can be a synonym for it. Sometimes *chchow* is replaced by *eningngaw* (stomach pains after indigestion), but not by *mékúrochchow*. Its opposites are *mecheres* and *chá*.

The unpleasant SEIC movements classed under the umbrella term *chchow* are:

aapaap: resentment, self-seeking, selfishness, meanness; the fear of losing out; people who do not let others do or have what they themselves do or have are reckoned *aapaap,* e.g. not being prepared to budge up to let somebody sit down; hence it is distinct from *nónówó* (envy) because with *aapaap* people have something they are unwilling to give or share. Thus *aapaap* often means envy, even in relations between the sexes.

Aapaap evokes the meanings of partisanship and group-centredness, involving the feeling of having to mark and defend one's own territory carefully against others. It denotes the feeling which stirs a Chuuk Islander to favour the advantage of his own social group, and to prioritize it.

Synonyms of *aapaap* are *apangngaw* and *nokonok*, the opposite is *apeyééch*; *aapaap* should not be confused with *apaap* (invoke spirits, entice).

fén: feeling injured, feelings of hurt stirred by unjust dealings or harsh words (*kkapas péchékkún*); always linked with hostile feelings; literal meaning of *fén* is the stabbing pain of touching a new wound (*éfénú*); *chchúng* means the same; important compounds are *éfénútip* and *fénúkkáy* (sensitive, not tolerating fun, easily made cross); not to be confused with *ffén*.

fitikopwut: upset over being disturbed by noise, mosquitos or children; jumpiness associated with it; contains the element *opwut*; opposite *kinamwmwe*.

kkowumw: grievance; caused by discrimination and similar issues; it is likely that pouting of the lips (*owumwuumw*) underlies this concept.

mángngaw: the anger brought on by feeling powerless, when one cannot respond; *mángngaw* is stirred by insults and scornful words; the idea of paralysis (*má*, also death) may underlie this concept; compound is *takirin ámángngaw* (scornful laughter, giving rise to *mángngaw*).

ningeringer: blazing anger, blind fury; the feeling that takes hold of a person wanting to smash everything around them.

nónówó: envy; begrudging people what they own because one has not got the same; *aapaap* is when one begrudges others what one also has oneself; opposite is *menemen* (contentment).

opwut: aversion, rejection, hatred; jealousy between same sex; opposites are: *chchen, efich, ttong*.

soong: anger, fury; rivalry between those of same sex (e.g. *soongen wóón feefin*); jealousy about food; *soong* is the most commonly used term for feelings of aggression; compounds *soongokkáy* (quick to lose temper, killjoy, prone to outbursts), *nisossoong* (continually cross, irritable; certain insects like moths flitting round a light and knocking into it are called *nisoong* (*nikamwúnúmwún*).

The generic category for a broad group of SEIC movements is headed by *mwechen*, whose meaning is: striving, longing, wanting; the transitive *tipeni* is a common synonym; *mwechen* itself is ethicaly neutral, yet some of its subsidiary terms are considered immoral SEIC movements (*mwecheyisow* covetousness and the like). Types of *mwechen* are:

ánáán: long-cherished desire; a wish that is voiced as a request is *tingór*.

mááyicha: covetousness, greed over possessions; unlike *mwecheniyá* the word only applies to material things (*pisek me mwéngé*); this meaning of *mááyicha* only applies on the western Chuuk islands (*Fááyichuk*); on the eastern (*Nómwoneyaas*) it means avarice, and covetousness and greed are called *mwárá*.

mwecheniyá: a more all-embracing sense of covetousness; the meaning of greed is secondary; a synonym is *tipemmóng*; the opposite is *menemen*.

mwecheyisow: covetousness in the sexual sense.

mwóón: longing, craving; often after certain foods that one would happily keep consuming even though one is full; *mwóón* is obviously largely a physical sensation, but there are contexts applying to a SEIC movement (*neetipey aa mwónneyiti ...*; compound *ómwmwóón* (inducing a craving, bait or lure).

nóchcheey: requirement, striving; strongly felt desire leading to actions bringing about its fulfilment; a transitive; synonym *ekimmóngeey*.

nómwunaawit: expectation, eagerness; feeling of a person seeking praise; to crave for attention; *nómwunaawit* does not apply to rich people; similar in meaning as *ssiyé*, but much less intense; *aawit* means a meal prepared for expectant guests.

sóssót: temptation; the feeling of being tested or put through one's paces; *sóssót* is not just being tempted to do bad things; pupils have this feeling before a test; a car engine is *sóssót* when going through checks; *sóssót* thus sometimes also means to make an effort.

ssiyé: to plead, to demand attention and help; what one feels in a dire emergency.

tawaat: sensation of having to hurry; disquiet stemming from time pressure or from several things needing one's attention at the same time; synonyms: *atapwan*(*apwan*) and *páchew*.

The penultimate group of unpleasant SEIC movements is headed by *neetipeta* (a SEIC which is destroyed, broken, smashed). It means bereavement, arising primarily from the death of a dear friend, or from other significant losses, but can also simply mean sorrow. Synonym is *chúpwpwún* (broken bones), its opposite is *chip*. Types of *neetipeta* are as follows:

chéféné: depression, the result of a minor disappointment; weaker in meaning than *neetipeta* and *nóniinen*, but like the latter.

chchúng (*ssúng*): a SEIC movement which is hard to understand and describe; as a metaphor of movement *chchúng* is the feeling of having been dealt with unjustly or in bullying manner (see 17.2); Chuuk Islanders consider it an outrage to hurt a person by *échchúngú*.

Chchúng however also applies to feelings such as wanting to look after someone, being compassionate and concerned, being moved and thoughtful concerning somebody; from an ethical viewpoint it is a virtue to share one's fellow feelings in *chchúngúúw*; linguistically a distinction arises in the use of the classifier for general possession (*ááy chchúng*, my personal distress) and the relational suffix *chchúngi* (commiseration for myself); both terms are kinds of *neetipeta*.

énúúki: disappointment of a woman who is pregnant or has just given birth when a present (usually of a store of food) has been taken away; people assume that the child will get sick as a result of the mother's setback; as an antidote to the consequences of *énúúki* a special medicine is prepared (*sáfeen énúúki*); in all other instances *nichippúng* denotes the feeling of disappointment.

mengiringir: pangs of conscience, guilt feelings, bad conscience; does not mean remorse or regret.

mitingngaw: feeling of being publicly disgraced; arises through criticism or rebuke in front of a third party.

mú: stirred emotionally; full emotional joy at remembering something; not longing for something, but similar intensity; compounds are *kkéénún mú* (a song sung with great inner conviction); *tunomúúmú* (tearful talk).

mwún: feeling of being overruled or rejected, of unrequited love; hurt at being abandoned; parents experience *mwún* when their children run away, and a husband feels it when his wife leaves him.

This emotion has a special significance for Chuuk Islanders who fear it for being the greatest cause for suicide. Suicide is practised most commonly because people seek to avenge themselves for a stinging rebuke. The rebuker is meant to experience *mwún*. The term thus conveys a very specific kind of remorse which can be triggered by the act of running away or suicide (*amwúnúmwún*: the action triggering *mwún*). Compound is *tipekkamwún* (the disposition of a person who constantly exerts his willpower and in an unspoken way threatens others to experience *mwún*).

nikamwúnúmwún is a night moth which flies into a naked light. Its action is compared to a person committing suicide to enforce the experience of *mwún*.

nameni: memory full of feelings, homesickness, longings linked with memories; happy memories indulged by older people; a transitive.

nameni belongs in context with some terms from the realm of the intellect: *namengeni* (remembered), *nameseni* (forgotten), *namónóóseni* (lost), *namanaman* (his/her way of thinking, behaviour) *namanamangngaw* (bad attitude); conversely *aan namanam* (his belonging to a religion).

nichippúng: disappointment; except the meaning of *énúúki*.

niyamaam: regret, remorse, self-accusation, crossness with oneself; *niyamaam* is a step further than *mengiringir* (pang of conscience); similar in meaning to *chiwichiwinó*, *ekiyekinó*, *namanamónó* and *nemenemenó*.

nóniinen: worry, affliction, grief, sadness from taking something to heart; unlike *éwúrek*, the reason for this should lie in the present or past: death, loss of a job, an engine that doesn't run smoothly, a child's illness; proverb: *aa ééch nóniinen me mwirin* (what is the use of worrying when the misfortune has already happened?).

ósoonapa: regret at a loss or a failure; hurt. The transitive *ósoonapa* is used rather surprisingly as a waste, of material and time; synonym of *áchchika*.

pwpwos: longing, homesickness; Chuuk Islanders tend to sing with devotion when they are full of *pwpwos*.

siit: feeling of rejection, of rebuke; feeling criticised; the feeling is triggered when one has been criticised verbally or when something has not been accepted unreservedly; *siit* is experienced in a small group setting, *mitingngaw* on the other hand is where the rebuke is more public; my informants could not define *siit* clearly as *neetipeta*; *esiit* (*siit* giving rise to criticism) is a compound; (see *ffén*).

The last group of unpleasant SEIC movements goes under the generic heading *niwokkus*, meaning fear and dread. The word has a suffix indicating intensification. The simple form *niw* is less common. The compound *eniwokkusu* (causing fear) can be used to mean to warn. The opposite of *niwokkus* is *pwara* (courage), the transitive *kkaweri* is a synonym. Types of *niwokkus* are:

éwúrek: despair, affliction, hopelessness, constant fear and concern about the future; soldiers facing the prospect of dying experience *éwúrek*; *éwúrek* is also the Chuuk Islanders' constant worry about perhaps having nothing to eat for the following day; a significant feature of the word is that it is focussed on the future; this distinguishes it clearly from *nóniinen*; the opposite is *épinúkúnúk(ééch)*, *sé*.

kker: timidity, uncertainty, fear; not being trusting because of previous bad experiences (e.g. at the dentist's or when gambling); fear that something might go wrong; coyness about meeting somebody's gaze; the word particularly applies to animals, notably to birds; opposite is *pwara*.

máyirú: fright, dismay, unpleasant surprise; amazement and consternation brought about by shocking behaviour; *máyirú* results from shocking news; Chuuk Islanders accompany this feeling with the cry of *ek*, as with *ruk* and *nenneyiruk* (*ek fóósun máyirú*).

nisiin: feeling of timidity, despondency, fear and nervousness; the timidity shown by children; *nissiyá* is a synonym.

niweniw: feeling of being unsettled looking down from a tall tree, or on a moving boat; feeling giddy as a non-physical phenomenon; physical giddiness *mwáániyen*; *niweniw* is evidently the redoubled form of *niw*.

piireyir: tense excitement, nervousness as of stagefright; *piireyir* occurs when meeting important people or before important tests at school, or when a young man first talks to a girl to invite her to dance, and anywhere one feels under the public gaze; people drink alcohol to avoid feeling *piireyir*, or else they rub themselves with an ointment whose effect derives from a spirit being called *Pwó* and which supposedly prevents an attack of *piireyir* (*sáfeen* or *epiten Pwó*); opposite *mesemaaw*.

rúng: panic reaction, fear of dying for example on spotting a shark nearby; physical reaction is to jump or start (*nupuffengenniiy, weyitiffengenniiy*), also to tremble and twitch in panic.

rúúké: terror, sudden shock experienced as a sensation in one's limbs; *rúúké* is experienced when one's hair stands on end, when dreading an encounter with an animal or a food one dislikes intensively, or when one believes one is seeing a ghost.

Chapter 19
The Characteristic Make-up of the
Terminology Describing SEIC Dispositions

19.1 A System for Analysing Their Structure

At the outset I maintained that the concept of the soul is something to-tally beyond description. This quality of being unfathomable is a feature of that realm of terminology which I have chosen to call SEIC. What Chuuk Islanders understand by the label SEIC is so exclusively non-intuitive and fully abstract that it can only be appreciated via the language and its struc-tures. Investigating and describing the SEIC necessitates applying method-ologies pertaining to linguistics, especially semantics. Right from the prac-tical fieldwork stage a combination of various approaches and methods were involved.

As a point of departure the researcher can choose a situation (an argu-ment for example) which he explains to the local informant, linking it with the question: What feelings are involved in this situation? In this way the researcher obtains a term opening up a host of other situations for further enquiry where the same feelings occur. Equally effectively, a term that the researcher has obtained can serve as a starting point to an enquiry. Both methods of proceeding will highlight why a series of situations and the accompanying feelings are experienced in the same way or differently. In an advanced stage of the questioning – when numerous terms have been investigated – there will be an increasing number of generic umbrella terms with whose help the common characteristics of several terms can be as-signed to the various categories. The result is a structure of concepts as set out in chapter 16.3 Table 3.

19.2 Issues Arising

This diagram of concepts is however incomplete in the form presented. Some of its deficiencies can be mentioned briefly. In truth, it does not dis-close all the terms contained within it. Yet there are good reasons for sup-posing that the most important terms have been incorporated in sufficient quantity to permit reliable conclusions.

Furthermore, most of the terms of level 6 are missing; formed from terms of level 5 (bottom level in Table 3) with the help of numerous suf-fixes, they offer a multitude of expressions for features. Some (not many) important word formations from this level 6 category are incorporated in the description of their basic forms.

A further issue is the order of terms within the table. The sequence of the columns from left to right is quite arbitrary; the priority was based on the way it looked. Those terms on level 5 are rather to be thought of as horizontal; their sequencing is alphabetical to facilitate easy reading. It is important to realise that terms with similar meaning are sometimes very far removed from each other.

A purely linguistic study of this diagram of concepts ought to acknowledge the fact that it is really a three-dimensional illustration. Developing this further would, however, go beyond the remit of what is basically an ethnological study.

19.3 Consequences

The storehouse of terms that Chuuk Islanders possess to express mental and emotional issues is astonishing by its numerical dimensions alone. The previous pages of vocabulary exceed 200 terms. If, for each of these terms (in level 5) we assume three more derivations using suffixes (level 6), we arrive at over 600 terms expressing the SEIC dispositions. This is a conservative estimate.

Studies of vocabulary structures which have become readily available for numerous languages show a link between the make-up of the terminology for a specific cultural area and the meaning that this area has for those living in the culture. Much simplified, the relationship can be explained thus: the larger the number of terms for a cultural area and the larger the number of levels to which terms are assigned, the bigger the need perceived by members of the culture to be able to speak in a nuanced way about that cultural area.

Berlin, Bredlove und Raven (in Tyler 1969:62) write as follows: "There is a strong positive correlation between cultural significance and degree of lexical differentiation ..."; Frake (in Hymes 1964:199) wrote in similar vein: "To explain why some areas of a folk taxonomy subdivide into a greater number of superordinate-subordinate levels than others, we advance the following hypothesis: the greater the number of distinct social contexts in which information about a particular phenomenon must be communicated, the greater the number of different levels of contrast into which that phenomenon is categorized."

These statements suggest that we are dealing here with a similar link or correlation. It seems to me that the doubtless conservative estimate of 600+

terms for expressing SEIC dispositions is impressive proof of the demonstrable and acute need the Chuuk Islanders have to communicate all their mental and emotional experiences with all their nuances.

So, of particular interest is the make-up of the terminology for SEIC dispositions listed under the sub-group *meefi* (SEIC movement). Within this sub-group the sub-headings form a clear hierarchy of five (six) levels, each subordinate to the one above, each one of which signaling a definable feature of the terms contained therein. In the other sub-group not classed under the generic heading *meefi* there is almost no hierarchy in the structure; consequently the terms grouped have fewer features and are thus less clearly differentiated.

The contrast in the degree of differentiation among terms in each sub-group suggests that the one headed *meefi* is the more significant word field for Chuuk Islanders' thinking which supports mental and emotional communication. The SEIC movements with their allied vocabularies give the Chuuk Islanders the opportunity to express and communicate precisely. The fact that we are dealing with a defined need echoes fully the observation made right at the outset that Chuuk Islanders speak and write about their feelings with greater readiness and spontaneity than Europeans.

The need for differentiated means of expression in the area of SEIC movements reveals distinctions that are nevertheless great, within this group. Of the 108 terms for SEIC movements (including *meefi* itself) 69 are labelled unpleasant (*weyires*); much more than half. The pleasant SEIC movements (*mecheres*) number 19 terms, as also the value-neutral ones which describe processes largely involving the intellect (each 22%). In addition, within the group of unpleasant SEIC movements, the hierarchy is maintained more consistently and fewer logical possibilities remain unfilled.

Here also it emerges from the varied degrees of differentiation in the vocabulary in each group *mecheres* and *weyires* that it is the unpleasant SEIC movements (feelings!) in particular where the vocabulary gives the Chuuk Islanders the potential to express themselves and communicate precisely. In other words, the main emphasis of the mental and emotional dimensions of their thinking is on what they understand as unpleasant SEIC movements.

Does what I have just stated justify us in concluding that they tend to rate the threatening aspects of their lives more strongly and experience them as insecurity? In my view this conclusion would be to go too far. A diagram of terms like this can scarcely lead us to read anything more from it than the interest a culture invests in one of its areas of expression. Even the issue of the origins of this interest cannot be answered from the diagram.

That there must be an emphasis towards the unpleasant SEIC movements can be clearly observed in the behaviour of my various informants. In the first stages a whole series of terms for SEIC movements could not be classified as pleasant, value-neutral or unpleasant. In the following second and third stages the informants tended quite strikingly to allot these unlabelled terms to the unpleasant (*weyires*) group, even those terms they had first supposed might belong to the pleasant (*mecheres*) group.

The mental and emotional sphere (in the European/Western terminology, the psychic sphere) is by definition something completely immaterial, abstract, conceptual. The occurrence of such realms in the European/Western way of thinking caused in the past various authors to suppose that so-called primitive peoples were unable to develop clear notions and concepts. The fact that in the Chuuk Islanders' mind there was such a pronounced and well-defined structure of concepts is impressive proof of how untenable this assertion is. The clarity of thought and the precision in defining terms which are recognisable features of this structure are no less highly prized than the clarity and precision of European and Western thinking in this area.

Frake points to the fact that it would be wrong to conclude from the numerically and structurally varied differentiation in the vocabulary for one and the same cultural realm as used by two different ethnic groups that the groups' cognitive competencies must be different in quality. He writes (1964:199): "If the botanical taxonomy of tribe A has more levels of contrast than that of tribe B, it means that the members of tribe A communicate botanical information in a wider variety of sociocultural settings. It does not mean that people in tribe A have greater powers of 'abstract thinking'. As a matter of fact it says nothing about general differences in cognition, for when it comes to fish, tribe B may reveal the greater number of levels of contrast."

Chapter 20
The Emergence of SEIC Dispositions

20.1 The SEIC and Its Openness to Change

All dispositions embraced by the SEIC make for a conceptual change in its nature. With the sheer quantity of the possible mental and emotional dispositions which it can absorb, the islanders must have a notion of its great susceptibility to change. All the more so because the SEIC reveals simultaneously such a host of dispositions: capability in the intellectual realm; character traits which come to the fore at a specific moment rather than as a result of adaptation; and movements such as joy and thinking which are revealed as changes to a SEIC so disposed to change.

Changes like these in the SEIC dispositions can arise in many ways. Every day the Chuuk Islanders observe that all the events occurring around them, impacting on their world and their mindset, give rise to changes in their SEIC dispositions. This makes them content, angry, or thoughtful. In addition there are a number of changes whose emergence is due to special root causes.

20.2 Spirit Beings as the Cause of SEIC Dispositions

Describing notions concerning the origins of SEIC dispositions arising from spirit beings (*énú*) presupposes that the Chuuk Islanders' use of the term spirit being is clear. This term is a significant component of their notions of the soul as a spirit-like being assigned to the person's physical self and enduring beyond death. Corresponding notions are dealt with in chapter 24. To understand how the origin of certain SEIC dispositions is perceived we need first of all to distinguish between good spirits and evil spirits.

Two opposing notions underlie the involvement of spirit beings in the formation of SEIC dispositions. Benevolent spirit beings (*énúúyééch*) cause the SEIC to become bright (*saram*), malevolent ones (*énúngngaw*) on the other hand make it dark (*roch* etc.).

Influence over the SEIC caused by spirit beings occurs when the particular spirit being is near the person or is in indirect physical contact. If it is a good spirit being, then the person gets dispositions which a bright and illuminated SEIC has: competence of the intellect, a positive prevailing mood and particularly harmonious, conformist behaviour (*miriit*).

A positive influence on the SEIC is also exercised by that same spirit being assigned to the person and prolonging his personality (*ngúnúyééch*) after his body has died. The spirit gives him a premonition (*meefi*) of dangers and witnesses his life-experiences as dreams (see ch. 25).

Evil spirits (*énúngngaw*) can target SEIC dispositions with devastating impact, especially when the person comes into physical contact with them, or when he is bitten (*wochooch*) by them or when they enter his body by force. The consequences are panic-like reactions. The person targeted begins to shriek and thrash about, becomes aggressive or exhibits other kinds of strange behaviour. His SEIC has darkened (*aa rochonó*). The consequences are a lessening or a failure in the functioning of his intellect, a prevailing negative mood, frenzied behaviour, mental derangement and abnormal behaviour (*wumwes*). Evil spirit beings form the causal element in a Chuukese theory of mental illness and personality disorder.

The features of behaviour that can be explained away as a darkening of the SEIC by evil spirit-beings include impaired speech and unexplained convulsive body movements, paralysis, etc. which in reality are symptoms of a stroke.

Details about the type of physical contact a spirit being seeks with a person, about the role of the *ngúnúyééch*, about notions of demon possession and the activity of mediums, with all the arising SEIC dispositions can only be understood within a discussion of the notions held concerning spirit beings. This discussion is also set out from chapter 25 onwards.

20.3 The Emergence of SEIC Dispositions through the Magical Medicinal Practices ("Psychopharmacology")

Regarding spirit beings' involvement with the occurrence of SEIC dispositions, there is a further important aspect of the notions held by Chuuk Islanders concerning mental and emotional phenomena. Evil spirit beings are not just assumed to cause unwanted SEIC dispositions, but also a range of physical illnesses which can be treated using "medication" (*sáfey*). This kind of *sáfey* also exists to combat unwanted SEIC dispositions caused by evil spirit beings, dispositions which are not dissimilar in concept to physical illnesses, and which like these can be treated by therapy.

Chuuk Islanders mean by *sáfey* not just items and substances which remove symptoms of illness, but also those which give rise to such symptoms. The principle underlying treatment by *sáfey* is the idea that the constituents of the items and substances call forth similar – and occasionally contrasting – constituents in the sick person. Moreover *sáfey* these days also means disinfectant and insect repellent, and cosmetics like hair dyes, injected medicines and all kinds of pharmaceuticals. Details about this concept and the general medicinal knowledge of the islanders can be found in the detailed study by Mahony 1970.

When a person's SEIC has darkened as a result of contact with an evil spirit being or by its bite, the victim must be treated with "illumination medicine" (*sáfeen asaram*). This is prepared, like most of the islanders' medicine, from parts of plants being boiled and sieved to give a juice extract to drink. Its "illuminating" effect on the SEIC is based on a simple analogy: *sáfeen asaram* displays gleaming colours, with red and green dominant (Mahony 1970:135). This medicine treats outbursts of anger and mental derangement (*wumwes*), and also symptoms which indicate the onset of a stroke. Fishermen who set out to sea at night are in particular danger, because of the sea spirits (*énússet*) lurking there, of lapsing into such negative SEIC dispositions. That is why the men take "illuminating" medicine as a precaution.

Because of its positive effect on a person's intellectual capacity, it is used before all those undertakings which require a "clear head".

For the Chuuk Islanders there are no tasks for which the illuminating medicine would *not* be useful. A canoe-builder does not like starting his work without it. With it, his concentration levels are higher, and it reduces the risk of his wasting the trunk of the valuable bread-fruit tree (from which he fashions his canoes) by wielding the axe carelessly.

It is also important for all experts in matters of magic (*sowuroong*): for bread-fruit magicians (*sowuyatoomey*), magicians of mischief (*sowuppéwút*) and many other sorcerers. Just one careless slip in the sequence of a magic ritual can signify a failed crop or can direct the harm back on to the sorcerer himself. Without *sáfeen asaram,* the expert medicine-men (*sowusáfey*) if they err in their preparations run the risk of directing the symptoms of illness they are meant to be banishing back on to themselves.

Medicine of illumination is undoubtedly all part of the medium (*waatawa*) and his preparations if the procedure for contacting the spirit of the deceased (*énú*) is to be a success. After taking it the medium is enabled to report clearly and correctly about the deceased's wisdom, advice and intentions; in short, to play his part in the community by ensuring its harmony (see ch. 27).

Medicine of illumination can bring about a change in the disposition of the SEIC of a spirit being. For this reason it was in the past a regular component of the sacrifice to a benevolent spirit; the intention was to facilitate clear advice in family matters or to appease the spirit's anger and prompt him to positive and benevolent behaviour.

Because *sáfeen asaram* has a positive impact on the achievements of the intellect, it is used even by normal people requiring to demonstrate shrewdness (*tipáchchem*), a good memory (*chchemekkáy*), acute perception, and clarity in thought and word. In days gone by, such medicine was taken when planning hostilities, and these days it is taken prior to important decisions and when learning magic incantations by heart, where accuracy is paramount for the outcome to be positive. Because of its beneficial effect on the life of the emotions, the medicine increases motivation, patience and self-control. In the past it was even imbibed before dance performances; in the present it helps boost sporting prowess.

Abnormalities in the SEIC such as mental deficiencies present even before birth cannot be treated successfully with *sáfeen asaram*. People with such symptoms are not considered human beings, but as evil spirit beings (*énúngngaw*, *soope*).

Of all the medicines designed to bring about specific SEIC dispositions or to alter them, the illumination medicine is clearly the most important. Yet there are a number of other similar medicines of lesser significance.

Mahony describes one such by the name *rocoon Sáát* (Mahony's spelling). It works in quite the opposite way to *sáfeen asaram*, by making the SEIC dark and causing *wumwes* (Mahony 1970:152).

A different medicine called *sáfeen Pwo* helps build confidence. *Pwo* is the name of the spirit being which provides the required effect according to plan. It is akin to a cosmetic oil, being rubbed all over the whole body. That is why it is also called *epiten Pwo*. In the past it was used regularly at dance celebrations. Its role now is to prevent one feeling panic (*piireyir*) and shame (*sááw*) on public occasions.

Medicine to arouse sexual feelings of attraction (*sáfeen omwmwung*) is also among the magic means to summon the dispositions of the SEIC. This medicine consists of a pleasantly smelling lotion for the body, which is why it is also called *néén* or *epiten omwmwung*. The way it works is very different from the medicines described above which conjure up the SEIC's dispositions.

The word *omwmwung* means "to produce *mwmwung*, to stimulate sexual attractiveness". The islanders use *mwmwung* (and occasionally *féng*) to describe a situation where a woman finds herself loved and sought after by a man (and conversely). This is why it is not correct to equate *mwmwung* to "sexual love" (Elbert 1947:124), because the term does not indicate a SEIC disposition as the Chuuk Islanders know it. If a man wishes to become *mwmwung* he must attempt to arouse in a woman the love disposition (*ttong*). This occurs with the help of *sáfeen omwmwung*.

To this end he seeks out an expert (*sowuwomwmwung*) who can prepare him this medicine. In its preparation the female spirit being *Inemes* plays a part, for if particular taboos (*pinin omwmwung*) are adhered to she endows the medicine with potency. One of the most important taboos in this respect is the ban on eating fermented breadfruit (*épwét, maar*); its smell is disliked by all benign spirit beings.

Producer and user are *fánnimar*, which means that they must avoid fermented breadfruit if the magic is to achieve its impact.

This medication is used generally without the knowledge of the person whose love the person seeks to win or to keep alive. In secret his/her body is brushed with it, or else something that he/she uses to sit on, or a place on the path he/she walks along. In doing so the user must take great pains that family members on which the incest taboo is to be used, do not come into contact with the medication. That is why it is only kept in safe places away from the home.

Mahony, after a brief mention of this medicine (1970:143), names another magic spell called *nukan* (Mahony's spelling) which is linked with the seat of the emotions. But it is harm-inducing stuff whose intention is to cause disfiguring skin diseases to help spurned lovers take revenge (1970:182-183).

Indications in early reports (e.g. Girschner 1911) lead one to suppose that in the past even more medicines were known about that called forth SEIC dispositions, for example one that undermined the courage of enemies in warfare, etc.

Psycho-drugs, which by their chemical make-up induce real psychotropic effects, are unknown to Chuuk Islanders (apart from alcohol made from the fermented sap of coconut spathes and similar); and even unknown to practising mediums (*waatawa*).

20.4 The Process of Learning

Islanders call special talents, knowledge and skills *sine*. Equally they are SEIC dispositions as well as character traits, both developing largely by themselves and independently from the influences of the (social) environment. This thought underlies in a particularly typical way the notions of a person's language acquisition, of which more later. Apart from this "natural" development of knowledge and talents, people can become *sine* through the learning process, and heighten and intensify these SEIC dispositions.

The learning process (*kkáyé*) is conceived as one of "hooking" on to (*éé*, fishing hook); so a song which has been practised and learnt by heart is hooked like a fish to a line (*aa é*). Learning and practice (*kkáyé*) are in this image conceived as one. When Chuuk Islanders learn a song they catch it from listening for a while to somebody who already knows it, then they sing along and repeat it until it is "hooked"; if necessary they sing for hours without pause. The result is knowledge and competence (*sine*).

Even the act of teaching somebody something is linked to the image of attaching and hooking (*áyééw*) the content to be learnt.

Chuuk Islanders notice that children learn more easily than adults. They explain this in terms of the childrens' SEIC being softer (*pweteete*) and hence more easily adapted than with adults; what needs to be learnt gets hooked in more easily.

20.5 The Development of the SEIC

A person's or an animal's SEIC is present from birth, but at that time has not assumed its final form. In fact, the SEIC cannot ever reach a final form; to the islanders' way of thinking it undergoes a continual process of change until death.

With animals the development of the SEIC goes through fewer stages of adaptation, but still has the same kind of process as humans. As regards the SEIC of spirit beings (*ngúún*, *énú*) completely different perspectives apply (see chs. 24.5.4 and 25.3.4).

Three notions dominate the progress of a person's mental and emotional development. At first his SEIC is small (*kúkkún*), soft (*pweteete*) and closed (*ppúng*). These three features mean that the SEIC in childhood is for some time only capable of functioning moderately. In due course it gets bigger, opens up and hardens, reaching optimum capacity in adulthood, then in old age reducing to a state of failing functionality.

The SEIC characteristics evident at birth, which change from that moment on, bring about the nuanced and integrated impact of personality that is particular to a person at his or her stages of growing up. The growth of the SEIC causes in the main an increasing differentiation within the realm of feelings; its hardening tends to a shaping of character and will-power; its opening sees competencies unfolding in the intellect. The influences of the three characteristics cannot be viewed in isolation, given that their mutation is simultaneous as they impact on one another.

A new-born baby's SEIC is small (*kúkkún*) and soft (*pweteete*). The expression of his will and his feelings are thus minimal, and his character traits are as yet unspecified. Because his SEIC is still closed (*ppúng*), no evidence of intelligence, consciousness or understanding can be recognised.

The word the islanders use for the closed quality of an infant's SEIC is *te* (sewn up); the word for a toddler until he starts talking is *tipáte* or *tipete* (SEIC-sewn up), or *setipeen* (without intention etc.).

A soft SEIC is easily distorted. This explains how a young child can be influenced so effortlessly, or easily frightened, or quickly consoled; for this reason young children are not unduly difficult to bring up.

With increasing years the SEIC grows. Character traits and tempera-
ments become more discernible. An older child's outbursts of will and temper show that his SEIC is quite quickly becoming harder.

The opening of the child's SEIC is brought about by the development
of intellectual aptitudes. His memory begins to function and the first memories of childhood are being etched. He is becoming intelligent (*weewe*),
aware (*sine*) and reasonable (*miriit*), i.e. he exhibits the sort of behaviour
which society around him deems appropriate.

The islanders use the word *ssuuk* for the openness of the SEIC; it means
an open door, an open book or a fully open blossom. When informants
were asked to describe how the SEIC opens they cupped their hands with
fingertips joining, then moved them apart, miming the unfolding of a hi-
biscus flower (*péen roowus aa ssukkunó*).

This process of opening is closely linked to the development of speech.
A child's SEIC begins to open and this is followed by it speaking the first
words. This means for the islanders that people can now begin to talk with
the child and explain things and give him instructions. They are convinced
that the child only understands the words that it uses itself. As a result for
them it is absurd to want to tell a child who is not yet talking to put down
something dangerous. So the object is taken away from the child in silence.
To the islanders' way of thinking a child can only be reared from the moment it starts to talk actively. Before this the SEIC is not yet in a position
to understand (*weewe*), so is incabable of identifying with what needs understanding (*weewe reen*).

It follows from this that for the Chuuk Islanders a child's language acquisition is not so much a learning process, more the natural development
of a physical function which is not dependent on the influence of the social
and linguistic milieu.

The language that a person uses would by this theory be acquired even
if he were to grow up in complete isolation. Islanders are convinced that
one of their children who grew up in a linguistic milieu not their own would
learn its language but would inevitably also speak and understand
Chuukese. A person's mother tongue is understood as a feature of race or
nationality.

The opening SEIC reaches its optimum blossoming when a person
reaches about thirty. Around this age men and women leave the life stage
énúwén and *féépwún*, and are classed as *mwáán* and *feefin*. The only feature of this stage of maturing is that the SEIC disposition is fully able to
demonstrate *miriit* (reason, a sense of duty, appropriate behaviour and maturity), which is based on a fully open SEIC.

The feature is evident at earlier stages. Even children can exhibit *miriit,* distinguishing between good and evil, what is mine and what is yours. Yet one cannot rely on them at all. Their age-group until about 13 is called *semiriit* (roughly translated: not reasonable).

The boundaries of age are fluid. Nowadays there are no rites of transition which might point to boundaries. The term *semiriit* is no longer applied to the age-group of the children, but reaches a fair way into the *énúwén* and *féépwún;* until the age of 18 the law labels all young people of Chuuk *semiriit.* Furthermore, they are not ready for marriage on being considered *miriit* – quite the contrary. The marriage experience and responsibility for their own children are thought of as factors which hasten attaining this quality and bring it to fruition.

The full opening of the SEIC coincides with its optimum hardness and size. At this point all a person's characteristics and competences (*tiip*) are clearly formed.

Individual differences demonstrate that the SEIC's development has resulted in varying degrees of openness, size and hardness. Somebody displaying at this stage a greater ability to cope with frustration, whose SEIC has attained a greater size than other people's, is mature. Malformations of the SEIC are evident in people having faulty personality profiles, deficient intelligence, less knowledge and competence, absence of self-control, etc.

At this point the SEIC has evolved to a point of stability for several years. During the life of an adult no noteworthy change takes place.

When a person gets to 40 or so, a change begins: the SEIC starts to close down, getting smaller and harder. Intellectual abilities wane, especially the memory. The person doesn't learn anything more. As the SEIC gets smaller both his tolerance of upset and his emotional stability dwindle. That is why old people (*chinnap*) lose their composure more easily than younger people. As the SEIC gets harder its original steadiness and strength of will turn into dourness and self-will. In the final stage of this decline the SEIC may lose its viability completely. Those affected become *wumwes* (opposite of *miriit*).

A few people never experience these symptoms of decline; their SEIC remains open, large and soft. They retain to a great age their mental abilities such as a good memory and their extensive knowledge. Their behaviour demonstrates a SEIC of great brightness (*saram*) and common-sense (*miriit*). The Chuuk Islanders consider them the epitome of wisdom (*átámiriit* or *niyemiriit*).

When the body dies all SEIC function ceases. In the view of the islanders, what a person has thought, striven after and felt is wholly physical.

The features and functions of the SEIC are related to the body, and thus ephemeral. A human's (physical) personality consisting of numerous dispositions (*tiip*) of the physical SEIC (*neenuuk, neetip, tipey*) embodying him has no existence beyond death.

Nevertheless a human's personality continues to exist. During its lifetime there is a SEIC (and thus a personality) which is the counterpart of the corporeal one in every respect. This SEIC belongs to a being which is fully similar to the human being, and associated with him, but with no material dimension: it is a spirit double. The following chapter deals with this spirit double and the conceptual realm of its existence.

Chapter 21
The Term "Spirit Double"

21.1 Introduction

If a Chuuk Islander is asked what happens when a person dies, he replies that the body decays, but the *ngúún* lives on. This statement holds the key to a multitude of notions about a being that survives the death of a person and perpetuates that individual's personality. The investigation of this range of concepts has to begin with the term *ngúún*.

21.2 The Term *ngúún* and Its Meanings

In the world of the Chuuk Islanders there is a group of phenomena which, despite all its variety, reveals a common feature and on the basis of this common feature all these phenomena are delineated by the term *ngúún*.

One of these phenomena is the shadow of an object or a being. However, a shadow can only be called *ngúún* if it reveals the form of the object that has cast it: *ngúún* is the silhouette of an object or being.

By contrast the shadow that produces a shaded place is called in the Chuukese language not *ngúún*, but *nnúr*. This is the shadow, for example, which offers protection from the sun when you sit "under it" (*fáán nnúrún*), but it is not the silhouette (*ngúún*) of the object in question. There is complete absence of the criterium of (recognisable) form in the concept of shadow as a shaded place (*nnúr*).

In the dialect of the island of Toon such a silhouette of an object or being can also be given the term *ngúnúwan*. (Its forms contain an obligatory suffix of relationship and are cited with the 3rd person singular unless otherwise indicated.)

A further phenomenon called *ngúún* is the mirror image of an object or being. This reveals the form of the object being reflected much more clearly than in its form as a shadow or silhouette.

Like the silhouette the mirror image can also be called *ngúnúwan* (etc.) on Toon. Both terms, *ngúún* and *ngúnúwan*, are used as terms in the language when situations to do with reflections are involved: *aa ngúnúwénú wóón sáát* (the surface of the sea is like a mirror), *emén aa éngúnúwa* (someone is looking at his reflection), *emén aa éngúnúwénúwa* (someone has put so much oil on that he is shining). However, events involving the forming of shade or shadow cannot be designated with terms derived from this word form.

A third phenomenon called *ngúún* is the notion of the Chuuk Islanders that the objects in their world do not just exist in their material form but have in addition a second form of existence. This second form of existence called *ngúún* is so completely identical in form with the object it belongs to that people who are able to perceive the normally invisible *ngúún* of objects can confuse the two. However, the way of existence of the *ngúún* of objects is fundamentally different from the material object to which it belongs. It is incorporeal, non-material, spirit-like.

Two of the most important qualities of this *ngúún* are its spirit nature and its likeness in form to the material object it belongs to, so that it appears as its double. For this reason I describe this *ngúún* as the "spirit double" of that object.

H. Fischer proposed the term "spiritual double" for describing his understanding of the "appearance in non-corporeal form" of people, animals and objects in certain regions of Oceania (1965:255-273), drawing on Crawley (1909, 1911). Certainly this description is better suited to these notions of the Chuuk Islanders than the term "image soul" (Bildseele) which has become the norm in the literature since Ankermann (Hirschberg 1965:47-48), because it excluded the associations of meaning of the European/Western concept of the soul. However, it is advisable to speak of a "spirit double" (or "spirit-like double") rather than a "spiritual" one, because meanwhile the adjective "spiritual" has undergone a change of meaning. It no longer means simply "spirit-like"[8]. Badenberg still used Crawley's term in his 1999 publication, but subsequently (2003, 2014) changed to "spirit double" like other more recent authors (e.g. Venz 2012 b).

Although the three phenomena described above are given one and the same term, *ngúún*, it should not be concluded that silhouette, mirror image and spirit double are considered by the Chuuk Islanders to be identical. These are three separate and distinct notions with clear differences as well as commonalities, as can be described by informants. The reason they are given the same term lies in two features that all three have in common: their non-materiality and the fact that the form by which the material object or being is recognised is that of the silhouette, mirror image or spirit double.

There is nothing unusual about this. No language can provide a discrete term for every individual phenomenon without inflating its vocabulary to such an extent that the language capacity of every human memory would

---

[8] With regard to the use of the term "spirituality", in the context of North American Indian ethnic groups, Feest (1998:32) commented ironically, but pointedly: "… a term which has emerged in the last 20 years as an attempt to avoid the word 'religion', as being too strongly associated with Christianity."

be overloaded. Hence languages behave economically, by grouping the "most varied" phenomena in classes represented by a single term, mostly on the basis of one feature common to that group of objects. The English word "key" can mean a metal object for opening doors, a symbol in music signifying the pitch of the various notes, and a booklet containing the rules for decoding a secret written message. Underlying the common linguistic term is the equally understood function of the three kinds of "key". The considerable differences between them have no linguistic role. It would be absurd, however, to conclude from this that the three "keys" were identical or indistinguishable. In the process of conscious, deliberate communication the speakers of that language are not aware of being hindered from also perceiving the differences in the objects which appear to be conceptually grouped together in this way. (Things are somewhat different when speaking without conscious reflection).

The same is true of the term *ngúún* and its meanings. Unambiguous statements show that silhouette, mirror image and spirit double cannot be identical. People, animals and objects always have a shadow and a mirror image, even when their spirit double is not (no longer) present, is stolen or otherwise removed. Shadow and mirror image can neither be lost nor stolen. Even objects and beings not having any material equivalent, i.e. doubles which are exclusively in spirit form (*énú*), have a mirror image.

Sometimes the Chuukese language reveals a conceptual separation, even if only between the spirit double on the one hand and the shadow or mirror image on the other. A Chuuk Islander can use the term *ngúún* for all three concepts, but the term *ngúnúwan* only for the shadow and mirror image, not for referring to the spirit double.

Soil from the place where a person's shadow has fallen can (like fingernails, hair etc.) be used to do physical harm to that person, using magic (*ppéwút*). However, such magic has no connection with the spirit double of that person. Comparable magic with the mirror image is not known among the Chuuk Islanders. Such facts show that the three notions are not conceptually identical.

Serious errors are inevitable if it is assumed that the concepts of shadow, mirror image and spirit double are identical and interchangeable simply because they are given the same word. There is a need to verify from this perspective whether it is indeed true for Oceania "that many ethnic groups […] designate their mirror image as their soul" (Hirschberg 1965:47). Information in the ethnographic sources currently available is too vague to say anything definite about it (H. Fischer, 1965:255 ff.).

An additional phenomenon called *ngúún* is conceptually closely related to the concept of the spirit double. The objects and beings which a person "sees" when dreaming are spirit doubles for which a material counterpart does not necessarily have to exist, but which nevertheless is considered by the Chuuk Islanders as existing. Images in dreams are identifiable. The person dreaming recognises in them objects and beings familiar to him. Here also the fact that their form is recognisable and that they are not material in nature is the reason for conceiving them to be *ngúún*.

Dream images also evoke the question of how pictures in the memory or the visual perception one has of objects or beings is understood. A canoe builder in the process of constructing a canoe from the trunk of a breadfruit tree has from the beginning a notion of the finished object before him as an image (*niyoos*) in his SEIC, determining the material form that is emerging. When asked about this informants confirm that this visual notion and a corresponding picture in the memory can be called *ngúún*. However, this by no means proves that this is what actually happens. There is much that contradicts the assumption that this has to do with a real concept in the world as perceived by the Chuuk Islanders. The two concepts do not appear to be consciously present in their thinking and are at most peripheral phenomena in the range of notions termed *ngúún*. What is certain is that, unlike images in dreams, images in the memory and visual perceptions are not to be identified with the spirit double of what is remembered or visualised.

As well as the spirit doubles which have a material counterpart, whether object or being, there are beings without any material counterpart, or that no longer have one. They are called *énú* (spirit beings), but exhibit basically the same characteristics as spirit doubles. Such beings "are not *ngúún*", but they "possess the *ngúún* form of existence", according to what my informants said.

The capacity of the term *ngúún* to carry the meaning "form of existence of the non-material beings", derives from establishing that the expression *emén énú (iiy) ngúún* represents an acceptable context, as opposed to the expression *emén énú (iiy) emén ngúún*.

And finally *ngúún* signifies the condition of the person after death, i.e. the condition he finds himself in when all that remains of him is his spirit double. Here *ngúún* is used in the sense of "life beyond".

The linguistic contexts relating to this are unambiguous. Chuuk Islanders call life after death *nóón* or *nupwen ngúni* (in my *ngúún*, when I am [only] *ngúún*) and *manaw nóón ngúún* (life after death).

From all this there are five meanings of *ngúún* which are clearly recognisable: 1. silhouette or shadow, 2. mirror image, 3. spirit double, and related to it 4. dream image, 5. form of existence of the person after death.

Two features are typical of these meanings. Essentially they involve phenomena with no material form. In this they differ fundamentally from the material phenomena assigned to them. Nevertheless they do posses a form which is the same as or similar to the material phenomena assigned to them and by which they can be recognised. They are copies, out-of-body manifestations, a kind of double of all objects and beings.

There are some other conceivable non-corporeal manifestations or doubles of objects which the Chuuk Islanders do not include within the concept of *ngúún*: *niyoos* (image, two-dimensional), *sasing* (photo), and *wunuun* (sculpture, model, three-dimensional).

It should be particularly noted that neither a silhouette nor a mirror image of an object or being can be identical with its spirit double, whereas the dream image of an object or being and its spirit double are regarded as one and the same. This fact results in far-reaching consequences.

Among the possible meanings of the term *ngúún* the concept of the spirit double certainly occupies a central position. Its scope will become evident from the numerous aspects which characterise it.

Right at the beginning of my inquiries I realised that it had to be given special weight, because questions about the range of meanings of *ngúún* resulted in many more spontaneous statements about the notions of the spirit double than, for example, about the concepts of the silhouette or mirror image.

However, before the individual notions of the spirit double can be analysed there is an additional term to be investigated, the linguistic features of which, together with the various notions connected to it, are closely related to the concept of the spirit double.

21.3 The Term *ngúnú* and Its Meaning

When someone remains thin despite eating regularly and substantially it must be assumed that the food he is eating is not *ngúnú*. Acquaintances concerned about his health then ask him what makes up the content of his meals (*ifa ngúnúwen onomw?*). The term *ngúnú* (rich in content) signifies the characteristic of food which helps the body to put on weight quickly.

The word *ngúnú* is adjectival and describes exclusively one quality (rich in content). By contrast its inflected forms are nominal, indicating an independent object of some kind. But it makes no difference whether you say a particular food is *ngúnú*, or whether it possesses *ngúnúwan*.

What is noteworthy about the term *ngúnú* is the fact that its inflected forms which are used for conveying the content of food are identical with the forms of *ngúnúwan*, which can denote (instead of *ngúún*) the silhouette and mirror image of an object or being.

The objects which can be *ngúnú* or possess *ngúnúwan* include first and foremost starchy tubers (*mwéngéén nóón pwpwún*) such as taro, tapioca, sweet potatoes etc. Meat is particularly *ngúnú*, and in recent times through European/Western influence all those foods known to contain a high level of vitamins. Drinks are not *ngúnú*, but all kinds of highly fragrant liquid cosmetics (*néé*) are, whether of local or foreign production.

Tubers can be more, or less *ngúnú*. If starch is to be gained from *mwékúmwék* (Tacca leontopetaloides, Mahony 1970:103), the tubers are kneaded to a fibrous mass, water is added and the mixture passed through a sieve. If a lot of starch is deposited (*soon*), the tubers were *ngúnúmmóng* (rich in content), otherwise *ngúnúngngin*. A detailed description of the procedure for obtaining curcumin can be found in LeBar (1964:49-50).

The quality of being *ngúnú* or possessing *ngúnúwan* is not transferable, neither by contact nor by using magic. People and animals who eat such food do not thereby become *ngúnú*, but *kitinnup* (fat). There is also no perception at all that the content of plant food can be enhanced by the use of manure.

Only with revulsion do informants make any reference to being forced under Japanese occupation to dig human or animal excrement into the soil and cultivate plants in it.

The number of objects able to possess content in the sense of *ngúnú* and *ngúnúwan*, is relatively very small. By contrast the number of objects possessing a spirit double in the sense of *ngúún* is enormously large, but phonological and morphological criteria reveal clear connections between these word forms. The fact that their meanings (content and spirit double) are also related to each other will become clear when discussing the consequences resulting from the separation of material object and spirit double. This will also involve discussion of the issue of whether or not the Chuuk Islanders have concepts of a "soul-like substance".

Chapter 22
The Spirit Double of Objects

22.1 Characteristics

Spirit doubles of objects have the same form as their material counterparts, but are themselves not material, but indeed spirit-like. Usually they are invisible. People who are dreaming see them so clearly that they can describe them afterwards. Certain people like mediums (*waatawa*) and seers (*móngupwi*) are able to see spirit doubles even when they are not dreaming, but awake.

A material object and its spirit double are not only identical in form but also in colour, smell, taste and the other senses. Even the effects they can bring about (e.g. the effects of a drug) are the same for both.

Medicine of illumination (*sáfeen asaram*) as an offering to the spirit of a deceased person is based on the notion that the latter only absorbs the spirit double of the medicament and that alone is sufficient to acquire an illuminated SEIC.

The identity in form of the material object to its spirit double applies also to their ontogenesis, which is believed to unfold in parallel. Thus the spirit doubles of plants, animals and people undergo all the changes in form which their material counterparts do in the process of development.

However, this identity, which characterises not only the form but also the changes in form of both the material object and its spirit double, does not continue unlimited. In all respects the double has the same form as that which the material object has or should have in normal circumstances, in order to function properly and efficiently. It only changes when its material counterpart changes in ways which are expected or intended. If the material object suffers damage or is destroyed this does not necessarily mean the destruction of its spirit double. Chuuk Islanders acknowledge that it is difficult to be sure about this, but are inclined to the view that if an object is damaged or destroyed its spirit double remains unharmed. Hence the material object can sometimes exist in a different form from that of its spirit double.

This throws up a whole series of questions which are difficult to resolve. If a bowl breaks in pieces its spirit double remains undamaged. Yet the fragments of the bowl are material objects with a form, for which a spirit double must exist. These could not come from the original spirit double of the bowl, for that has remained undamaged.

One possible explanation for assuming that the spirit double remains whole is as follows: linguistic research has shown that Chuuk Islanders are unable to disconnect the term "matter" from some kind of form. For them matter (*meen, mettóóch*) appears to be always coupled with the meaning "thing, object" (i.e. something with form). Fragments of a bowl are objects with no definite form, and have no use or meaning compared with the intact bowl, so that the Islanders would rather assign a spirit double to something recognisably meaningful, i.e. the intact bowl. Nevertheless they are quite able to follow this train of thought ad absurdum and to recognise its illogicalities.

The recognition that damage and destruction affecting a material object does not necessarily affect its spirit double leads to an important conclusion.

22.2 Separability of a Material Object from Its Spirit Double

The spirit double has an existence independent of the material object. In reality the spirit double is independent of its material counterpart in a way which permits it to spatially separate the two.

Before Christianity was accepted the Chuuk Islanders used to prepare presents for the deceased, which were placed as *owun ménúmá* on the grave of the one who had only recently died, and offered as *ósór* to the important ancestors who had died long ago: food, fragrant liquids, items of jewellery etc. The things which the deceased (the surviving spirit doubles of the deceased) took to themselves were simply the spirit doubles of the presents. Their material counterparts remained undisturbed where they had been placed.

Offerings to the spirits of ancestors who died a long time ago are no longer made. Also no *owun ménúmá* is any longer laid on the grave of the recently deceased; instead it is taken into the house of the relatives of the deceased.

22.3 Consequences of the Separation

Chuuk Islanders say that at first no changes of any kind can be perceived in objects whose spirit double is no longer present. However, they claim that one can soon notice that they no longer fulfil their purpose as well as before, become blunt and break more easily than those whose spirit double is present. Food set before the deceased as a gift and, as a consequence, without a spirit double dries up or rots more quickly than other food. Most striking was the finding that such food offerings do not make those who eat them put on weight, however much they might have consumed. Having lost its spirit double, such food was no longer *ngúnú*, had lost its nutritional value, its content.

22.4 "Soul Substance"?

In this connection some ethnographers writing about ethnic groups in South East Asia and Oceania speak of "soul substance". Whether indeed such a concept is present in those ethnic groups seems at least doubtful or must for the time being remain an open question (H. Fischer, 1965:299-313).

When Chuuk Islanders refer to certain objects as possessing *ngúnúwan*, it may well appear that they mean something material, which is removed along with the spirit double. There are several reasons against this assumption: 1. Whatever soul substance might be, it would only be present in a few objects such as tubers. 2. The concept of soul substance then lacks the recognisable form which has to be present in order to be able to call a phenomenon *ngúnúwan*; 3. The attitude of the informants shows that this cannot actually be a concept in their thinking.

22.5 Origin and Fate of the Spirit Double

Notions of the origin of the spirit double of material objects and beings are only defined in a few areas. People are mostly satisfied with the assertion that they have one, if they exist, but in some instances notions are revealed claiming that spirit doubles are pre-existent and bring about the origin of their material counterparts. Such notions are closely bound up with observations of the growth of plants.

Somewhere in the south of Chuuk lies the isle of *Éwúr*. People cannot reach it, for it only exists as the spirit double of an island (*náán, piis*). No material counterpart to it exists. Even the plants and beings there are exclusively spirit doubles. *Éwúr* is famous among the Chuuk Islanders, for it has food galore. Nowhere else do the coconuts, bananas and taro flourish so well, and nowhere else can one catch such magnificent fish. *Éwúr* is a kind of Cockaigne.

On some islands of the Chuuk lagoon there are certain places considered to be particularly fruitful, and they are called *Neeyéwúr*, e.g. near *Wóónipw*, a settlement on *Toon*, and on *Paata*.

The lord of *Éwúr* is the mighty spirit *Sowuyéwúr*, an *énúúsór*. When the breadfruit trees (*maay*) on the islands of Chuuk show signs of forming breadfruits the time has come for *Sowuyéwúr* to send countless spirit doubles of breadfruits which settle on the trees and produce edible breadfruits in the same form. If no spirit doubles arrive from *Éwúr* the harvest will fail and there will be famine.

In earlier times the fear that *Sowuyéwúr* might hold back the spirit doubles of the breadfruit (and other plants used for food) was a matter of great concern to the islanders, leading to the establishment of the office of bread-fruit sorcerer (*sowumey*, *sowuyatoomey*), whose task it was to ensure the process of fruit formation by means of certain rituals.

Notions of the fate of the spirit double of objects when its material counterpart no longer exists are just as vaguely defined as the notions of their origin. It seems that what happens to it is of little importance for the Chuuk Islanders. Its fate does not interest them. However, it is part of the nature of the spirit double that it can continue to exist, even when its material counterpart is no longer present. It is still called *ngúún* and undergoes no change (*wutumas*), like the corresponding spirit double of a person when it becomes a spirit of the dead (cf. ch. 26.3.2).

Bollig's claim (1927:13), that the "souls of objects" perish along with their material counterpart is shown to be incorrect after examination of the facts.

22.6 The Significance of the Spirit Double for Its Material Counterpart

Summarising the above observations on the relationship of the material object to its spirit double leads to the following conclusions:

Destruction of the material object has no effect on its spirit double.

The two can be separated without any immediate effect on either. Some time after the separation the material object shows signs of (accelerated) decay and loss of its original or customary efficiency, but not the loss of its shadow/silhouette or mirror image. By contrast the spirit double suffers no ill effects.

Many objects which undergo development, e.g. plants, possess a pre-existent spirit double, the final form of which they eventually assume. However, this pre-existence is not presumed for all objects.

One can deduce from these conclusions that for the Chuuk Islanders the spirit double occupies the prime position, exercising a determining effect on its material counterpart. This determining effect emerges particularly clearly in the relationships between the person and his or her spirit double.

Chapter 23
The World Beyond of the Chuuk Islanders

23.1 The Spirit Double and the Structure of the World

For the Chuuk Islanders each object and each being exists at the same time in two forms, a material one and a spirit-like one. This means that alongside the material world as the totality of all material objects and beings there is a second world as the totality of all related spirit doubles, having the corresponding characteristics.

Since material objects and their spirit doubles have the same form, the material world and the spirit-like world, each in their totality, ought likewise to possess the same form. That is not the case. In the spirit-like world objects are imperishable. By contrast in the material world new objects and beings provided with a spirit double continually arise and pass away. When material objects and beings pass away their spirit doubles are preserved, thus increasing the number that already exists.

Here, too, the theory is confronted by contradictions. If all spirit doubles are preserved, then over the course of time this spirit world would not have enough room to accommodate all the objects and beings in it. Only in rare, exceptional cases and within a very limited framework were informants prepared to admit the possibility that one spirit double could be assigned to a material object or being several times over (ch. 26.3.12)

All this means that the imbalance of the material world and the spirit world is based on the simple fact that while (to all intents and purposes) no material object or being can exist without a spirit double, there exists an abundance of spirit objects and beings without (any longer) a material counterpart.

23.2 This World and the World Beyond

Since all material objects and beings, after the loss of their material form of existence, continue to exist in the form of the spirit double, particularly the person after the death of the body, the world of the spirit doubles appears to correspond to a certain extent to the "life beyond" of European/Western society. Its counterpart, the world of material objects and beings, can be compared with life on "this side".

The terms "this world" and "the world beyond", as applied subsequently to the contrasting pair material world and spirit world, serve to define clearly the notions held by the Chuuk Islanders concerning the structure of their world. All objects and beings materially present exist simultaneously in this world and the world beyond; objects and beings having no (longer any) material counterpart only exist in the beyond.

For the Chuuk Islanders this world and the world beyond exist alongside each other at the same time and in the same location. The only difference is in their way of existing (material and spirit-like).

In the Chuukese language there is no actual term meaning "this world". But in certain contexts *ngúún* would seem to signify the "beyond" (cf. 21.2).

This world and the world beyond are not as sharply separated as these two expressions might imply. They interact in numerous ways. The determining effect that an individual spirit double can exercise on its material counterpart emanates from the beyond into this world in a comprehensive way. There is a reciprocal influence which this world has on the beyond, but only to a limited extent.

23.3 Structure of the Beyond

23.3.1 Spirit-like Locations (*náán*)

The disparity between this world and the beyond also affects the notions of how they are structured. It is thought that in the beyond there are areas, regions, locations and places with no counterpart in this world. They are called *náán* (*nenin énú*).

A *náán* in its broadest sense is the spirit double of a location (*ngúnún neeni*), an abode of spirits where benevolent spirit beings (*ngúnúyééch, énúúyééch*) are accustomed to socialise or reside (Mahony 1970:136 "spirit homes"). Normally malevolent spirit beings (*énúngngaw*) are denied access to such abodes. Nevertheless they are always trying to gain entry.

In order to distinguish the various *náán* from each other they are given individual names reminiscent of the names given to certain places on the islands in the Chuuk lagoon, e.g. *Féwúkasé* (stone of rest), *Neechuunap* (place of assembly) or *Ppiyeyireng* (saffron-yellow sand). Using a collection of these names one could draw up a detailed topography of the world beyond.

Goodenough (1966:95-129) has made a general collection of these place names and set out the individual locations on a map.

There is an extraordinary large number of these *náán*. Each island and each village usually possesses several. Above all they are the abode of the benevolent spirits of the dead (*énúúsootupw*) of the deceased inhabitants. Sometimes a new *náán* arises near the grave of an important deceased person, and it is believed that his benevolent spirit will remain permanently at that place (e.g. *Neekuchiyón* for the village of *Chukiyénú*).

Spirit beings like remoteness and quiet, so *nάάn* are particularly abundant in regions where no one lives, i.e. on uninhabited islands, on the barrier reef of the Chuuk lagoon, in the atmosphere above the earth and the sea, possibly even under the earth. Basically there is no place where one could not presume a *nάάn* to be present.

Among the innumerable *nάάn* there are some renowned ones where many and mighty spirit beings prefer to reside. One such *nάάn* is *Tupwuniyόn* (Sunset), which is thought to be "somewhere in the west", and is famed because of his shining red and yellow colours. Another famous *nάάn* is the already mentioned island of *Éwúr*, the Cockaigne of the Chuuk Islanders.

As a purely spirit-like location a *nάάn* is normally not visible. It can be that a path or a canal crosses it. People and other beings make their way through unnoticed and have nothing to fear, because when one is in the area of a *nάάn* one is always in the vicinity of benevolent spirit beings.

However, when one is dreaming the world of the *nάάn* becomes "visible" in all its strangeness. The dreamer recognises and experiences details about the objects and beings that are there. The Chuuk Islanders derive most of their knowledge about the nature and characteristics of the *nάάn* from their dreams. Thus one knows, for example, that in the *nάάn* and quite generally in the world beyond it is always day, for no one has ever had a dream experience in which it was night.

Only the medium (*waatawa*) has special knowledge about where certain *nάάn* are located and what happens in them, for he is the only person to whom the ability is attributed of seeing *nάάn* when awake. Through him it is known that most *nάάn* move around freely and can betake themselves at lightning speed to wherever the inhabiting spirit beings desire them to go. *Nάάn* are thus just as independent of time and place as all other spirit doubles.

Sometimes the mobility or fixedness of a *nάάn* is indicated in its name: *Nenifάtάn* (the moving one), *Nenichchang* (the hovering one), *Nenisú* (the hurriedly departing one), *Nenippόs* (the immoveable one) .

There are special *nάάn*, where only the spirits of the dead of women, men, famous warriors or sorcerers reside. Of particular importance for a Chuuk Islander are the *nάάn* of his clan or extended family (*nenin eyinang* or *faameni*), because these are the preferred abode of the spirits of his ancestors, who care for the spirit doubles of their future unborn family members.

Each *nάάn* is also the location of all the spirit doubles of all those objects and beings which spirit beings are accustomed to surround themselves with and engage with. Here are the practical items of daily life, houses, boats, good food, and also all kinds of amusements, competitions, dance festivals etc. and all in abundance and of best quality. A *nάάn* is a kind of paradise.

23.3.2 Spirit-like Landscapes (*piis*)

Larger *náán* have landscapes conceived as spirit-like and are called *piis* (*pisin énú*). They contain islands, lakes, the sea, luxuriant vegetation and much more. The Chuuk Islanders also conceive *piis* to be the levels of the sky (*sássárin nááng*).

The sky (*nááng*) comprehends the whole air space above the earth, understood to be a finite hemisphere of great height. The actual boundary ("the blue, where the stars are") is called *fachcham* or simply *nááng*, like all the space below it. But this is not the limit of the cosmos. Above it lies the actual *Fachcham*, the abode of the Great Spirit (*Énúúnap*), the Supreme Being of the Chuuk Islanders. The *Fachcham* is a gigantic *náán* with many *piis*, a paradisiacal land with a great variety of regions, inhabited by countless spirit beings.

Bollig's account (1927:3 ff.) of the world view of the Chuuk Islanders in general and of their notions of the sky or heaven in particular has meanwhile been strongly influenced and altered by Christian ideas and the general knowledge of astronomy. Not all of the names of the individual levels of the sky and their order were familiar even to my almost ninety-year-old informant *Wupwiini*.

23.3.3 Places of Offering (*faar*)

The *faar* (*fárin énú*), the place of offerings to the spirits of deceased family or village members (*neeniyen ósoomáá ngeni énú*; Mahony 1970:136 "spirit altars") is a completely different kind of *náán*, because it also exists in material form.

Today the *faar* has completely disappeared. It used to exist in various forms, as shown in Krämer's illustrations (1932, 1935).

The most widespread was the *faar* in the form of a double canoe made of wood (usually breadfruit tree wood), the two hulls being held together by a box-like centrepiece. Sometimes the box would have a lid shaped like a roof, and in many instances the hulls were missing, leaving only a box. There were also small ones 30 to 50 cm long (Bollig 1927:31), but some were as long as an arm or up to the dimensions of a table. The size of the *faar* corresponded to the importance of the spirit of the dead being honoured, which also determined the wealth of its decoration and colouring. Its decoration corresponded to that of the seaworthy outrigger canoes and was coloured white, red and black. Sometimes a dance stick was laid across it from which additional offerings could be hung. The dance stick indicated an important activity of all benevolent spirit beings, who especially enjoy group dancing.

Usually the *faar* hung from a rope made of coconut fibre from the ridge beam of the house, but could also be found standing on the floor. (Illustrations Krämer 1932:240, plate 27; 256, plate 28: 283, Fig. 210).

The second type of *faar* consisted of a particularly large and richly carved dance stick, on both ends of which a piece of coconut fibre string was tied, somewhat longer than the dance stick itself. When hung up this string, decorated with fronds of young coconut palm leaves, formed a triangle with the dance stick from which offering gifts were hung. (Illustrations Krämer 1932:152, plate 14 c; 274, Fig. 207; 278, Fig. 208 and 209; 1935, Vol. 2:152, plate 1).

A third, apparently rarer type, consisted of a house-like structure veiled by a curtain made of plant fibres. (Illustration Krämer 1932:341, Fig. 223).

Sometimes the box of the *faar* also contained the bones of the deceased person to whose surviving benevolent spirit offerings were being brought. Its emotional attachment to the remains of its previously existing body obliged it to return again and again to its *faar*. In this way the living could rely on its frequent presence and call on its help more easily. However, burial at the *faar* was reserved for the physical remains of people whose surviving benevolent spirit was regarded as particularly powerful or possessing high status, i.e. an *énúúsór*. The large, ostentatiously furnished *faar* were located in the communal houses (*wuut*). Simpler designs, serving only as places of offering, were to be found individually in dwellings (*iimw*).

These were made by craftsmen who were also skilled in other kinds of woodwork (*sowufanafan*). Supervision was by the medium of the village or of the family in question.

Behaviour to do with the *faar* involved special taboo regulations (*pin*). Nobody apart from the head of the family or the medium would dare to approach it without risk of punishment in the form of disease or death by the spirit of the dead to whom offerings were being made.

There is no reliable information about the origin of the *faar* in the form of the double canoe and its connection with the origin of the "ancestral settlers". That which Böhme (1937:63) was able to extract from the sources consists only of assumptions by the ethnographers.

Later Damm (1954) evaluated the sources in more depth, compiled their illustrations and compared them with similar phenomena in South East Asia.

The *faar* constitutes a special case among the spirit-like locations called *náán*, because it is not exclusively spirit-like, and hence not conceived as being solely part of the world beyond. But it can only be a genuine *náán* if benevolent spirit beings are in the habit of socialising and residing there.

Chapter 24
Beings in the World Beyond

24.1 Introduction

In the earlier discussion of the world beyond and the spirit objects with no material counterpart, the spirit doubles of beings were tacitly implied. This was justifiable, for in principle the same phenomena are involved. However, spirit beings are furnished with qualities which differentiate them from spirit objects, and which need to be described separately, otherwise it is difficult to integrate and understand the concepts of the spirit doubles of living people.

The spirit beings which are now about to be discussed are exclusively those for which a material counterpart has never existed, or no longer exists.

24.2 The Term *énú* and Its Meanings

A being which only exists in spirit form, i.e. transcendent, of the world beyond, is called *énú*. This reflects the first difference from spirit objects, which are always called *ngúún*, even when they only exist in spirit form.

In addition a transcendent being differs from a transcendent object in that it has animal or human features, i.e. it can generate its own movements, indicating consciousness or a will of its own. Hence *énú* are (living) spirit beings, having a SEIC (*neenuuk, neetip, tipey*) and consequently a personality.

Although *énú* are not categorised as *ménúmanaw* (living beings) they are referred to as *raa manaw* (they are alive); also numerals referring to *énú* must carry the suffix for alive (*emén, rúwémén énú*).

In the anatomical terminology of the islanders the word *énú* also means the cervix, and according to Mahony 1969:209 the whole uterus (cf. 7.9); a connection with the notions of spirit beings cannot here be established.

24.3 Characteristics Common to all Kinds of Spirit Beings

24.3.1 General

Spirit beings have no material body, only a bodily form (*napanap*), but which they can change at will. The smallest aperture anywhere is sufficient for them to gain entry.

However, without such an opening it is for example impossible for them to get into a house. Chuuk Islanders cannot conceive of a spirit being getting inside a stone which has no hole or crack. This means that the spirit nature of an *énú* is perceived as having limited, not complete non-materiality.

The fact that spirit beings are not perceived as being totally spirit-like is also revealed by the very pronounced physical features, including associated physiological aspects, which are attributed to them. They do not cast a shadow, but it is assumed that they have a mirror image.

More details about their appearance are known from the descriptions given by mediums, from dreams, and encounters with spirit beings. Apart from dreams their visibility is dependent on special circumstances, which differ among the individual types of spirit being.

Spirit beings are independent of time and place. They can cover even the greatest of distances from island to island or from earth to sky without any elapse of time.

All spirit beings are capable of thought, feeling and will, i.e. they possess a SEIC, as described in chapters 15-20. This is constituted differently among the individual types of *énú*. Their variety is expressed in the predominance of certain typical dispositions of their SEIC, representing criteria according to which spirit beings can be divided into certain categories.

It is impossible for any person to injure or kill a spirit being. Nevertheless, despite their nature as spirits, they are not immortal, apart from spirit beings with special status (*énúúsór*). If an *énú* antagonises a high-ranking spirit being by failing to show the required respect it can reckon on being punished by death in *Neepwúnnúpis*.

Neepwúnnúpis is a spirit-like location in the form of a hole, from which there is no escape. Such holes exist exclusively in the beyond, but are present in large numbers, for the individual islands in various places, on the penultimate stage of the sky, (*Fachcham*), on the earth, particularly on uninhabited islands, under the earth or somewhere in the depths of the sea (*fáán fááyinón*). For the spirit beings of the island of *Toon* there is such a hole on *Wonnang*, an uninhabited island of the Chuuk barrier reef.

Neepwúnnúpis is not a *náán*. The information varies according to the informant. Sometimes there are the variant forms *Neepúnnúpis* and *Neepúngúnnúpis*.

If a spirit being has not made itself known for some time and has not permitted itself to appear despite the keeping of all the taboos and observance of the necessary rituals, then there is good reason to assume that it has perished in *Neepwúnnúpis*. Only in extremely rare cases has *Énúúnap*, the Supreme Being of the islanders, revoked the "death" (*máánó*) of a spirit being in this place of damnation, in earlier times.

Among the features common to all spirit beings there is also a quality or capability which can explain the unusual effects which emanate from them.

24.3.2 Mana (*manaman, iiman*)

The Chuuk Islanders' concept of mana is made up of so many individual notions that it is impossible to provide here anything approaching a comprehensive description. This has been done elsewhere (Käser 1991). Hence the following summary of the most important aspects provides only a rough survey of its linguistic and conceptual complexity, but is nevertheless essential for an understanding of the functions of spirit beings and beyond that of the world view of the Chuuk Islanders.

The concept of mana might well be called a classic problem of research into the religion and ethnology of Oceania. In the history of research into mana two periods can be discerned. The studies in the period up to the publication of Lehmann's dissertation (1915) tend towards speculation, conditioned by a lack of an adequate foundation in initial ethnographic and linguistic data, leading to unreliable generalisations and a one-sided grasp of the concept of mana. In his dissertation Lehmann compiled the available reports on the concept of mana up to 1915, compared them, and published an extended version of this study in 1922. His assertion that linguistic perspectives play an important part in understanding the concept of mana led in the following period to a whole series of empirical investigations, of which the essay by Firth (1940, 1970) counts as a prime example. My own results are based on the same methodic principles.

Mana is a factual attribute of events, objects and beings. This makes it fundamentally different from the concept of taboo (on which more detail under 24.6). Whether events, objects and beings "are" mana or "possess" mana is of no importance.

Word forms denoting the concept of mana are *man, iiman* (adjectival) and the (more frequently used) reduplicated form *manaman* (adjectival and nominal). There is no fundamental difference in meaning between expressions such as *óóch mettóóch aa manaman* (an object is mana) and *aa wor aan manaman* (it possesses mana).

From the external appearance it is not possible to discern whether an event, object or being possesses mana. This can only be concluded from their effects. They must prove themselves to be *manaman* in order to be accepted as *manaman*.

This can happen in various ways. A person who is uninjured after falling from a tree or is just missed by a falling coconut must be *manaman*. In the former his mana has preserved him from harm, and in the latter has deflected the coconut which would otherwise have hit him. People who have shown themselves to be mana in this way are called *átáman* or *niyeman*.

The usual way objects are revealed as being mana are through the help they give in achieving intended effects in an unusual form, or even effects which one would not normally expect of them.

A spear must possess mana if it is apparent that it hits the target more often than other spears, or impales bigger fish. In such cases the unusual effect could be brought about by the mana of the one throwing the spear. If the latter is true, the proof would be in the fact that the same unusual effect is achieved with other spears, not just with that particular one.

Not everything that achieves an intended outcome or proves to be especially efficient may also possess mana. A tool which does the job better than others is noticeably *túúfich* (suitable), but not *manaman*. Situations in which an object can be shown to be *manaman* are characterised by the small probability of actually achieving a desired effect. The smaller the probability, the greater the mana evident in such a situation.

This means that a spear is shown to be *manaman* not only in comparison with other spears but also, for example, by hitting the same spot several times in succession.

There are people whose presence has such an impressive effect on others that they command respect and obedience. The authority of such personalities (*manaman wóón aramas*) derives from the mana which they clearly possess, and is also inherent in the words they speak. The more unquestioningly their instructions are followed, the greater their mana must be.

Status and mana mutually determine each other. Those who are evidently *manaman* enjoy higher status, and vice versa those to whom mana is attributed are assumed to have status.

Terms such as *nemenem* (power, control) and *péchékkún* (force, energy) are not part of the mana concept.

Like all mana, the mana of the word spoken by such authority figures can become dangerous. If such people utter a curse on someone who is resisting their will, this will bring calamity on that person and can result in death. If people of high status even sense displeasure or the desire to punish someone, this can have the same consequences.

This aspect of the concept of mana plays an important part in the Christian thinking of the islanders. If a missionary or a local pastor as much as names something which is *ttipis* (sin), the one who has become *ttipis* must fear that he will become *feyiyangngaw*, i.e. that something will happen to him.

On the other hand the mana of missionaries and local pastors works mostly to advantage. The presence of such a person on board a canoe makes an accident at sea unlikely, so the islanders assume.

Associating with people whose mana can mean danger obliges one to observe a number of rules of behaviour. Those who enjoy special status because of their mana (or vice versa) are taboo (*pin*), meaning that one must show them respect, and that any violation of that can incur serious consequences. However, not every object or person proved to be *manaman* is thereby necessarily also *pin*.

The relationship between mana, taboo and the concept of the holy have been described in detail elsewhere (Käser 1991, 1994).

In and of itself *manaman* is a value-neutral concept, but looked at subjectively it is ambivalent: there is good and bad mana (respectively *manamanééch* and *manamanangngaw*), depending on whether the effects experienced are useful or harmful. A spell aimed to do hurt (*ppéwút*) is always regarded as containing evil mana.

Events for which one can find no explanation, happenings which surely could not occur like they have, are likewise *manaman*. It is possible that they could have been caused by people or objects with mana, but one is more likely to look for the reason among the spirit beings.

Such inexplicable events are likewise called *manaman* (miracles). They can happen (*óóch manaman aa fis*), and they can be performed (*fééri manaman*).

Not all spirit beings are proved to be mana, but those who possess it are mostly far superior to people and objects who also have it. Malevolent spirit beings (*énúngngaw*) are considered to have less mana than benevolent ones (*énúúyééch*).

Spirit beings regarded as especially *manaman* are called *énúúman*. In general everything said about people and mana applies also to spirit beings. The greater the mana of a spirit being, the higher its status among its kind.

If events, objects and beings are indeed *manaman*, it has to reveal itself. This means it is mostly discovered by chance (as is also the loss of it). However, sometimes objects and even people can be made *manaman*. This never happens through contact with an object or being possessing this quality, but always in the context of an action during which mana is not transferred, but arises.

For example the mana of a medicament (*sáfey*) arises in the process of production. The observance of certain taboos is merely a necessary prerequisite for it. The medicament becomes *manaman* in the sense intended when the individual actions are undertaken in the "correct" sequence and the accompanying words are spoken without error. If the maker commits a blunder the medicament will remain ineffectual or will become *manamanangngaw*, i.e. it will bring about in the maker the very symptoms it is supposed to remove (more details in Mahony 1970).

Mana as a feature of personality (authority) cannot arise within the context of an action, but the act by which a person is inducted into an office does indeed bring about heightened mana in that person. The prayer of a church elder who has been consecrated is regarded as more effectual than the prayer of an ordinary Christian. This effectiveness is not the result of a transfer of mana during the act of consecration but is believed to have arisen during the act.

Spirit beings can be involved when an object or being becomes *manaman*, but their cooperation is not absolutely required. As far as the Chuuk Islanders are concerned mana always means something unusual, out of the ordinary, but not purely of the beyond or bound to beings of the beyond. No proof can be found that in the final analysis mana could have or must have originated in the world beyond.

The extent to which the concept of mana is independent of notions of the beyond is illustrated by the following example. If a passport has not expired, it has *manaman* (validity), similarly a bank note if it is part of the official national currency, and a cheque becomes *manaman*, when it is signed.

For the Chuuk Islanders mana is essentially an effectiveness beyond the normal, integral to events, objects and beings, and able to manifest itself in terms of authority. Spirit beings are furnished with particularly effective mana, each according to status. At the same time it is not something expressly of the beyond, or attributed to religion. There is no evidence of any particular connection between mana and concepts of the soul.

24.4 Types of Spirit Beings

Spirit beings exist in immeasurable numbers, but the Chuuk Islanders do not have a single unified conception of their appearance. Using the features by which they can be distinguished they can be divided into categories as follows:

Feature	Term	Meaning
abode	*énúún nááng*	sky spirit
	énússet	sea spirit, reef spirit
	énúún	spirit that lives
	óroppeniinen	on the horizon
	énúún pwpwún	earth spirit
origin	*énúúsootupw*	spirit of a deceased person

Feature	Term	Meaning
sex	énúúfeefin énúúmwáán	female spirit male spirit
appearance	enú aramas énúmmóng	spirit with human exterior giant spirit
status	énúúsamwoon énúúsór	"chief spirit" or "titular spirit" mighty, effecting spirit
function	énúún fénú énúún sóópw énúún eyinang énúún faameni	guardian spirit of an island of a village of a clan of a family
special capacity	énúúman	spirit possessing mana
typical behaviour	énúúsowusow énúúwochooch	spirit that lies in wait for people spirit that attacks ("bites", or eats raw things)
character traits	énúúpwara énúúpweteete énúúroch énúúmwaken soope énúúyééch énúngngaw	adventurous spirit gentle spirit aggressive spirit lying spirit malevolent spirit (of the deceased) benevolent spirit malevolent spirit

Table 4: Types of spirit beings

In accordance with the last two characteristics all types of spirit beings can be summed up in two groups. An *énú* is either a benevolent (*énúúyééch*) spirit being or a malevolent one (*énúngngaw*).

The division of spirit beings into benevolent and malevolent ones is not so much made according to their usefulness or harmfulness towards humans, but rather on the basis of the character traits attributed to them. The Chuuk Islanders distinguish between benevolent and malevolent spirit beings according to the contrasting disposition of their SEIC (*tipeyééch* and *tipangngaw*), their positive or negative basic attitude.

The suffixes *-ééch* and *-ngngaw* do not just mean good or bad, as we understand it, but in quite general terms the contrast between higher and lower quality: beautiful and ugly, advantageous and disadvantageous, fitting and unfitting, appropriate and inappropriate.

24.5 Benevolent Spirit Beings (*énúúyééch*) and Their Features

24.5.1 Visibility

Like all *énú* benevolent spirit beings are normally invisible, but can sometimes make themselves visible or simply become visible. However, it is in their nature to reveal themselves rarely, in contrast to their malevolent counterparts.

It is not possible for ordinary people really to perceive a spirit being. Hardly any Chuuk Islander will claim to have ever seen one face to face when awake. Only the mediums, through whom one can make contact with them, have this capability.

However, in dreams anyone can see them, as dream images in human form, but even then they are only *énúúyééch* when the dream images are not those of living persons (*ngúnúyééch*). The dream images of animals are also generally not considered to be benevolent spirit beings.

24.5.2 Appearance

The feature which proves that a spirit being is without doubt benevolent is its total identification with a person's outward appearance. This is why *énúúyééch* are also called human spirits (*énú aramas*).

This designation, *énú aramas*, is certainly first and foremost an indicator of their outward appearance, but can also be regarded as related to their origin. Benevolent spirit beings are for the most part the spirits of deceased persons (*aramas*), but there are *énú aramas* which the islanders say have never belonged to a living person. Further evidence against their origin being the basis for the designation *énú aramas* is provided by the fact that a particular kind of malevolent spirit being (*soope*) cannot be called *énú aramas*, although they are also the surviving spirits of deceased persons.

Benevolent spirit beings never display any signs of disease, physical defect or malformation. In many ways they reflect the Chuuk Islanders' ideal of beauty. To the mediums their form appears so bright (*saram*), that even in daylight they stand out against the background. Nevertheless inexplicable manifestations of light are regarded not as benevolent spirit beings but as malevolent ones, because they do not let any human shape be recognised. Benevolent spirit beings wear clothes, decoration, and sometimes carry tools (in the form of spirit doubles of these objects), by which one can recognise them.

24.5.3 Physical Features

Physical height and weight correspond exactly to those of a person of equal size. Because of its weight a spirit being can leave footprints behind. Its bodily weight is yet more discernible when it is sitting on the shoulders of a medium and speaking to the living. If it is a man-sized spirit being the medium, who is crouching or sitting on the ground, groans under the load. By contrast spirit beings of the size of a child are felt by the medium to be light.

They have the same body temperature as a person, or warmer. This explains the medium's perspiration during any lengthy contact with the spirit of a deceased person, the two of them being in close bodily contact with each other while the spirit is being questioned.

Like all *énú*, benevolent spirit beings can exercise impressive bodily strength. If required, they can effortlessly uproot trees and move boulders from their location. In this they are always superior to malevolent spirit beings.

They can move about freely, run, climb, fly and swim. Dancing is one of their favourite occupations. They breathe like humans, but can cope without breathing for an unlimited period. When they sleep it is not because of bodily need but as a pleasant way of passing the time.

They can speak, sing and weep like humans. Dreams are the proof of this: many *énúúyééch* are considered to be excellent singers. However, people who are awake are never addressed by them directly, but always via a medium.

Their speaking ability differs from that of malevolent spirit beings, who sometimes appear in human-like form but cannot articulate properly. This is why only benevolent spirit beings can answer the medium's questions. A spirit being that does not speak or only makes incomprehensible sounds shows that it is malevolent.

Benevolent spirit beings can hear and see better than humans and animals. Their senses of smell and taste are particularly acute. Unpleasant odours have a repugnant effect on them, make them angry and drive them away. Pleasant ones attract them, even over great distances, and placate them.

They find human body odour repulsive. Anyone having dealings with them must pay the greatest attention to personal hygiene. No *énúúyééch* would approach a medium who placed no value on care of the body.

Among the odours that are repudiated by spirit beings are particularly that of human genitalia. Menstruating women are avoided by them and are then in great danger because without the presence of benevolent spirit beings they are exposed without defence to the malevolent ones, who feel themselves attracted by unpleasant smells.

Like all spirit beings, *enúúyééch* are not required to take in nourishment regularly, but now and again they do develop an appetite for something tasty. At the same time their sense of taste is very particular. They only eat food which is mild and quite fresh. Among the strong-tasting foods which they disdain are fermented breadfruit (*épwét, maar*) and high or salted fish, acidic fruits such as oranges (*kurukur*) or lemons (*siitor*), and all things bitter (*maras, pwáánu, kkipwin*). Anyone having dealings with *énúúyééch* or in need of their help in a special way must avoid these foods.

Énúúyééch are sexual beings, but their sexual interests are directed exclusively towards their own kind, and not towards humans and animals like their malevolent counterparts. However, female spirit beings to not become pregnant. Their sexual activities are part of their lifestyle, which is focused completely on pleasure.

24.5.4 Emotional and Mental Characteristics

Énúúyééch think, decide, have memories and desires, feel joy, love, sadness, fear and anger.

They do not fear light or fire, unlike the malevolent spirit beings who can be driven away by it. Light is their very element. However, they can be startled and chased away by sudden noises.

They behave with reverence and obedience towards spirit beings of higher rank (*énúúsór*), for they fear the anger they might otherwise incur.

Their psychic disposition is equivalent to that which the Chuuk Islanders understand by a bright, illuminated SEIC (*saram*). They are equable and serene (*pwaapwa*), polite and accessible (*pweteete*), helpful (*kirikirééch*), courageous (*pwara*), level-headed and discerning (*miriit*), composed (*soongommang*), conciliatory (*chákkáy*) and honest (*wenechchar*). They are viewed as industrious, persevering (*achoocho, nikiitú*), observing the same code of conduct as is appropriate for humans.

Their intellectual capacities are well developed and imbued with clarity of thought (*ekiyek mii ffat*), intelligence and knowledge (*tipáchchem*), with the gift of rapid comprehension and good memory (*chchemekkáy*). Here also they are far superior to their malevolent counterparts.

Despite their intelligence and positive mood it can sometimes happen that their SEIC is dimmed (*roch* etc.). They can then become so angry that they give the impression of being malevolent spirit beings. The reasons for an *énúúyééch* becoming angry and aggressive are unseemly behaviour by other *énúúyééch*, intrigues of their malevolent counterparts, and wrong actions of humans who do not respect their wishes and demands.

However, this ill-nature is temporary and rendered less acute by two conditions. Those who remain open to their wishes and submit to their demands have no need to fear their wrath. And those who have aroused their wrath can always rely on their being reconciled.

Many spirit beings recognised as *énúúyééch* can suddenly, for no apparent reason, only reveal their hostile side. These are assumed to have become *énúngngaw*. Spirit beings who were *énúngngaw* from the beginning cannot become *énúúyééch* (cf. Mahony 1970:133-134).

24.5.5 Relationship to Humans

With their intelligence and underlying positive attitude *énúúyééch* are kindly disposed towards humans. They are amenable spirit beings, desirous of maintaining an orderly course of events. This approach, a feature of their SEIC, is a key aspect of their appearance as benevolent spirit beings. Herein lies the difference from the *énúngngaw*, whose evil intentions are from the start assumed as given.

Chuuk Islanders have no fear of the *énúúyééch*, as long as they feel that everything has been done so as not to arouse their anger. One can expect their help in any of life's situations. There is no situation for which one or another spirit being is not qualified and competent to deal with.

Nevertheless the hope of help on the part of the benevolent spirit beings is bound up with a considerable element of uncertainty. There is no way of compelling them to help, or in any other way exercising control over them. A defensive spell (*ppéwút*) which is effective against malevolent spirit beings cannot touch an *énúúyééch*. Anyone with expectations from them must reckon on the possibility of refusal. Sometimes they also make decisions which do not correspond with one's wishes.

24.5.6 Place of Residence

For the Chuuk Islanders the expectation of receiving help in their problems from a benevolent spirit being is connected with the notion of its presence. When such a problem arises the benevolent spirit being is at once aware of it, even if it is a great distance away. However, they do not engage from a distance, but move to the location of the event.

Usually they take up residence in the *náán*. There they pursue their pleasures and deal with all kinds of tasks, and from there, whether by desire or necessity, they move into the proximity of humans.

24.5.7 Benevolent Spirit Beings as Spirits of the Dead (*énúúsootupw*)

The largest group among the countless numbers of benevolent spirit beings are the benevolent spirits of the deceased. As such they are called *énúúsootupw*. A distinction is made between the unburied deceased (*soomá*) and buried ones (*sootupw*); the corpses of animals are called *ménúmá* or *ménúpe*.

A benevolent spirit of the dead looks so completely like the dead person that the latter can be recognised in it. This is known through the mediums who can see them, and from dreams in which ordinary people can also get to see the dead and experience what they are doing in the beyond. The deceased person can be further recognised by the fact that his spirit wears the same clothes and ornamentation and carries the same tools, i.e. their spirit-like counterparts (*ngúún*). However, physical changes, such as the loss of a hand suffered by the deceased when alive, are usually not visible on the benevolent spirit of the dead.

A benevolent spirit of the dead stays forever in close relationship with the area where the deceased person formerly assigned to it spent his life. If it has been at some distance from these surroundings for any length of time it gets homesick and longs for the surviving family members and acquaintances of the deceased. The term the islanders give to this emotional attachment to the environment of the deceased is *ttong* (love, empathy, compassion etc.), denoting a disposition of the SEIC, a feeling typically characteristic of the members of a social group and essentially determining its cohesion and continuance.

In the reverse direction the same emotional attachment exists between the living members of a social group and the spirits of its deceased members. This means that benevolent spirits of the dead are still members of the social group to which the deceased persons belonged to, and whose personalities they are perpetuating. This is not only how the living members of the group understand them, but also how they understand themselves.

It is not just the family and clan groups that the islanders regard in this way. A whole village community can consider the *énúúsootupw* of their deceased village members as "their spirits of the dead" (*aar énú*). They are then called *énúún sóópw* (roughly: spirits of the village area or district). In the same way the inhabitants of several villages of a larger island, or whole groups of islands, feel a link with the benevolent spirits of deceased fellow inhabitants, which they call *énúún fénú* (island spirits). Even the representatives of the various "professions" such as canoe builders, breadfruit sorcerers etc. are felt to be a group whose members are in many respects dependent on the benevolent spirits of their deceased "colleagues in the trade".

If such *énúúsootupw* want to bring their influence to bear they have to be present or in the vicinity. Hence they usually have their *náán* in the region they are responsible for, or else they leave it more frequently in order to be where they are needed.

For the islanders the most significant aspect of the relationship between the living and the spirits of the dead is their solidarity with the spirits of the dead of their own family and clan, their *énúún faameni* and *énúún eyinang* (family and clan ancestral spirits). They are designated in a way that indicates common property *ááy kkewe neewo* or *énú* (my ancestors or my spirit beings). Consequently the integration of benevolent spirit beings of deceased members of a social group by its living members creates a considerable extension of its group structure into the beyond.

The emotional attachment of the benevolent spirit beings to the living members of their social group explains many aspects of behaviour of both sides. The influence of this attachment is clearly evident in the various relationships between the living and their benevolent spirits of the dead.

For the islanders the feeling of *ttong* (love, empathy, compassion), as mentioned briefly above, is the essence and the basis of all human relationships. It governs those between friends, spouses, parents and children. Those who are aware that nearby are people who feel *ttong* for them have a sense of security.

The Chuuk Islanders often clothe their sense of emotional insecurity with open requests that one might feel *ttong* for them. Letters are full of them. Walls of wood or tin, boulders beside the paths, even the backs of shirts are furnished with clearly visible invitations to feel *ttong* for that person. The reasons for it are seldom or never revealed. Everyone knows that there may be nothing more to it than the fear that their lives are of no significance as far as others are concerned, of losing the emotional bond others have for them, and hence of being isolated.

This emotional bond with others is regarded by the islanders as the essential force maintaining the cohesion of the social group, and especially of the family. *Ttong* is an important, even if not the most important relational virtue. The mutual emotional bond between family members and relatives results in quite definite mutual expectations. As a rule a relative does nothing that might harm other relatives. He helps them to prevent calamity, to deal with emergencies, and provides for their welfare, i.e. for the continuance of the group.

The islanders also confront the benevolent spirits of their deceased family members with these expectations and rely on them behaving like living relatives. Indeed more so. Since benevolent spirits of the dead, like all *énú*, are not limited to time and place, they have considerably extended opportunities at their disposal for caring for the living. They can easily find out where the most fish can be caught, where at that moment turtles can be found, where a lost canoe is drifting, and how its crew is faring. As beings of the beyond, benevolent spirits of the dead can recognise in advance whether malevolent spirits are plotting to inflict disease or other calamities on the living. If such is the case they are able to ask the mighty spirits (*énúúsór*) for their help and thus provide ongoing prevention of disaster on behalf of the living. They promote fertility of the gardens and ensure that plenty of children are born. In short, their chief aim is the preservation of the group.

This is also helped by the effect that benevolent spirits of the dead have on the SEIC of the living. When they are present among them they have a calming effect, so preventing the outbreak of open aggressive behaviour which would otherwise disturb or destroy the cohesion of the living community.

Their task of ensuring the continuance of a social group is a decisive influence on the behaviour of the benevolent spirits of the dead.

A society functions on the basis of rules which have to be observed by its members if the fabric of that social group is to be sustained. If one of its members disregards rules, the observance of which is necessary for the communal activity of all the members of the group, the fabric of that society must disintegrate. A head of any family who does not provide enough food endangers the welfare of the family and indeed its very survival. If it is to be maintained, the head of the family must observe the rules which are held to be prescribed to him. Rules determine the part that each individual member of a group has to play, and since the group can only operate effectively by observing those rules they take on the character of ethical norms by which the behaviour of the members of the group is to be directed.

The norms form a benchmark of values. By means of these the members of the group can evaluate their own behaviour and their attitude to one another. What is good is defined as that which corresponds to the norm and thus maintains the group. The bad is that which is contrary to the norm and hence directed against the continuance of the group.

For the islanders this raises the question of what happens if there is a threat to the norms which are valid in such an important social structure as the family, for without that validity the family cannot survive.

Every person presumed to possess *miriit* (reason, right behaviour etc.) knows what is good and bad in any individual situation. This is communicated to him by his SEIC (his super-ego, his conscience). In many instances this recognition is sufficient to oblige him to behave according to the norms. However, frequently this does not suffice, particularly if the interests of the individual conflict with those of the group. In such situations members of the group tend to act contrary to the norm and hence wrongly. Preventing this requires greater and more lasting security than can be provided by the recognition of the SEIC, including the super-ego or conscience of the individual.

This involves the second important task of the benevolent spirits of the dead of a social group. All actions directed against the community, theft, murder, deceit, breach of duty of care etc. are avenged by them. If a member of the community disregards the norms accepted in that community, he incurs the wrath of the benevolent spirits of the dead and must reckon on being punished by them for it.

Each individual member of the group is aware of this and the knowledge serves as a restraint against committing an offence against the norms. Thus the existence of the benevolent spirits of the dead guarantees the validity of ethical principles and norms in the broadest sense.

All those who commit offences against the norms are then in a condition which the islanders call *ttipis* (guilty, sinful). This term includes everything which must put the spirits of the dead in an ungracious mood and arouse their wrath (cf. also Käser 1994).

Actions which make a person *ttipis* include not just egregious crimes such as theft and murder, but in the final analysis any unfriendly behaviour towards members of one's own group. Even a completely unintentional insult affecting a member of the group can incur sanctions against the offender on the part of the benevolent spirits of the dead, particularly if the person offended is of higher status. This explains the conspicuous need the islanders have to reconcile someone of superior rank if they become aware that they have inadvertently insulted him; even the assumption of having caused such a higher ranking person to be resentful can trigger the attempt to reconcile him.

Goodenough (1951:111-119) has shown that "right behaviour" as understood by the Chuuk Islanders comprehends a whole range of norms which have to be heeded when in the presence of members of the group who are of higher or lower rank. Those who decline in any way to display respect (*mósónósón*) towards someone of higher rank infringes these norms. The same applies to distancing oneself sexually from all persons with whom such a relationship would be classed as incest according to Chuuk custom. Any violation of these behavioural norms makes one *ttipis* and can invoke sanctions.

One can also antagonise the benevolent spirits of deceased members of the group by not taking sufficient account of their personal interests, inclinations and wishes. For example, a benevolent spirit of the dead may put in a request via a medium for a particular meal to be prepared for it. If those requested do not take the desire seriously they become *ttipis* (guilty). Not only does their behaviour break all the rules governing the treatment of relatives, it must also be evaluated as an infringement of the demand for a respectful attitude towards someone of superior rank, for this is how the benevolent spirits of the dead regard themselves, being older and as spirit beings having more influence and power over the course of events than the living (they are *manaman*).

The requirement to display towards the benevolent spirits of the dead an attitude of respect, in the sense understood by the islanders, is further evidence that they continue to be regarded as members of the group and do not only constitute an extension of the group into the beyond but at the same time form an invisible superstructure over and above the hierarchical group structure of the living.

Islanders expect the attitude and behaviour of their relatives to be displayed substantially for the benefit of the group. Unjust treatment of an outsider has to be more or less accepted and is not considered as serious as it would be if committed against a member of one's own group. If a group member has committed an infringement against outsiders and has got into a difficult situation because of it he can count on the other members of his own group siding with him.

As relatives the benevolent spirits of the dead behave similarly. Their wrath and subsequent dealing out of punishment is only to be expected if someone has offended his own group. Usually violations of the norms against outsiders do not have such consequences. The offender's own benevolent spirits of the dead do not take any opposing measures and even defend the culprit in their own group against the benevolent spirits of the dead of others who are possibly seeking revenge against him. However, he does not remain completely free from fear of reprisals. It could indeed be that the benevolent spirits of the dead of the other group are more powerful than those of his own group. Nevertheless as a rule violations of the norms that people commit cannot be avenged by benevolent spirits of the dead which do not belong to the group. Overriding the powers which belong to another group would bring into play that group's own benevolent spirits of the dead. Such instances would cause strife in the beyond.

The benevolent spirits of the dead which regulate the behaviour of a social group in this way are exclusively responsible for that group. This is how the ethical principles directing this behaviour acquire their status and significance. They can only be understood with reference to the group.

When a benevolent spirit of the dead becomes angry it must be assumed that it will act accordingly. Whatever action it then takes is regarded as punishment for violation of the norms, whether those violations are known or remain unknown. The punishment consists in the infliction of some kind of harm (*feyiyangngaw*) happening at some unforeseen place involving the group.

The islanders consider *feyiyangngaw* to consist first and foremost of injuries to the body, but including also material damage and other kinds of misfortune.

Such calamity does not necessarily have to fall on the one who actually violated the norms and has thus become *ttipis*. The time gap between deed and punishment cannot be determined and can sometimes involve many years. Also the type of offence may bear no relation to the kind of misfortune to be expected. Following a violation of the norms there is always uncertainty as to which member of the group will be punished. The consequences of a violation of the norms are always to be born by the group collectively. For the individual who has not behaved according to the norms this constitutes a risk and a special responsibility. The knowledge of this risk is therefore a factor exercising considerable pressure on the group to keep to the norms.

The kind of calamity afflicting the group is almost always the illness or death (of one) of its members. A father who has endangered the existence of his family by immoderate consumption of alcohol can be the cause of his son/daughter falling ill, drowning at sea or coming to harm in some other way. Calamity can also befall the group through an outbreak of famine, because the benevolent spirits of the dead have destroyed the taro fields by flooding them with salt water or brought about a typhoon uprooting the breadfruit trees.

Whether famine, accident, disease, death or any other kind of calamity as a consequence of an individual's violation of the norms, the target is always the body, i.e. the destruction of the physical existence of the members of the group, but not their spirit doubles, which will be discussed later. In other words, the punishment for "sins" (*ttipis*) always affects one's form of existence in this world, not in the beyond.

24.5.8 Benevolent Spirits of the Dead with Special Status (énúúsór)

Not all the benevolent spirits of the dead of a social group are really significant for them. Some of them are better known than all the others. People speak of them, of their abilities and achievements, with adulation. These benevolent spirits of the dead are called *énúúsór*, benevolent spirits of the dead with special status.

It is difficult to describe the meaning of the affix *sór*. It is found not only in connection with spirit beings and places (*náán*), but also with people. These are men (*átásór, mwáánesór*) and women (*niyesór, finesór*), who are known for their intelligence, their knowledge, their predominantly positive disposition, in short for their illuminated SEIC as understood in Chuuk society. As prominent personalities, what they say must be taken seriously. They possess mana and hence authority (*manaman wóón aramas*). These qualities are the basis of their status within their social group. Material wealth is of no importance in this connection. Their status rests purely on mental and emotional aspects.

Among the benevolent spirits of the dead of the families and clans (*énúún faameni* or *eyinang*) the *énúúsór*, as spirits of the dead, perpetuate the personality of eminent relatives. Among the spirits of village districts and islands (*énúún sóópw* and *fénú*) it is mostly deceased title holders (*samwoon*) and famous sorcerers and mediums, who were of significance in one of these areas. All such people possessed when alive a special status (*átásór, mwáánesór, niyesór, finesór, sowusine* etc.) on account of their personality.

Even before they die it is said of such people that their benevolent spirit double will later become an *énúúsór*. Mediums can give reliable information about this because they know the benevolent spirit doubles of these people personally. The desire to become an *énúúsór* is widespread among the islanders.

The outward indication of this status is their name, which they make known via a medium after they change into a spirit of the dead. The other benevolent spirits of the dead who are not able to attain the status of the *énúúsór* keep the name of the person whose personality they are perpetuating. There are also malevolent spirit beings with individual names, e.g. the *soope Nimwootong*, but they have not acquired their names themselves but have been given them by the Chuukese people. If a spirit of the dead gives itself a new name and makes it known via a medium, the living have to regard it as an *énúúsor*.

The benevolent spirits of the dead are given various names according to physical characteristics, e.g. "Yellow Man" (*Reyiyón*); according to objects they are always supposed to carry around with them , e.g. "Fish Basket" (*Pacheniik*); according to typical ways in which they behave, e.g. "Mast Climber" (*Tééyéwú*); according to particular knowledge and ability e.g. "Dance master" (*Sowupwérúk*); and finally according to the aspect of human life they are responsible for, e.g. "Birth Instigator" (*Nikowupwuupw*), a female *énúúsór* who ensures that there is posterity.

The evidence that an *énúúsór* has special status is his ability to bring about extraordinary events. He succeeds in this because he possesses a lot of mana (*manaman*), because of which he can solve problems which appear hardly or not at all solvable. This means that he is able, more than other benevolent spirits of the dead, to mitigate emergencies affecting the living, to provide adequate food and offspring, cure diseases, ensure the success of all kinds of enterprises etc. *Énúúsór* know how to bring help in any and every situation.

The special abilities of the *énúúsór* depend in the main on the qualities with which his SEIC is equipped. The latter is described as specially rich in knowledge (*sine*), clever (*tipáchchem*), sensible and wise (*miriit*). The features of his character are courage and resolve (*pwara*), and equanimity (*tipeppós*). The SEIC of the *énúúsór* is more luminous (*saram*) than that of ordinary benevolent spirits of the dead, which means that his fundamental disposition is happy, content and cheerful (*kinamwmwe*).

Énúúsór speak lucidly and coherently, and their utterances are evidence of their honesty and incorruptibility. An *énúúsór* neither lies nor deceives. If any of his predictions are not accurate this shows that he can no longer hold the status of an *énúúsór*, but is a (malevolent) "lying spirit" (*énúúmwaken*).

Honesty and love of truth are in a special sense attributed to the benevolent spirits of deceased children. One can always rely on them proving to be *énúúsór*. Chuuk Islanders cannot conceive of a child's benevolent spirit of the dead having a "dark" SEIC with its necessary consequences.

Because of their vast knowledge and abilities *énúúsór* are considered to be much in demand as advisers in all of life's situations. Office holders (*samwoon*) inquire of them about political decisions and their consequences. One can find out from them why a member of the family has become ill and what medicine should be used for treatment. In essence there is no issue about which one could not appeal to an *énúúsór*. However, they never impart information directly, but always via a medium or in a dream.

In addition *énúúsór* are able to exercise influence over a person's body, SEIC and behaviour without that person's awareness. A medical expert (*sowusáfey*) can diagnose the cause of a disease particularly accurately when an *énúúsór* supplies him with the right ideas (*ámééfi*). A canoe builder who receives such unconscious help handles his tools more dexterously and is in less danger of ruining the valuable breadfruit trunk he is working on through carelessness. The *énúúsór Resiim*, who is regarded as especially bold and daring, can also engender these qualities in the living. And *Inemes*, a female *énúúsór*, can if she is so inclined make a person attractive (*mwmwung*).

This exertion of influence, experienced unconsciously by the living, is connected with the notion that the *énúúsór* active in this way is located close to the person involved or has physical contact with him. Such a person, noteworthy through special qualities or achievements, is described by the islanders as having an *énúúsór* "sitting on him, riding him" (*aa wááni*). This can be equated in a sense with the notion of the term "possession", albeit in every respect with positive outcomes, for the SEIC of that person is thereby illumined (*aa saram neenuukan*), with the result that *énúúsór* not only imbue the living with intelligence (*tipáchchem*), but also with all other qualities of character which are essential for living together in the community, the foremost of which is called *miriit* (rationality, right action etc.)

The qualities with which *énúúsór* are furnished do not only enable them to solve problems of daily human life. Some of the *énúúsór* have special gifts. Many of them can speak several languages, preferentially Japanese and English. Others are excellent singers. Many of the islanders' songs, particularly from earlier times, originate from the *énúúsór*. Also there is hardly one among them who would not excel at dancing. Indeed, all the dances of the islanders (*tokiyá, pisimóót* etc.) were invented by the *énúúsór* and communicated to people via the mediums (or in dreams).

This explains why earlier many of the mediums were both dance teachers and lead dancers (*sowupwérúk*) at big festivities. They were also commissioned by the *énúúsór* to arrange and organise dance festivals. An artistically decorated dance stick also graced the place of offering (*faar*) for an *énúúsór*.

The positive emotional and mental qualities and personality features of human beings are present in virtually ideal form in the *énúúsór* and are the basis of their status. In accordance with this status they exercise the functions as chiefs in the beyond. The benevolent spirits of the dead and even the spirit doubles of the living of any social group are subordinate to them and receive orders and commissions from them. *Énúúsór* are at the head of the hierarchical group structure, which is itself a counterpart of the group structure of the living. Even malevolent spirit beings have to obey the *énúúsór*. Their influence on this life and the beyond is all-embracing. The more *sór* a benevolent spirit of the dead is, the more it is also inclined (*pwaapwaa ngeni*) to help the living and meet their requests. For this reason it is necessary for the living to do everything they can to preserve or heighten this inclination. *Énúúsór* are only prepared to grant the living their support if one satisfies them in every respect, obeys their instructions and fulfils their wishes. This includes first and foremost observing the ethical norms accepted as valid in one's own group. It is essentially the *énúúsór* who pay attention to this. When there is an infringement they decide who has to be punished for it, and in what way. The ordinary benevolent spirits of the dead are usually the ones who execute the initiatives of the *énúúsór*. Even malevolent spirit beings can be ordered by them to e.g. bring about a famine or an epidemic.

A liar would have to reckon on being punished, but earlier one could invoke an *énúúsór* to affirm one's innocence. One swore (*ékképén*) on the name of an *énúúsór* to tell the truth. The proof became evident if after the oath no one in the group of the person taking the oath came to harm (*feyiyangngaw*).

When a member of the group becomes ill this is not necessarily a sign that the wrath of an *énúúsór* has been incurred by the guilt of the living. Sometimes, despite all the precautions of benevolent spirits, a malevolent spirit being succeeds in getting at a person and infecting him with its bite. This can be countered by medicine (*sáfey*) and healing procedures. If these means still have no success, or more and more members of the group get the same illness, then the suspicion arises that the wrath of an *énúúsór* has been aroused through the guilt of the living. The only way to avert the calamity that threatens, or redress what has already begun, is to placate that wrath.

It is said that many *énúúsór* can become so enraged that they become no different from a malevolent spirit being.

First of all one must find out which *énúúsór* is annoyed, and what he is annoyed about. If it turns out that a member of the group has become guilty (*ttipis*), he can change the mood of the *énúúsór* by admitting his error and reconcile the person offended, injured or otherwise affected, by means of gifts and expressions of regret. This process is called *omwusomwus* (resolution, exculpation). Until this takes place, the *énúúsór* will continue to deny the group his support and cause further calamity to befall individual members of the group.

If no one emerges as the guilty person, or the members of the group are unable to find him, not even through a dream, there remains the possibility of questioning the spirits of the dead via a medium. One either calls upon the malevolently disposed *énúúsór* himself, who will then name the reason for his anger, the guilty person, and his own demands, or one asks one of the other spirits of the dead for information, for it is assumed that they all know about the matter.

Énúúsór have no desire whatsoever to misuse their powers over the living simply to torment them or kill them. Nor do they enjoy what they are doing. This would be against their nature. Their only intention in punishing error is to cause the living to be rational and act rightly (*miriit, emiriiti*).

When the living need the help of the benevolent spirits of the dead they should not simply expect them to take the initiative themselves. Frequently they have to be asked to do so. This can happen simply by calling (*kkééri*). One speaks the name of the *énúúsór* expected to help, asks him to come and presents one's request. This is how it is done when sudden danger occurs, e.g. when under attack by fighter planes during World War 2. The *énúúsór* can hear such a request even over long distances, but must still move to be close to the person seeking aid.

Such a request can run as follows: *Póróchaap, kepwe feyitto!*" The Christian prayer that has extensively superseded the call for help to the *énúúsór* is called *iyóótek*.

However, such a call for help is only possible in immediate emergencies. *Énúúsór* and other spirits of the dead normally only act on requests from the living when the latter have fulfilled a number of conditions.

Goodenough (2002) made an interesting proposal for a pertinent translation of the term *énúúsór* into English. He called this special kind of benevolent spirit "effecting spirit".

24.6 Taboo (*pin*)

Énúúsór do not only reject infringements against ethical norms. They also require human beings to observe some of their own idiosyncrasies. Everything which can incur the displeasure of such a spirit being and deter him from assisting the living is "taboo" (*pin*).

The concept of taboo and the history of its research is similar to the concept of mana (cf. 24.3.2). Again it was Lehmann who in his professorial thesis "Die polynesischen Tabusitten" ("Taboo customs of Polynesia") laid the foundations for empirical research and further investigation of the concept of taboo in Oceania. It contains the proposition that the word form *pin* (in the Mortlock islands *fel*), while probably having no connection with the Polynesian *tapu* (*kapu*), is possibly retained on Chuuk in the form of the negating particle *-sapw* (Lehmann 1930:310).

Objects, locations, actions and people can all be taboo. However, *pin*, unlike *manaman*, does not denote an objective quality which an object, place, action or person possesses, but a relationship between a particular person or group of persons and that which is taboo. Food which at a particular point in time is *pin* for a particular group of people, and must therefore be avoided, can quite happily be eaten by others or, at a later time, by that same group of people.

E.g. fermented breadfruit (*épwét*) need only be avoided by those wishing to ensure that a love spell (*omwmwung*) is effective. Others may eat it with no ill effects.

Indeed, relativity is one of the principles of the taboo concept. Someone for whom a particular food is taboo may nevertheless partake of it if he takes measures which counteract the effects of breaking the taboo.

During the production and application of medicine the maker must not eat certain marine animals. If he does, his medicine is non-effective, or he himself will fall victim to the disease his medicine is supposed to cure. If he has nothing else to eat but the marine creatures which are taboo for him he first of all applies the medicine to himself, so that he can then enjoy the forbidden food safely (Mahony 1970:129).

The Chuuk Islanders' concept of taboo includes not just avoidances and vetoes but also all actions which have to be undertaken with reference to matters under taboo, i.e. also conditions which have to be observed.

For example, although for a group of men going fishing it is *pin*, and hence forbidden, to sleep at home (*woneyimw*), the opposite command, to sleep in the community house, is likewise a "taboo", i.e. *pin* or *pinin attaw*. This means that the term "taboo" is only a partially correct rendering of the Chuuk concept, to say nothing of "translations" such as "holy, sacred" or "sanctity".

The concept of taboo plays an important part in social relationships, where it governs the behaviour among members of the group. Children learn to understand their position in the kinship system as their parents explain to them which relatives (mother's brother etc.) are *pin* with regard to themselves, and for which relatives they themselves are *pin*. The outworking of the taboo grading of a person among the members of a social group in terms of showing respect or of sexual relations has been described in detail by Goodenough (1951:111-119).

The extent to which the concept of taboo is involved in the most everyday aspects of human relations can be seen in the fact that even infringements against elementary rules of decency or tactlessness can be called taboo. E.g. terms to do with sex are *pin* (inappropriate) when women are present (*raa pin neeyin mwáán me feefin*).

When someone distinguishes himself by demonstrating special abilities such as intelligence, courage and authority (*manaman wóón aramas*), he becomes *pin* in as much as others show him respect, because otherwise they fear that that person and his mana combined with his own superiority will be directed against them. This reveals a connection between taboo and mana, although this connection does not have to be present. An object which proves to be extraordinarily efficient (*manaman*) does not thereby necessarily become taboo, even if it concerns a cheque which has become *manaman* when signed.

The islanders do not understand the concept of taboo as something religious, for it influences all aspects of life. Observing its rules is necessary for the smooth functioning both of the relationships between the living and between the living and the benevolent spirits of the deceased. Only those who keep them can be sure of success. Disregarding a taboo leads to failure and incurs sanctions. Those who break a taboo arouse the displeasure of their fellows, and also in the final analysis the hostility of the spirits of the dead of their group.

Even today many activities of the islanders are bound up with the observance of quite definite taboos. Their variety is great. Many taboos are valid everywhere and always, e.g. the rules governing the behaviour of the individual within a social group. Others only apply at certain times and in connection with certain activities, of which they are so typical that they constitute regular complexes of taboos. Such a taboo is also characteristic of the behaviour of the living towards the benevolent spirits of the dead of their group, especially towards important spirits of the dead. The rules governing behaviour towards the latter are termed *pinin énú* or *pinin énúúsór*.

In matters of smell and taste benevolent spirits of the dead are considered to be extremely choosy and sensitive. Someone who eats food which they have an aversion to cannot rely on their presence in the vicinity and hence on their assistance. This is why it is taboo for pregnant women to eat fermented breadfruit (*épwét, maar*), particularly around the time of the birth of their children, when they are relying more seriously on the help of benevolent spirits of the dead. Similarly mediums must avoid such food at least some time before making contact with an *énúúsór*.

The command to avoid fermented breadfruit is an important taboo in connection with the love spell (*pinin omwmwung*), for the success of which the help of the female *énúúsór Inemes* is required. This taboo is named after the forbidden food: the one who has to avoid it is *fánnimar*. In addition the spell is only successful if the person involved is careful about physical hygiene and fragrance.

Odours which the *énúúsór* finds unpleasant endanger the success of all significantly large undertakings. The reason given for prohibiting sexual intercourse before sea journeys, fishing, boatbuilding, sport competitions and (earlier) military campaigns was the repellent effect that the odour of human genitalia has on the *énúúsór*. Men to which it adheres offend them and drive them away, thus preventing them from offering assistance and moreover enabling malevolent spirit beings to have access to the undertaking and to endanger its success. This is why the participants are strictly ordered to sleep in the community house (*pinin wonowut*). For the same reasons a medium must abstain completely for several days before making contact with a spirit of the dead. A female medium is not able to function as a medium during menstruation.

However, observing all these taboos is more like a prerequisite for ensuring the help of an *énúúsór* on behalf of the living. Requests to him have an increased prospect of being fulfilled if they are accompanied by a gift. Such a "present" can put an *énúúsór* under an obligation.

24.7 Offerings (*ósór*)

The Chuuk Islanders make a distinction between two kinds of gift or present. The one is called *kiis* and refers mainly to an exchange between a husband and the brothers of his wife. There is no obligation to give something in return. The other kind of present is called *niffang*, can be exchanged by anybody, and plays an important part in the economy because it entails an obligation to make a reciprocal gift. A *niffang* renders the recipient *kinissow* (grateful, obligated). The islanders use this term to describe a sense of compulsion to respond equally, whether in material terms or with acts of service.

There are two reasons for an islander to make a *niffang*. He may wish to respond to such and so free himself from the feeling of being *kinissow*, or he may simply wish to express his liking for the giver. However, a *niffang* is often given with the intention of making the recipient *kinissow* and in this way preparing the ground for later making a request which he already has in mind, calculating that the recipient would be embarrassed if he did not fulfil the request (Goodenough 1951:37-61).

The reality of this situation was brought home to me in rather unpleasant circumstances during my research there. One day an acquaintance brought me a splendid fish, explaining that it was a *niffang*. It seemed that the giver wished to express his appreciation, since a reciprocal gift was not possible. However, it turned out later that it was intended to make me *kinissow*, for the following day the giver appeared again, wanting to "borrow" a fairly large sum of money.

Offerings to spirits of the dead and especially to an *énúúsór* also have to be understood as *niffang*, for even spirit beings can feel *kinissow*. Such an offering is called *ósór* or *ósoomá*. It is a gift by means of which the benevolent spirit of a deceased family member or village friend can be made favourably inclined, or as a way of conveying gratitude for a service rendered. The term *ósór* literally means "rendering favourable". The morpheme - *sór* which it contains is also present in forms such as *átásór*, *niyesór*, *énúúsór* and indicates the link between benevolent spirits of the dead with special status and the offering. No satisfactory explanation of the term *ósoomá* could be discovered (*ósór* + *má*, death?).

Offerings to spirits of the dead are no longer made. Before the adoption of Christianity all conceivable kinds of work, undertakings and events in the lives of the islanders constituted occasions for *ósór*: making medicine, building a canoe, starting and finishing building a house, birth, illness, and many other matters. The intention was to oblige one or more *énúúsór* to favour such undertakings and events and ensure their success.

A pre-emptive *ósór* prevented an *énúúsór* from losing his good mood and becoming angry, or one could placate his wrath subsequently if there were any signs that he had lost his good mood. In such instances the *ósór* was an offering of entreaty.

The services of the *énúúsór* are also a *niffang* to people, who thereby become *kinissow*. Hence fairly large *ósór* were to be brought as thank offerings after the completion of all these undertakings and events. A breadfruit sorcerer who had brought a petitionary offering to the *énúúsór* of a deceased "work colleague" at the beginning of the breadfruit ripening, in order to ensure a good harvest, felt the need to bring him a further *ósór* offering after the harvest, consisting of the first of the breadfruit (*mwmwemey*) as an offering, as an expression of gratitude. There was no requirement for a special "priest" to bring the *ósór*. Anyone wishing to obligate an *énúúsór* made the necessary preparations. The family members cooperated in preparing an offering to their benevolent spirits of the dead. The men procured the necessary food, the women took care of the wreaths of flowers and other décor. If a house or a canoe had to be built, the artisans and employers shared in various ways the preparations for the necessary *ósór*.

The overall responsibility was born by the oldest man in the family or work group (*mwáániichi*), and for offerings only brought by women the oldest woman (*finniichi*).

All participants had to observe strictly all the taboos generally demanded by all *énúúsór* and these were occasionally extended by an additional taboo: sexual abstinence, avoidance of certain foods, physical hygiene. Younger people (*énúwén* and *féépwún*) were regarded as hardly suitable for preparing *ósór*, because they were not unconditionally trusted to keep the rules of taboo, particularly the sexual ones.

The time and place for the *ósór* were not prescribed. If it was brought in the open air it was laid in a place that was clearly visible, during sea voyages on the deck, on the prow or stern, when fishing on calm water above a shelf, on land on stones, boulders and under trees. In whatever locations cleanliness of the place of offering and security against encroachment by animals were essential.

For important *énúúsór* and on very special occasions the offering was prepared in a house. In the case of spirits of the dead of one's own family it would be the home of that family (*iimw*), in the case of the village spirits and similar it would be the community house (*wuut*). Here also no particular place was prescribed. However, the offering was not placed on the floor or in the actual living room, but on the raised beams under the roof. This avoided it coming into contact with people for whom it would signify danger because of the taboos connected with it. Such a raised place also formed the *faar* of the *énúúsór* for whom the offering was intended.

Offerings consisted of anything and everything which could please the *énúúsór*. This meant that they had to satisfy aesthetic demands and include all kinds of decorative items (*fowut*), combs, necklaces, ear pendants, superb mussel shells etc.

Because of their highly developed sense of smell *énúúsór* placed great value on all kinds of cosmetics, fragrant plant extracts (*néé*), yellow turmeric (*teyik*), as well as fragrant blooms and herbs, e.g. *sowur* (Fragrea sp., Mahony 1969:97) and dried tobacco leaves (*suupwa*). Blooms and herbs were woven into magnificent garlands (*mwárámwár*).

Medicine of illumination (*sáfeen asaram*) was also used as an offering, to brighten the SEIC of the *énúúsór*, convey to him clarity of thought and heighten his mood.

The main part of the offering consisted of food of various kinds (*fééten énú*). Sometimes an *énúúsór* would convey via a medium or a dream a desire for a particular meal. However, usually the offering was made up of a kind of standard menu: shelled coconuts for drinking (*kituun*); taro (*pwuna*) and breadfruit (*maay*), both cooked; fresh unsalted fish (*iik*); added pressed coconut milk (*aarúng, eyiwu*) and mild spices; fruit such as bananas (*wuuch*), mango (*mangko*); sugar cane (*sápúk*) and many other items.

All food of strong taste and odour were forbidden (*pin*), food which people also had to avoid if they needed the presence of benevolent spirit beings. In addition acidic fruit such as pineapple (*pweyinaper*), orange (*kurukur*) and lemons (*siitor*) were totally unsuitable as offerings and would have aroused the wrath of the *énúúsór*.

The significance of food as part of the offering is explained by the attitude of the islanders to food as such. Despite adequate means of obtaining food they have a predominant fear of not getting enough food for the next day, a fear which is internalised in children quite early on (Gladwin/Sarason 1953). During their social development they subconsciously learn to equate food with security of existence, and this leads to food becoming later on a *niffang* of great value. A gift of food indicates a sign of affection and family care. The greater the amount of food, the greater the care to be shown towards the recipient. For famous and important *énúúsór* a correspondingly generous meal is prepared. But in all cases quality was more important than quantity. Offerings had to be new, beautiful, valuable, fragrant, mild yet tasty.

After completion of the preparations for the offering one of the offerers, usually one of the older ones, called out the name of the *énúúsór* for whom the *ósór* was designated, bade him come, invited him to eat, and named the request which he should consider.

Everything further remained hidden from the offerers. The *énúúsór* took to themselves the spirit doubles (*ngúún*) of the gifts offered, which then soon revealed the subsequent effects: they lost their food value, rotted, dried up and were no longer useable. After some time the remains were thrown away. Removing them too early would indeed have had serious consequences: an *énúúsór* would regard it as an unfriendly act, similar to an insult.

Énúúsór never demanded human sacrifice. One could, however, win their favour by recommending to them a child from one's own family, which they in a sense adopted (*néwúnéw*), and then cared for it in a special way.

As with all other benevolent spirit beings, an *énúúsór* can never be compelled by the living to meet a request, whether by observing the taboos, by making offerings, or even by a magic spell. However, the living can expect him to respond accordingly, otherwise he would endanger his honour as an *énúúsór*. If he took no action he would have to reckon with curses and scorn (*óttek, óttekiiy*). His reputation as an *énúúsór* would be so ruined that the living would not even fear his revenge any more.

24.8 Special *énúúsór*

A number of *énúúsór* are not spirits of the dead (*énúúsootupw*), because they were never assigned to a living person. These beings possess all the qualities of the *énúúsór* in such complete measure that they enjoy the highest status among all the *énú*. Their permanent abode is in the heavens (*nááng*), more precisely on the second highest level (*Fachcham*). Accordingly they are called sky spirits (*énúún nááng*). Included among them is *Énúúnap* (the Great Spirit), the indolent Supreme Being of the Chuuk Islanders, surrounded by the members of his family. These sky spirits appear in the mythology and in numerous tales of the islanders as the agents of natural phenomena and inventors of tools, work techniques etc. They are rarely concerned about people and what is happening on the earth. Even the relationships of people to themselves are a long way from reaching the intensity of those with the ordinary *énúúsór*. As a rule no *ósór* is brought to them, and they never use a medium to communicate with the living. If the sky spirits want to make contact at all with people they employ the other *énúúsór*, for they only have dealings with them. If a benevolent spirit of the dead desires access to the sky spirits it must be accompanied by a particularly mighty *énúúsór* or itself be an *énúúsór*.

The Christian islanders have incorporated many of these notions into their form of Christianity. God (*Koot*) and the angels (*chóón nááng*) are regarded as *énúúsór*, on account of many of their features.

The Christian offering is presented in the form of money, but it still has the functions of the former *ósór*. It is largely regarded as a gift intended to oblige God to reciprocate with some kind of service.

The ethical integrity of these special *énúúsór* is so flawless that it is impossible to imagine that they could ever go against the demand always to treat the Supreme Being *Énúúnap* with respect. Hence they never give occasion to be punished with "death" in *Neepwúnnúpis*. However, one is aware that even special *énúúsór* can be forgetful in their dealings with people. In many cases it happens because an *énúúsór* is shown to be no longer capable and hence dismissed, or because he has failed to report via his medium for too long. There are *énúúsór* who, following the death of their medium, do not look for a new one again or despite intensive efforts no longer report. A further factor is that after some generations following the death of famous people (*átásór*, *niyesór* etc.) new *énúúsór* have arisen who are closer to the living and themselves have a more intensive relationship with them.

The fact that at the present time *énúúsór* are no longer a talking point is attributed by the islanders to the widespread disappearance of the old practices of offerings, taboo regulations and rituals since they turned to the Christian faith.

24.9 Visual Depictions of *énúúsór*

... today no longer exist on Chuuk. They used to be familiar in two forms of wood carving (*wunuun*), mostly in breadfruit wood.

The first kind had the form of a person standing upright, as in the illustration of the *énúúsór* Reyiyón (Yellow Man) in Krämer (1932:67). Such statues stood in the open or in the community houses (*wuut*) and were regarded as the likeness of an important *énúún sóópw* or *énúún fénú*, i.e. referring to the benevolent spirit of the dead of an important person or sorcerer in that region. Offerings were laid in the immediate vicinity of these statues and dance festivals were held in honour of that spirit of the dead (further illustrations in Krämer 1932: plate 30 b; 1935:118).

The second kind was a human face in the stylised form of a mask. The representations of male *énúúsór* as masks reveal on top, whether on the right or left, a bulbous extension indicating the knots (*réét*) of the former hair style among the men. Masks without *réét* are representations of female *énúúsór* (illustrations in Krämer 1935: plates 8, 119 etc.). These masks hung on the gable uprights of the community houses and were of considerable significance on the Mortlock Islands south of Chuuk, where they were called *tapwpwaanú*. On Chuuk itself they seem to have been rare and were apparently not used to the same extent in rituals for defence against storms and corresponding dances as on the Mortlocks. Secret societies connected to masks were unknown.

The illustration in Krämer (1935:118) shows the combination of statue and mask as representing a male *énúúsór*.

The human form of statue and mask indicate that the *énúúsór* thus portrayed is a benevolent spirit being. There were no representations of *Énúúnap*, the Supreme Being.

24.10 Malevolent Spirit Beings (*énúngngaw*)

24.10.1 The Term *soope* and Its Meaning

Énúngngaw consist of two groups of malevolent spirit beings. The largest by far are the *soope*. The other group has no separate designation. *Soope* reveal the typical features of malevolent spirit beings in such complete measure that they must be regarded as representative of the category *énúngngaw*.

The term would appear to consist of the two morphemes *so-* (in compounds *soo-*) and *pe*. Similar forms are apparent in *soomá* (unburied corpse) and *sootupw* (buried corpse). *Pe* means "dead, totally exhausted, finished", and sounds vulgar when used with reference to people. A deceased person is referred to as *má* (dead). Since *soope* usually describes one of the two surviving spirits of the deceased person there is possibly a connection between the term "dead" and the spirit being called *soope*. For a long time it was not clear how the syllable *soo-* should be interpreted. Elbert (1947:197) links it together with *so*: "alight, land, settle". However, his literal translation ("alight-dead") cannot be satisfactory. The explanation given by Bierbach and Cain (1997) seems to me to be correct.

They prove convincingly that *soo-* is a morpheme occurring in numerous Austronesian languages with the meaning of "person" (in a very general sense). Combined with the morpheme *pe*, which when applied to people carries a vulgar overtone, it produces in Chuukese the word *soope*, originally used to designate a dead person, in a pejorative sense, because one had to fear his spirit of the dead, because he had died a so-called "bad death", befallen him by violence, an accident, or in foreign parts. *Soomá* and *sootupw* by contrast indicate the deceased who had died an "acceptable death", in their own social environment and following traditional ritual. The change in meaning of *soope* from "bad death" to malevolent spirit of the dead follows naturally from this understanding.

24.10.2 Names

Many *soope* bear individual names in the same way as other kinds of *énú* do. These names are also known to the Chuuk Islanders through those spirit beings who speak to people via a medium, something which malevolent spirit beings themselves are unable to do. Usually the names indicate conspicuous traits or aspects of behaviour e.g. *Soopepwech* (White *Soope*), but they often seem to be meaningless, e.g. *Nimwootong, Neyimeefi* etc.

24.10.3 Visibility

Like all spirit beings *soope* are usually invisible, but have the ability to make themselves visible. In contrast to their benevolent counterparts neither dreams nor unusual abilities are required in order to perceive them. Hardly any islander claims never to have seen a *soope* and be unable to give a detailed description.

24.10.4 Appearance

Soope have the physical form of animals, of people with body parts missing, or look like a mixture of animal and human. When Chuuk Islanders encounter an animal they are unable to say with certainty whether it is a *soope* or not.

Soope appear in every conceivable animal form, but certain ones are preferred. These are ugly animals, carnivores such as cats and dogs, essentially those which are a danger to humans, wild and voracious (*maan mwacho*). Danger, savagery and voraciousness also betray the *soope* if it adopts the form of an animal known to be tame and harmless, such as the *soope Nimwootong*, said to look like a chicken.

Moreover all animals of a grey or dark hue, active and audible at night, are regarded as *soope*: bats and flying foxes (*péwúte*), birds such as sandpipers (*kuning*) and herons (*kawakaw*).

Soope come in all sizes. Some are giants (*énúmmóng*) and some are dwarfs.

One typical feature of human-like *soope* is the lack of bodily proportions. Only in rare cases are *soope* described as good-looking. Most of them are viewed as decidedly ugly. They are described as monkeys or apes (*raa mesen mwóngki*), with deformed tongues hanging out, oversized noses and pendulous ears. Physical abnormalities and mutilation are predominant in such descriptions. There are *soope* with only one arm or leg. Many have a surplus of limbs. Their skin is usually of dark hue: green and black. This could be the origin of the (rare) term *pwoochón* (.?.black) for *soope*. They can use camouflage colours in order to get close to humans unobserved. However, there are also *soope* who stand out in white, red or many colours. They can change their colour at will.

24.10.5 Other Physical Features

As with all spirit beings *soope* are not weightless, and leave footprints in soft ground. They have enormous physical strength, which is, however, inferior to that of benevolent spirit beings. Their body temperature is lower than that of humans and animals. Their skin feels damp and cold. They emit a repulsive body odour. An inexplicable stench is a sign that a *soope* is nearby.

Soope sleep from time to time, particularly during the day, but do not require regular sleep.

They can move about freely, run, climb, and fly, even if they do not have the form of an animal that flies.

Like all malevolent spirit beings *soope* are not able to speak coherently. You can hear them knocking, whistling (*owuwá*), grunting, muttering and groaning (*ngúúngú*) like animals. Among themselves they frequently grumble (*nan ffengeen*) and quarrel loudly, mostly about food. Sometimes a few words might be understood. However, they never address people directly.

Soope sense feelings of hunger and take in food. They consume indiscriminately whatever they find, even stuff beginning to rot or lying in the dirt. Their voraciousness is insatiable and they steal like crows. They digest their food and leave excrements behind.

They have sense organs. Their sense of smell is highly developed. They can pick up human scent over great distances. Pleasant fragrances attract them in the same way as a stench, in contrast to benevolent spirit beings.

Nevertheless their sense of taste does discriminate. Although they like things which are obnoxious to humans, they are so repelled by anything bitter (*maras, pwáánu, kkipwin*) that those things can be used effectively to drive them away. They even decline acidic fruit such as lemons (*siitor*) and oranges (*kurukur*).

Their hearing and sight are as good as those of nocturnal animals. It is said that their eyes gleam like light bulbs (*wusun tengki*).

Soope are sexual beings. There are male ones, female ones, and hermaphrodites. Sexual intercourse, which they practise both among themselves and with animals, does not result in pregnancy. Male *soope* sometimes attempt to approach women for the purpose of sexual intercourse. It happens mostly at night, or when women are alone. Usually the women are unaware of it, but can still become pregnant and give birth to deformed children. The reverse situation, a female *soope* having intercourse with a man, is not known.

24.10.6 Emotional and Mental Characteristics

Soope also possess a SEIC, i.e. they are capable of thought, feeling and volition. They experience both joy and anger, have memories and desires. They are afraid of mighty spirit beings, dreading their mana and also the magic spells (*ppéwút*) which humans know how to make in order to repel them. Most of all they fear fire and light.

The features of their character, their overall emotional and mental state reflect that which the islanders understand by a dark SEIC. *Soope* are continually in a petulant mood (*rochongngaw*), raging (*chchow, soong, ningeringer* etc.), impudent (*namanam tekiya*), full of guile (*sooná*) and meanness (*kirikiringngaw*). They are lazy (*chipwang*) and quickly lose interest in what they have begun (*achaanú*).

Their intellectual capacities are limited to a minimum. *Soope* are regarded as stupid (*tiparoch*) and hence unable to learn anything or focus on anything for any length of time (*chchemeni, chechchemeni*). They lack any kind of common sense and awareness of "right action" (*miriit*). Because of the darkness of their SEIC, their malevolent basic attitude and intentions, they are also called *énúúroch*.

24.10.7 Relationship to People

Their malevolence and aggression can render them dangerous. Certain *soope* are known to lie in wait (*énúúsowusow*) for people in order to throttle them, scratch, bite and consume them. There is a particular concept of eating (*wochooch*) which is typical of such *soope*. They are also called *énúúwochooch*, indicating "raw eaters", or "meat eaters". To be eaten is indeed what one has to expect from them. This is what the islanders most fear about a *soope*. To be bitten or eaten by a *soope* and to be attacked or waylaid by a malevolent spirit being are identical expressions in the Chuukese language.

The islanders make a general distinction between taking in liquid nourishment (*wún*, *wúnúmi*) and solid food (*mwéngé*). Liquid nourishment includes everything drinkable, soup and gravy, but also all food which only becomes liquid in the mouth, such as sugar, salt, honey etc.

Solid food is divided into two groups. The eating of cooked plant food and cooked fish is called *eni*, the eating of all other kinds of meat and raw plant food is called *wochooch*, *wocheey*. The two terms not only denote how they behave regarding taking in food, but also how they (and all other malevolent spirit beings) typically behave towards people.

A bite from a *soope* mostly leads to a swelling around the bite, and pains or disease of the body generally. Usually one is unaware of being bitten by a *soope*. As spirit beings they are also quite capable of causing pain in this way inside the body. An unborn child bitten by a *soope* in the womb will enter the world with a birth mark, deformities, or stillborn, depending on the severity of the attack.

Many *soope* aim to jump on people, climb up them (*téétá*) and cling round their body. This causes a panic reaction in that person. If someone begins to scream, rage or behave in some other odd way the reason can only be that a *soope* (or another *énúngngaw*) has that person in its grip, although it remains invisible. The victim becomes *wumwes* (mad), a term the islanders use to describe not only abnormal psychic behaviour but also all forms of extreme emotion, excitement, anger etc.

The notion here is rather not that a malevolent spirit being has "entered into a person" and is controlling his behaviour from "inside". This kind of possession has more to do with the notion of external contact with a malevolent spirit being which climbs on to its victim and " sits on him, rides him" (*émén soope, énúngngaw aa wááni*).

The overwhelming majority of *soope*, which are countless in number, do not cause such mischief. They are not actually dangerous and also play no serious part in causing disease (see also Mahony 1970:135). Usually they take pleasure in stealing from people, playing tricks on them, scaring them by throwing sticks and stones at them, confront them in nightmares (*ttanen soope*) or annoy them by multiplying the pests in their plantations.

Adults like to use the fear of all kinds of *soope* to persuade children to change their behaviour. If a child is bothering a group of adults in some way they threaten that a *soope* will come and do it harm.

24.10.8 Place of Abode

Soope fear the light, and so during the day they mostly remain invisible. They spend this time sleeping or lazing in dark places in the mangrove swamps, in holes in the ground, caves or under large stones. As twilight approaches they come out of their hiding places, flit around people's houses and move about on the islands during the night, before creeping back to their corners again as dawn breaks. Hence they can easily be confused with harmless nocturnal animals.

24.10.9 Protection against *Soope*

The most important safety rule for protection against *soope* is very simple: never remain alone. *Soope* have an aversion to groups of people and only attack isolated individuals.

Those who have to be alone at night should carry a burning torch or some other kind of light, because *soope* fear fire and light. Sometimes they can also be driven away by throwing stones at them.

They also permanently avoid houses if the walls and posts are painted with the juice of bitter plants such as *maras* (Soulamea amara, Mahony 1970:96) or bile (*maras, pwáánu*). This kind of "bitter-making" preparation (*amarasen soope*) also applies to long journeys in open boats. One rubs one's body or at least the arms and face with *kurukur* (Citrus aurantium, Mahony 1970:95) and *siitor* (a kind of orange/lemon growing on Chuuk). If children are on board the application is repeated in order to be quite sure that the bitter taste makes them safe against any attack by a *soope*. They also rely on certain medical drugs (*sáfey*) and other magical means of defence (*ppéwút*) for effective protection. In addition holy water and the mana of Christian prayer (*iyóótek*) are further means of protection against *soope*.

24.10.10 *Soope* as Spirits of the Dead

When people die they leave behind not only a benevolent spirit of the dead (*énúúsootupw*), but also a malevolent one. The latter, called *soope*, is revealed in all its characteristics as *énúngngaw*. It is said that it possesses the sex and approximate physical size of the deceased, but no longer its outward appearance. Any physical defects of the deceased such as missing limbs are said to be retained by the *soope* as that person's spirit of the dead, in contrast to the benevolent counterpart.

As malevolent spirits of the dead *soope* do not belong to the social group of the deceased person, i.e. they are not *énúúsootupw*. Nor can they be *énú aramas*, because they lack human form. It is impossible, and because of their inability to speak also pointless for them to communicate with them via a medium.

Being spirits of the dead *soope* frequently abide near the grave of the deceased, since it contains the body to which they had been assigned (as *ngúnúngngaw*) while that person was alive. This means that the area around a grave can constitute a danger. The fear of a gathering of many *soope* has (according to Bollig 1927:20) been a powerful hindrance to creating Christian cemeteries. Even today most burials take place on one's own land. Even in the (no longer usual) home interments this fear was still at work. It was, however, lessened by limiting home interments to deceased with special status, whose benevolent spirits of the dead, being *énúúsór*, could easily hold malevolent spirits of the dead in check.

This indicates the position that the *soope* occupy as spirits of the dead among the other spirit beings. Benevolent spirit beings are superior to them, give them orders and can drive them away.

24.10.11 Mortality

As spirit beings *soope* are in principle immortal, but they can also "die" in *Neepwúnnúpis*. More malevolent spirit beings end up there than benevolent ones, because their malevolence more often creates conflict with benevolent spirit beings, incurring the punishment of "death".

24.10.12 *Soope* as an Explanation or Comparative Description of Phenomena

24.10.12.1 for Inexplicable Manifestations of Light

Marine luminescence and insects that glow (*nikámáráyiyá*) are not considered to be caused by animals. They are evoked by malevolent spirit beings (*énúngngaw, soope*), or they are the actual glowing eyes of swimming and flying *soope*.

Another kind of *nikámáráyiyá* creates certain kinds of fungi and lichens which glow in the dark. Because of their strange form and the putrefaction of the locations they prefer they are called *seningen énú* or *seningen soope* (spirit ears) (cf. Mahony 1970:90).

Meteors are also *soope* (or *énúngngaw*). The Chuukese have no other term for them.

24.10.12.2 for Malformations

Soope are the cause of birth deformities and miscarriages, both human and animal. If a woman brings into the world a child with extra fingers or toes it must have been engendered by a *soope* (*aa wupwun wóón soope*). This is also how a very obese child ("without bones") is explained, children with an unusually light skin and those with hermaphrodite features and Down's syndrome. All these are predominantly externally visible deformities. Children with mental handicaps, which only emerge later on, are not classified in this way. Suddenly occurring emotional and mental abnormalities are not actually explained in terms of being fathered by a *soope*, but as the consequence of a bite or other kind of bodily contact with one, or simply as the unsatisfactory development of the opening of that child's SEIC.

Deformed children are not regarded as proper human beings. They are immediately designated as *soope* and feared and shunned accordingly. Being neglected, they fall victim to death early or are dispensed with by abandoning them, throwing them into the sea, or burning them.

For the islanders *soope* are the quintessence of all that is deformed or distorted. Cartoon representations of people in European newspapers are designated as *soope*. Ugly people are described as looking like a *soope* (*aa mesen soope*).

24.10.12.3 for Bad Features of Human Character and Behaviour

People of a dissolute way of life are also called *soope*. Of vagrants it is said that they wander around like a *soope* (*raa soopefátán*). Selfish, vulgar, treacherous people, deceivers, thieves and liars have the SEIC and hence the thinking of a *soope* (*raa tipen* or *ekiyekin soope*). The behaviour of an uncaring mother belongs in the same category: they have the empathy of a *soope* (*ttongen soope*).

24.10.13 The Other Malevolent Spirit Beings

What is said about *soope* is in the main also true for all other spirit beings, of which there are countless numbers.

One feared group among them consists of those named *énússet*, a term which reflects their preferred abode (sea and reef spirits). They usually reside near the coast on the edge of the island reefs. Among them the *Chénúkken* ("Saltwater") are regarded as particularly dangerous.

The appearance of the *énússet* is described as being fairly similar to that of humans. There is no mention of them having any animal-like features. However, their aspect is just as horrifying as that of many *soope*.

When they enter a house at night in order to have sexual intercourse with women they always change their ugly form into that of a beautiful person. As infamous fathers of deformed children their notoriety exceeds even that of the *soope*.

The *énússet* possess a pronounced sense of smell (cf. Mahony 1970:148). They are drawn especially to human (feminine) genital odour. Men who have had sexual intercourse and women who are menstruating run the danger of being bitten or eaten by an *énússet* while fishing. The danger is all the greater because by contrast well-intentioned spirit beings are repelled by genital odour, distance themselves and so no longer offer protection against attacks by evil-intentioned *énússet*. This is why before a large joint fishing expedition the men of the village sleep in the *wuut* (community house). Anyone not observing the taboo *wonowut* (sleeping in the community house) would not only put themselves in danger but also the whole enterprise.

Indeed the islanders hold the bite of the *énússet* to be the cause of all kinds of diseases. As spirit beings they can instigate not only external pains but also inside the human body itself. The results are considered to be chiefly still-births, epileptic seizures and symptoms indicating a stroke: paralysis of individual parts of the body, loss of the ability to speak etc.

Among the Chuuk Islanders the *énússet* and many other *énúngngaw* are the causal factor in a comprehensive theory of disease and its treatments, as described by Mahony (1970).

Moreover the *énússet* are not just feared because of the consequences of their attacks. They outdo most other malevolent spirit beings in terms of their evil disposition and pleasure in attacking, i.e. for humans they constitute altogether one of the most dangerous kinds of malevolent spirit beings.

Those who go out at night on to the sea to fish put themselves in particular danger of coming to grief on account of an *énússet*. Effective protection against them includes all those means which also help against *soope*. One should at least take some kind of light and never stay unaccompanied in the area where there are *énússet*. Ignoring these elementary safety rules would be tantamount to committing suicide.

Gifts in the form of offerings have no long term effect on malevolent spirit beings. Because of their emotional and mental disposition they are hardly likely to feel any gratitude (*kinissow*). Even if they were unable to suppress a feeling of obligation their spiteful nature would gain the upper hand. No amount of gifts would stop them from being hostile to people.

Nevertheless it is not completely hopeless to try to appease them by placing before them a *niffang* of something edible. This, too, is an offering (*ósór*), aimed at achieving the same effect as with benevolent spirit beings. However, it is not necessary to take anything like as much care over the preparations as for a benevolent spirit of the dead (*énúúsór*). Also no special place of offering is required. If you want to prevent the *énússet* from begrudging you a large catch, you lay a few fish on a stone, or simply throw them into the sea, drawing the attention of the recipient to them by calling out ("*ósórumw, Chénúkken, pwe kepwe eniyapaakeem!*").

Énússet and all other malevolent spirit beings are not surviving spirits of the dead like most of the *soope*.

24.11 Summary

Benevolent spirit beings (*énúúyééch*) are all spirit-like beings of the beyond, whom a person can encounter with confidence. If one has to fear them, it is mostly one's own fault. As a rule they possess good qualities, a human appearance, a high degree of intelligence, a friendly disposition and temper. Their presence can evoke the same attitude and mood in people. As benevolent spirits of the dead (*énúúsootupw*) they perpetuate the personality of deceased people and as such constitute a part of the social group (family, clan etc.) to which those people belonged when alive. As benevolent spirits of the dead with special status (*énúúsór*) they watch over the preservation of the group by taking comprehensive care of their food and progeny. Infringements of the group norms put them at odds with the group, leading to calamity as a form of punishment. However, it is not their intention to endanger the physical existence of the living. If people behave appropriately (removing the cause of their anger, making gifts, offerings etc.) they respond with a change of mood and a favourable attitude. In other words they can be either benevolent or malevolent depending on circumstances.

They are placed in the category of benevolent spirit beings (*énúúyééch*) not so much on account of their outward human appearance but rather from the perspective of their positive emotional and mental disposition (*tipeyééch*), i.e. their SEIC is known for its brightness. They constitute a kind of sustaining principle in the world of the islanders.

Malevolent spirit beings (*énúngngaw*) are spirit beings of the beyond whom people must encounter with suspicion. The qualities they possess are decidedly bad. In form they are like animals, and sometimes like humans. Their appearance is ugly and terrifying, they are of very low intelligence and of a spiteful, malevolent disposition. Their presence can evoke the same attitude and mood in humans. As the instigators of disease and emotional and mental disturbances they constitute a threat to the physical existence of people which is difficult to control. The range of possible dangers emanating from them extends from the harmless to the fatal. They live like animals and populate preferably the natural human environment (bush, mangrove swamp, reef, mountains).

As malevolent spirits of the dead (*soope*) they have scarcely any similarity with the former people whom they represent as spirits of the dead, nor do they belong any more to their social group.

Among the malevolent spirit beings most *soope* are regarded as rather harmless creatures, who find satisfaction in playing tricks on people and scaring them. They make up the large group of nature spirits, goblins, ghosts etc.

Likewise they are placed in the category of malevolent spirit beings not so much on account of their outward appearance but rather from the perspective of their negative emotional and mental disposition (*tipangngaw*), i.e. their SEIC is infamous for its darkness. They constitute something like a destructive principle in the world of the islanders.

They believe that many spirit beings have "always" been benevolent or malevolent spirit beings in the sense of *énúúyééch* and *énúngngaw*, with no actual history of origin. However, *énú* as spirits of the dead, both benevolent and malevolent, "came into being". The story of their origin is inextricably bound up with the origin of the person and his or her destiny in life. This complex of notions is the subject of the following chapters.

Chapter 25
The Two Spirit Doubles of a Living Person

25.1 Introduction

The transcendent beings called *énú* which were described in the previous chapter are either spirit beings for which a physical or material counterpart never existed, or for which a physical counterpart no longer exists. Apart from these exclusively transcendent beings, there are at the same time in the other world beings having a physical equivalent in this present world. These are the spirit doubles of living humans (and animals) that are called *ngúún* just like the spirit double of objects.

The concepts that Chuuk Islanders have of the spirit doubles of human beings far surpass their ideas of spirit doubles of objects, in precision, complexity and significance. We assume at the outset that a human in his lifetime has a body (*inis*) and (at least) two spirit doubles, a benevolent one (*ngúnúyééch*) and a malevolent one (*ngúnúngngaw*).

25.2 The Terms *ngúnúyééch* and *ngúnúngngaw*, and Their Meaning

Describing the two human spirit doubles as benevolent and malevolent follows the same criteria as for those spirit beings for which there are no longer any material equivalents. They differ by their contrasting mental and emotional dispositions, i.e. by their positive or negative basic behaviour.

Although *énú* do not belong to the category *ménúmanaw* (living being) like humans and animals, one hears the phrase *raa manaw* (they are alive), and the numerals relating to them require the suffix appropriate for living creatures (*emén ngúnúyééch*).

As a rule the words *ngúnúyééch* and *ngúnúngngaw* mean only the two human spirit doubles. A person's other out-of-body manifestations such as mirror and shadow images cannot be described with these words. But comparisons are available. It is said that the benevolent spirit double is as clear as the mirror reflection with colours and other clear details. In this respect the mirror image keeps its outline shape, unlike a shadow changing shape with the sun and having blurred outlines and lacking details. This is why a shadow can be compared with the malevolent human spirit double. It is also said about these comparisons that both the mirror image and the shadow reveal injuries and deformations and loss of a limb, but that benevolent (and malevolent) spirit doubles cannot do this. We are dealing with three distinct notional entities. In the light of this the Chuuk Islanders do not think that their mirror image is their soul (cf. 21.2).

Of course, *ngúnúyééch* and *ngúnúngngaw* also occur in contexts whose classification within the framework of a spirit double poses a number of problems. In the production of starch (see 21.3) and liquid perfumes (*néé*) the ingredients lie at the bottom of the receptacle. The desired end products, i.e. the starch and the perfume, are called *ngúnúyééch*, the waste *ngúnúngngaw*. When fishermen melt lead to make weights for throwing nets, the unsightly grey dross (*ngúnúngngaw*) floats on the surface of the gleaming liquid lead (*ngúnúyééch*). Similarly with the digestion process, where the stomach separates the "good" elements of the food from the "bad".

These perceptions are difficult to classify because *ngúnúyééch* and *ngúnúngngaw* do not refer to spirit doubles but to qualitative contrasts in the material world. Yet they are mere marginal phenomena in this realm of concepts, and only a few islanders, it seems, are aware of them. Moreover, as regards objects, no distinction is made between a benevolent and a malevolent spirit double.

25.3 A Person's Benevolent Spirit Double (*ngúnúyééch*)

A development in the person's *ngúnúyééch* is noticeable for having three more or less distinct phases: a pre-existing one (i.e. existing before the body), followed by the person's lifetime, and finally the phase a few days after bodily death involving the start of the change of the benevolent spirit double into a benevolent spirit of the dead. For reasons of intelligibility the chronological sequence in the following presentation cannot be maintained. It must rather begin with the notions of the benevolent spirit double during a person's lifetime.

25.3.1 Appearance

The benevolent spirit double so completely resembles the person to whom it is assigned that it can be mistaken for him, both in newborn babies and in very elderly folk, with the limitation, however, that injuries are not visible on him and non-functioning organs are not to be found. A blind person has a seeing *ngúnúyééch*.

As a person's benevolent spirit double, the *ngúnúyééch* has this identity in common with the *ngúún* pertaining to objects.

The identity of the *ngúnúyééch* with the person is also valid for the clothing he wears: his clothes are the spirit doubles (*ngúún*) of the clothes the person wears. People seeing a spirit double cannot distinguish between it and a person merely by external appearance but by specific behaviour. It suddenly looms out of nothingness, in a closed up house for example, and merges back into nothingness, or it doesn't answer when one talks to it, even though it can hear and speak.

25.3.2 Visibility

Benevolent spirit doubles are visible to anybody in dreams, but the only people who can see them when awake are those with a special gifting. Apart from mediums (*waatawa*) this is the preserve of people who are considered seers (*móngupwi*).

When a living person's benevolent spirit double is visible to a medium, or to a seer or – on rare occasions – to the person it is assigned to when it seeks out that person in his home or encounters him at his place of work, then it has a specific intention behind the visit: to point out that the person will shortly die. On rarer occasions the spirit will appear with a wound, for example, to indicate a threat or to draw attention to a real accident.

My informant *Wupwiini*, who is considered a *móngupwi*, reported that one morning at the jetty he met a man from his own village suffering from serious leg injuries that had been clearly caused by a shark. Suddenly the man, namely his spirit double, was nowhere to be seen. Several hours later the man himself was brought back by boat from fishing; a shark had mangled one of his legs.

25.3.3 Physical Attributes

By the same token, benevolent spirit doubles do not have a body (*inis*) any more than *énú*, but they certainly have physical attributes; their size and weight (even footprints) correspond exactly to those of their designated person. Their physique means they can even lift and move heavy objects. In their manoeuvrability they differ from living people in being able to fly. Like spirits, they are not bound by time or space. They don't need to eat or sleep; when they sleep they do so independently from body sleep. They can manage for a long time without breathing continuously, but strangely they cannot sneeze. Spirit doubles weep just like people, and occasionally they wash. They are either right-handed or left-handed like their designated person. They have sexual intercourse with other spirit beings, but mostly with their own kind, but they are unable to conceive or become pregnant.

A benevolent spirit double goes through the same physical stages as his person. It grows until it has reached full adult size; in other words a person's physical body follows the growth of his benevolent spirit double.

There is some doubt whether it continues to grow if the person has supposedly died in childhood.

Benevolent spirit doubles are able to talk, but only do so in the person's lifetime to mediums and similar, i.e. they converse with other *ngúnúyééch* and *énúúyééch*.

Their sense organs, seeing and hearing at great distances, far exceed the capacity of a physical human. A baby acquires these faculties a few days after birth, yet a benevolent spirit double has them fully developed from day one.

A benevolent spirit double has a particularly remarkable sense of smell and taste. No other physical attribute is so marked – in fact in this area one may justifiably speak of a super-sensitivity. It is repelled by bitterness. Its ability to detect smells at a great distance gives a person the opportunity of recalling it to himself by means of its own fondness for sweet-smelling perfumes. Although food-related taboos, along with others, must be observed because of the sensitivities of smell and taste of benevolent spirits of the dead, the taboos are without significance as far as the benevolent spirit double is concerned.

Its sense of touch and its sensitivity to pain mean that it needs to take care near fire. Nevertheless, it is able to move among a pile of burning wood without harm; its resourcefulness finds ways of avoiding being burned.

25.3.4 Emotional and Mental Characteristics

The benevolent spirit double has its own SEIC which functions just like the physical equivalent. It can frighten, can feel homesick, and can grieve. Yet its SEIC is not identical to that of the physical body; the benevolent spirit double thinks, feels and expresses its will quite independently from the physical body.

Whereas a person's SEIC develops from birth until seniority, a benevolent spirit double's SEIC is fully developed (*ssuuk*) from the beginning; that is, it already exhibits all the emotional and mental adult characteristics only acquired by the physical body after a lifetime of many years. Thus a new baby's benevolent spirit double can talk and has nothing whatever to learn.

Evidence comes from the fact that benevolent spirits of dead children, which were in the children's lifetime their benevolent spirit doubles, talk like adults via a medium and show knowledge about things that only adults know.

In its characteristics and intellectual prowess it is no different from benevolent spirit beings. Its SEIC is bright, and its fundamental mood is positive. Without its intelligence (*tipáchchem*) it would be unable to fulfil its obligations to the physical body. For example, it would not be in a position to recognise the first sign of disaster and to avert it.

As well as having these general mental and emotional attributes, benevolent spirit doubles also have numerous personality traits and giftings which make them individual. Some are more courageous and intelligent than others. Some have particular expertise in building canoes, in treating illnesses, or in having magic powers to determine the ripening season of breadfruit.

A person having a benevolent spirit double with this kind of gift will demonstrate it over a lifetime, given that his own personality develops in all respects according to the model of his benevolent spirit double. Together with his physical self, his SEIC dispositions are also determined by the pre-existing characteristics of his benevolent spirit double.

The ramifications of this notion are such that Chuuk Islanders will attribute a person's habit of smoking to the same tendency in their benevolent spirit double.

In all situations the benevolent spirit double's SEIC is independent of the physical SEIC. If a person's SEIC darkens to the extent of behaving abnormally and showing signs of mental confusion (*wumwes*), his benevolent spirit double's SEIC remains unaffected. Conversely the physical SEIC is only initially uninfluenced if that person's benevolent spirit double's SEIC is darkened by specific harm-inducing black magic (*ppéwút*). Because it is then no longer able to fulfil its duties towards the body, the malevolent spirit beings (and the malevolent spirit double of the person affected) can without opposition bring about illness and death, and the darkening and confusion of the body's SEIC.

Mental and emotional defects which become apparent in somebody over time are reckoned to be caused by malevolent spirit beings, yet a benevolent spirit double does not necessarily exhibit the defects. If they are linked with such physical disabilities as Down's syndrome, for example, the person is not considered to be a person, but a malevolent spirit being, a *soope* in material guise.

The benevolent spirit double is superior to its attached person, knowing always what the person thinks, feels and wants. This again shows its independence from the person it is assigned to. Its very independence is, however, restricted in one quite specific respect.

25.3.5 Relationship to the Person

The benevolent spirit double usually has a strong sense of responsibility towards the body it belongs to. This feeling of responsibility is accompanied by emotions which ensure cohesion between members of a social group and which are also present among their benevolent spirits of the dead. One of the strongest feelings binding the benevolent spirit double to the body is in turn what the islanders understand by *ttong*. It causes it to behave towards the body like a close relative.

Yet another feeling imputed to the benevolent spirit double relating to the body is *chchopwa* (*aa chchopwaangeni inis*), that nervous anxiety felt when one is on tenterhooks; *chchopwa* is also the term for a hen's behaviour when refusing to let her chicks out of her sight.

The benevolent spirit double sees its task primarily in terms of maintaining the physical existence of the body. As a being from the world beyond, it is able to predict in time whether calamity threatens from malevolent spirit beings, causing sickness in the body and darkness in the SEIC. It is usually superior in intelligence, and possesses greater physical strength and greater mana, a combination which is able to render the malevolent spirit beings harmless.

A person's benevolent spirit double also is aware in good time if a dangerous animal intends attacking. It either acts upon the animal by preventing it from becoming aggressive and detracting it from its purpose, or else it influences the person's SEIC, making this aware of the threat and acting as a prompt to seek safety. The benevolent spirit double can even achieve this if the body is asleep, by evoking a dream of impending danger, or simply by waking the sleeper. In these circumstances the benevolent spirit double personifies the functions of the subconscious.

The impact on the SEIC, which the person is unaware of, is called *ámeefi* (to feel, to sense, to insinuate). By this is meant to hint broadly at something, and non-verbal communication by typical mannerisms and facial expressions and the like.

It is able to fulfil its objective of properly ensuring the physical existence of the body. It achieves this because, as a transcendent being, all avenues are open to it that are accessible to any benevolent spirit being. The benevolent spirit double knows beyond the immediate what is going to happen; it can – if required – summon help from benevolent spirit beings, without being bound by time and place.

When a person comes to grief despite the presence of his *ngúmúyééch* it can be because he has done something bad: he has become *ttipis* and needs to be punished by the benevolent spirits of the dead in his family. In such a case the *ngúmúyééch* cannot intervene to be protective, since it is required to be subject to the benevolent spirits of the dead of his family members.

The benevolent spirit double is usually only responsible for the particular individual. However, its involvement and care can extend to benefit his children: were one of them in mortal danger the benevolent spirit double of the father and mother would try by all means to draw their child's attention to the imminent danger.

Occasionally the benevolent spirit double can, by influencing the person's SEIC, attempt to bring about change in his mood or his thinking without his becoming aware; it will calm him if he is worried about a sick child, or it will dissuade him from a plan to harm somebody. In this respect the benevolent spirit double is a kind of warning voice of conscience. It can even get angry if the person is unwilling to alter his own response. Of course, punishments for wrongdoing are not at the behest of the spirit double but are the preserve of the person's benevolent spirits of the dead, to which his benevolent spirit double owes obedience.

The way the benevolent spirit double behaves is conditioned by its emotional relationship to the body, which involves a distinct interest in the body, and which the person cannot reciprocate. It emanates unilaterally from the benevolent spirit double, which remains invisible and inaccessible and above any influence he might bring to bear. Physical bonds between them are non-existent; the benevolent spirit double's SEIC with its disposition is the sole link binding them.

25.3.6 Place of Abode

Despite its emotional link to the body a person's benevolent spirit double is a fully autonomous person, leading a largely independent existence separate from the body. At any time it is able to distance itself as far and as often – but not for as long – as it likes, without the person knowing and without any impact on him. Yet because it is emotionally linked to him it does generally stay close, so that it can see him. It is his constant companion through life. In this way it discerns what is happening in the person's immediate surroundings, whether his body is threatened by being involved in some dangerous activity or because malevolent spirit beings are prowling round. Because it is aware of likely dangers and feels responsible for the physical person, wanting to prevent harm, it is usually loath to stay some distance away from him.

Chuuk Islanders have no conception of the benevolent spirit double living within a person's body (even though this is not excluded as a possibility). If it does come into contact with the body then the notion is that it is over the person or on him. In which case the person feels that his benevolent spirit double is with him; he feels heavier. If the spirit is merely close then it cannot be physically sensed.

If the benevolent spirit double returns to the body after an absence, the saying is *ngúni aa niwitto wóóy* (my benevolent spirit double has come back to me). Even if it were deliberately to find its way into the body or seek to leave the body, it avoids choosing a specific opening (airways, fontanelle, etc.)

Because one cannot generally sense the presence of the benevolent spirit double, a person is rarely aware if it is around one, or where it is at any given time. Benevolent spirit doubles have their own ideas, intentions and wishes. Just like people, they enjoy meeting for specific purposes. They especially like going to the *náán*, enjoying fun with the benevolent spirit beings living there, or meeting the benevolent spirits of the dead in their family circle or their village and swapping news with them. Quite often they also visit the medium responsible for the locality of the folk they belong to. Sometimes they inform him that they will be absent for some while; they request the medium to tell them if the person is anxious about something or discovers symptoms requiring the benevolent spirit double to return to him.

Uncertainty about where it may be can sometimes be allayed for a short while. If a benevolent spirit double is present locally the medium can, of course, see it and relay news of its whereabouts. Over greater distances the medium can only find out through a dream just where the absent benevolent spirit double is. Such a dream can even be experienced by people.

25.3.7 Dream (*ttan*)

Sleep (*méwúr, annut*) is a purely physical process; the benevolent spirit double is not involved. The fact that the spirit double may leave doesn't result in the person falling asleep. As a rule the benevolent spirit remains very close to the person asleep, in order to watch over him. Conversely, the fact that a person wakes is not a sign that his spirit double has returned.

Furthermore, a person's dreams (*ttan*) are not caused by his benevolent spirit double departing on some journey or other; the person is also able to dream when the spirit is close. Chuuk Islanders consider dreams to be short extracts from the on-going life experience of their benevolent spirit double. While he is asleep a person has the opportunity of experiencing what is occurring in the realm inhabited by his benevolent spirit double. A dream is a kind of window giving a person in this life an insight into the next; it shows him things and events unknowable except by dreaming. Thus dreams are the ultimate source of knowledge about the world's general dual structure and about the nature of the spirit double and specifically about the complete otherness of the world beyond.

The fact that a person also dreams when his benevolent spirit double is with him is evidenced by the many dream experiences in which the action unfolds in the immediate surroundings of the person asleep.

Dreams show that benevolent spirit doubles resemble very closely the people they belong to, both in form and behaviour. Dream experiences give one to understand that they must indeed relate very closely to coherent experiences in the life of the benevolent spirit double: it is possible to resume dreaming an interrupted dream soon after falling asleep again. Finally, dreams clearly show that benevolent spirit doubles (apart from individual differences) do not differ in any way externally from benevolent spirits of the dead of deceased friends and relatives that the person dreaming has known.

A person's experiences of dreams and the corresponding experience of his benevolent spirit double occur simultaneously. In the dreaming process there are thus always two participants, the one experiencing and the other sharing the experience. This is a significant aspect of the theory of dreams. Yet it can only be a causal explanation of dreaming, since linguistically the process is so conceived that the person himself appears as the subject and not his benevolent spirit double: people say (*ngaang*) *wúwa ttan* (**I** have had a dream). This is a clear indication that for the islanders the personality of the physical person is conceptually identical to the personality of his benevolent spirit double.

H. Fischer has declared that (1) the conceptual identity of the benevolent spirit's personality with the respective person's personality and (2) its function as a being who experiences what happens in dreams are two important characteristics of a single "soul perception" which occurs within Oceania as a whole, the Austronesian and the non-Austronesian (Papua) groups; a perception he thus calls the "dream ego" (1965:243 ff.). In this context he discusses other terms from the soul typology of anthropology, justifying why he does not wish to retain the term "free soul" (Arbmann) for Oceania. Without reservation, his arguments and results are pertinent for Chuuk in relation to the concepts of the benevolent spirit double: it is the Oceanic conception of "dream ego". Yet reasons of terminology and reasons inherent in the structure of thinking for the area of my research persuade me to avoid this term and to continue to use the phrase "benevolent spirit double".

A person's SEIC is however only indirectly involved in dreaming. The person is experiencing, in a manner that cannot be explained any more closely, what his benevolent spirit double is going through; and later he can remember it. This act of recall is the only role his SEIC can have.

Memories of dreams are mental and emotional dispositions, the dreams themselves are not.

Research into the structure of the vocabulary for mental and emotional dispositions demonstrate this. If the dream were a process or a circumstance conceived as being a function of the body's SEIC then *ttan* would have to represent a kind of *tiip* (SEIC disposition) as well as a kind of *meefi* (SEIC movement). Both are ruled out by informants. The islanders do not consider dreaming as a concept belonging to the mental or emotional realm.

For that reason even new-born babies can dream. The fact that nothing can be discovered about it from them is explained in terms of their SEIC not being open (*ssuuk*) and therefore their capacity for remembering and for speaking are not yet developed. It is even supposed that animals dream.

Chuuk Islanders declare that they often dream if they have fallen asleep with a particular worry or an unfulfilled wish on their mind or heart. Interpreting dreams of this kind involves the notion of a being reliving a dream. The benevolent spirit double, aware of the cause of the worry or wish, feels sympathy with the person it relates to. It sets about creating a remedy, sharing in a dream its efforts to console him and restore his hope.

A person going to sleep hungry witnesses that his *ngúnúyééch* somehow knows where fish can be caught, or where a group is having a meal he might get invited to join. A person's homesickness for familiar surroundings is able to prompt his benevolent spirit double to set off and bid him accompany it on his journey. If a woman who has had a stillbirth dreams that her baby is still alive and pining for her, this shows that the baby's *ngúnúyééch* is so deeply sympathetic to the woman that it is trying to console her through such dreams.

However, dreams are not just attempts by the benevolent spirit double to allay fears or fulfil wishes. Through dreams it finds an effective means to point the person to any threatening dangers; its function as a personification of the subconscious is most clearly manifested here.

If somebody needs to climb a tall tree, not suspecting that its branches are rotten, his *ngúnuyééch* alerts him in a dream of him climbing it, then falling because of a branch breaking. Similarly even the *ngúnúyééch* of one of his children is able to act out in a dream sequence what dangers it will run into, in order to persuade the parent to be vigilant.

Dreams acting as pointers from the beyond are not always clear enough to be immediately understandable. They need to be decoded, because the benevolent spirit double, full of tact, wants to spare the person unpleasant things or make pleasant news more interesting through veiling the actual circumstances. The supposition is that it wants to make use of stereotypical scenarios for specific messages. This is why even seemingly meaningless dreams can be variously interpreted.

For this purpose the islanders use a proper dream typology. For example, a *ttanen mooni* (a dream to do with money) means that the dreamer is about to experience a disappointment.

The islanders' theory of dreams is, of course, not without its inconsistencies, yet it does explain the process of dreams in a vivid and plausible way. It shows especially that dream processes, broadly speaking, need to be treated for real.

How dreams are experienced as reality can be understood from the fact that Christians among the islanders consider that offences committed in dreams against the Ten Commandments are sins.

Because dream experiences are seen as real, people can infer from them where a benevolent spirit double is located when there are signs that it has been keeping its distance from its assigned human being for some time.

25.3.8 Causes and Consequences of *ngúnúyééch* Being Absent from the Body

The further the benevolent spirit double is from the body, the less it is able to carry out its protective role. Its absence always signals a considerable threat hovering over the person: malevolent spirit beings can have unimpeded access to him, and he can find himself in mortal danger without realising it. The worst aspect is that he is alone with his malevolent spirit double (*ngúnúngngaw*), which can have devastating consequences. The *ngúnúngngaw* operates in a way that is contrary to what is expected of the benevolent spirit double. It will divert people from being aware of likely dangers; its sole aim is to cause the person harm.

As a rule people assume that the emotional bond between the benevolent spirit double and the body generates such a great sense of responsibility and duty that it feels compelled to fulfil its actual tasks and stay close to protect the person. There are various reasons why the benevolent spirit double occasionally has to distance itself from him. It possesses its own will, has intentions and wishes. Its curiosity and its lust for life cause it to participate in activities with other spirit beings, or else to meet its peers and its friends from among the benevolent spirits of the dead. In the beyond the same obligations exist as in this life to care for one's relatives; tasks that a powerful spirit of the dead or effecting spirit (*énúúsór*) assigns to the benevolent spirit double need to be carried out promptly if it wishes to avoid danger. Occasionally, the functions that a person is fulfilling in the community require his benevolent spirit double to move far away from him. So it is assumed that the *ngúnúyééch* of a breadfruit sorcerer (*sowuyatoomey*) occasionally travels to the *Éwúr* island to fetch the *ngúún* required to bring the breadfruit to the ripening stage. A boat-builder's *ngúnúyééch* can feel the need to seek advice from an *énú* of an ancestor or of a deceased fellow-craftsman.

On the other hand it is impossible for a person himself to send out his benevolent spirit double or to chase it away for whatever reasons. Even mediums cannot achieve this, despite fewer restrictions being placed on their dealings with the spirit world. Neither does it happen that the benevolent spirit double distances itself from the body because it feels animosity towards him or because of a dispute with him. It cannot surrender its emotional tie to the body during the person's lifetime.

It leaves the body usually when the person is in an extreme physical or mental and/or emotional circumstance. Sudden shock sends it fleeing, for example when it sees a malevolent spirit being, or when somebody is being beaten up. For this reason mothers are careful to avoid their child seeing its own reflection in a mirror at a young age, for fear of it shocking the child. It is not good either to wake a person abruptly: its benevolent spirit double, which may be present, could be driven away by the shock. Usually it returns once the person has calmed down.

When the islanders want to say that they have been scared witless, their phrase is *aa súúnó* or *ássinó ngúni* (my spirit double has fled or flown away). Whenever it returns after such a shocking experience, the person cannot help sneezing; he then declares *wochonapey aa niwitto*; *wochonap* is a rare word that cannot be analysed any more closely; it means the benevolent spirit double during the person's life and a spirit of the dead.

In catastrophes where a person is badly injured it sometimes happens that his benevolent spirit double absents itself because it cannot watch and see him suffer. This happens with men even when they are just suffering from toothache. Pregnant women reckon that their benevolent spirit double leaves at the onset of labour pains. At this stage they are defenceless targets for attacks by malevolent spirit beings and need protective magic (*ppéwút*) to a special degree.

Sometimes a person's benevolent spirit double is persuaded or pressured by a powerful spirit being (*énúúsór*) to keep somebody company. In most cases when a benevolent spirit double is forced to stay away from the person himself the reason has to do with a crime which the person or a member of his family has committed and needs to atone for. There are even cases where a benevolent spirit double itself is guilty of something similar and behaves in a high-handed and reckless manner. The punishment for this lack of respect towards an *énúúsór* may involve captivity or in extreme circumstances "death" in *Neepwúnnúpis*.

The punishing *énúúsór* lures the offending *ngúnúyééch* into an ambush and tips a great traditional ceremonial bowl (*wuunong*) over its head (for an illustration see LeBar 1964:15). The bowl crashes over him with a thunderous din that echoes around the whole neighbourhood. If unexplained noises of thunder can be heard locals are on the alert to see if a victim is showing signs of his *ngúnúyééch* having been captured.

Finally, the benevolent spirit double may be persuaded by some bad magic (*ppéwút*) to stay far away from its body. It is unheard of for a spirit being to be stolen.

If the spirit was on him, the moment of its disappearing can only be noticed by the person feeling suddenly rather lighter. This is a rare event because the physical person and his *ngúnúyééch* are not usually in such close contact with one another.

The benevolent spirit double can definitely be absent from the body for several hours without there being consequences, after which time specific signs suggest that the spirit has not been around for a while. One sign is a sense of weariness (*ménú, ménúúnú*) occurring just when one would not expect it, such as waking from a deep sleep. If the benevolent spirit double does not return to the body, its condition worsens: tiredness becomes weakness, sickness, apathy and even unconsciousness. This inevitable process results in the person dying. Failing physical powers are often accompanied by deep mental disturbance, where the person can become aggressive, wild and even mad (*wumwes*). It is, of course, true that malevolent spirit beings can be responsible for these symptoms, easily overcoming the person in the absence of the protecting *ngúnúyééch*. They can, however, manifest themselves merely because the spirit double is absent.

Inexplicable tiredness need not be a cause for alarm. In a breadfruit magician (*sowuyatoomey*) it may just betoken that the *ngúnúyééch* is about its business of bringing ripeness, and will return in due time.

Unconsciousness (*masaroch, má, pe*) may just be prompted by something physical; it may not be a reliable sign, any more than sleepiness is, that the person's *ngúnúyééch* has deserted him.

The consequences of a benevolent spirit being's long absence from a person tend to match completely the consequences of objects being separated from their spirit doubles. In both instances the effects of separation are not immediate; yet after some while both exhibit signs of decline and loss of functionality and integrity. These consequences lead to collapse.

Only rarely does the absence of a benevolent spirit double signal doom like this. Empathy for the declining person mostly encourages the spirit to return; death is averted. However, nobody can know this for sure. Fear of having an unpredictable spirit double forces a person to take action.

25.3.9 Calling the Benevolent Spirit Double Back to the Body (*amwééngún*)

If one is forced to accept that the bad circumstances facing a person were caused by his *ngúnúyééch* being absent, and if, moreover, dreams reveal that its whereabouts are unknown, then there are several options for calling it to return. One can use a medium to enquire of the relevant spirits of the dead and ask where that person's benevolent spirit double has gone, requesting it to speak with the absentee and remind it of its duty. In this way it can be discovered whether the missing spirit double has been captured, which *énúúsór* has captured it and what ploys can be used to change its mind.

One dream prompting the thought that a benevolent spirit double's absence must underlie a person's bad circumstance runs as follows: somebody is dreaming he wanted to visit the sick person at home, but didn't find that person (nor his benevolent spirit double).

The least elaborate way of fetching back an absent *ngúnúyééch* is to use a medicine (*sáfey*). The whole process of assembling the ingredients, preparing them and then administering them is called *amwééngún*.

The word involves a causative conveyed by the term *ngúún* (in its basic form), and its meaning cannot be determined fully (literally something like: to cause the spirit double to adopt a cowering position); inconsistencies in meaning abound even with the transitive usage *amwééngúnú* or *amwééngúnúwa* (to fetch a spirit double). For some of my local contacts the word means precisely the opposite – namely to drive away a spirit double!

The *amwééngún* involves a *roong,* i.e. a combination of magic rituals that the medium (*waatawa*) is primarily responsible for. Further specialists in the medical arts may also be involved, because the procedure is not essentially different from therapies for other illnesses.

A fairly large container (*péén amwééngún*) is required, such as the huge shell of the mollusc *tridacna gigas* or an ordinary enamelled bowl (*waaspeesen*). It lies on a bed of fragrant and tasty leaves from the *sowur* plant *(Fragrea sp.)* with their white perfumed blossom so beloved of spirit beings. In the shell itself there is a leaf of the taro plant *óni* (*Colocasia esculenta*).

Boiling and sieving ripe coconut meat (*taka*), mixed with parts of the clerodendrum plant *aapwech* (*Clerodendron inerme*), and with *ééwúr* and *kúchún* (kind of turmeric) produces a reddish, strongly aromatic herbal brew. The standard equipment and ingredients allow for a practitioner to vary the process.

The most important factor here is the smell of the finished product. The smell is the means to attract back (*apaapa*) the absent benevolent spirit double, even from afar. Its highly-developed sense of smell lures it compellingly.

My informant *Wupwiini* explained the *amwééngún* process involved for his relief when he fell seriously ill: the medium visits him at home in the evening and asks for a freshly cut bamboo cane to be brought. He carefully chooses a length between two nodes and cuts it so that the dividing membranes at the nodes remain intact. He decorates this length at both ends with two loops of young coconut leaves (*wupwut*), ties a piece of string round its circumference and hangs it up. The medium warns the occupants of the house not to touch the bamboo and to keep completely quiet during the night.

The next morning the medium arrives with the ritual *amwééngún* container. The sick patient's family bring out prepared coconuts (*kituun*) ready to drink from, and arrange sweet-smelling blossom and ornaments. (This seems to be the only occasion where a living person's benevolent spirit double receives a kind of offering. Yet it is not called *ósór*). The medium pours into the container various liquids he has brought, and gives them a stir. Then he unties the bamboo and shakes it vigorously. A slopping sound from the liquid inside is clearly audible. The medium cuts into the bamboo in such a way to make a small hole for pouring out the liquid. When it mixes with the contents of the container they become blood red.

When preparation of the medicine is complete, the medium sits down in front of the container and stares silently into the liquid for a long time. If he sees nothing the benevolent spirit double is doomed, and the patient will die. Sometimes the medium realizes what is happening to the absent *ngúnúyééch*. If the medium eventually sees its face in the liquid it means that the benevolent spirit double has returned. The patient is required to drink it and then announces with relief: *ngúni aa niwitto wóóy* (my benevolent spirit double has returned to me). The improvement to the patient is immediate.

Krämer mentions (1932:309) a variant on this procedure, where the inside of a coconut half is smeared with fat. If the medium sees the face of the absent *ngúnúyééch* looming in this hollowed out mirror, it is reckoned to have returned. If on the other hand the medium sees the back of the head of the *ngúnúyééch* it is reckoned to have perished.

It may happen that not just a single *ngúnúyééch* returns, but several, all having been attracted by the smell of the medicine. Opinions are then divided as to how to proceed. The medium can fish out those unwanted *ngúnúyééch* using the mid rib of a coconut pinnate leaf (*soow*) and "cast it away" (*péwútóónó*). Then the patient can drink the liquid without any harmful effects. Many people think that drinking the *ngúnúyééch* of one's relations produces the same impact in them as in the patient.

The *amwééngún* is unable to force the benevolent spirit double to return if it is unwilling. The medicine is ineffective as well if the spirit double is countermanded by a hostile magic (*ppéwút*) and banned, or when it is captured by powerful spirit beings or has died in *Neepwúnnúpis*. Benevolent spirits of the dead do not respond to this. Nor can the medicine be used to prevent a benevolent spirit double from distancing itself and staying away; except for new-born babies whose benevolent spirit double used to be firmly tied to the body in a process involving smoke (Krämer 1932:249-250). This method had no effect on older children and adults.

25.3.10 Origins

Before his birth a person's benevolent spirit double dwells in one of those spirit-like places (*nááŋ*) home to the benevolent spirits of the dead belonging to his family. The spirit takes the form of an infant, and the spirits of the dead care for its wellbeing.

Notions regarding its origin are mere speculation. Some folk believe that *Énúúnap*, the Supreme Being, or *Semekóóror,* a member of his family, or indeed (the Christian) God is responsible for the pre-existence of the spirit double. The most widespread view is that it has "always been present".

The pre-existence stage generally lasts until the birth of the person to which it will be assigned. During that time it stays in its *nááŋ*.

A woman's pregnancy (*pwoopwo*) is merely physical and has no causal relationship to the expected baby's *ngúnúyééch*: she became pregnant when the blood in her uterus became mixed with sperm.

Details about the form and function of the male and female sex organs have already been studied in chapter 7; now it is appropriate to briefly expand and summarize the significant features within the present context.

In the islanders' understanding the sperm originates in the spine whose fluid is similar in colour and consistency. In men, over-frequent sexual intercourse gives rise to back pain because increased outflow of sperm leads to the spine drying out. Until the menopause the uterus is always full of blood, which is renewed regularly every four weeks from the menarche onwards. Pregnancy can sometimes occur before the start of the menarche, because there are girls who fall pregnant even before their first period. A woman cannot become pregnant during her period, because there is no blood in her uterus.

When blood and sperm mix in the uterus during sexual intercourse a foetus results from this kind of clotting process. Blood and sperm need to be present in roughly the same quantities. Usually the amount of sperm released in intercourse is smaller than the amount of blood in the uterus. For this reason pregnancy requires repeated acts of intercourse. The gender of the baby cannot be influenced.

Around the time of the baby's birth the benevolent family spirits of the dead come to the woman's home to help her and to protect her against malevolent spirit beings who have been targeting her and her baby.

Because the fear is inevitable that the mother's benevolent spirit double may distance itself at the birth, and because she is thereafter so much more vulnerable to attack from the malevolent spirit being *Sowumwerikes*, she is particularly beholden to the presence of her family's benevolent spirits of the dead. Before the birth, therefore, care must be taken that nothing startles her. Additionally, for pregnant mothers all foods are taboo that benevolent spirit beings are inclined to refuse (*épwét* etc.) The birth is accompanied by magic rituals featuring fragrant herbs.

The baby's benevolent spirit double comes with the benevolent spirits of the mother's family ancestors. Sometimes it will have made its way to the baby by itself, because it already knows the little person to whom it is assigned. The precise moment of its arrival cannot of course be determined; the time may drag on. When a new-born baby has settled and is no longer screaming, then it is clear that the benevolent spirit double is present and intends staying.

A new-born baby is not really meant to scream. If it does there are reasons for supposing that a malevolent spirit being has got hold of it in the absence of its *ngúnúyééch*. Even then a new baby needs to have all its physical functions if one is to be quite sure that its *ngúnúyééch* is not yet present. The fact that the baby is breathing is not by itself a sign that the *ngúnúyééch* is present. In the islanders' view the breathing process is a function of heart activity and thus a purely physical process (see 7.17); if it is failing, then the baby must be massaged or shaken. Methods for compelling its *ngúnúyééch* to be present are unknown.

The baby is fully identical to its benevolent spirit double. For this reason one can determine from specific physical features quite where the *ngúnúyééch* had been until the baby's birth. Children whose hair has a reddish or blond colouring have a benevolent spirit double from the *náán*

Tupwuniyón area in west Chuuk where the sun sets in a glow of red and yellow. These children are called *ménúkónen Tupwuniyón*.

The benevolent spirit double is given the same name as the child and responds to being called by this name.

25.3.11 "Rebirth"

If a malevolent spirit has designs on a pregnant woman her baby may well be stillborn. Its benevolent spirit double knows this in advance, yet is nevertheless present at the birth. Even at this moment it feels such a strong emotional bond to the little baby that it grieves at the loss. Not only does it stay by the corpse but it also attends the mother to comfort her. It causes her to dream that her dead baby is still alive and wanting her to suckle, and so on.

It is quite common for it to remain with her some time, until she is pregnant again. A new pregnancy occurs even more promptly, because the child's benevolent spirit double commits itself especially to the family's benevolent ancestral spirits. The baby born as a result resembles the previous stillborn infant in all respects, because it has the same *ngúnúyééch*.

Wupwiini reports that his son *Iro* died soon after birth. He and his wife had dearly loved the child and felt the pain of his loss acutely. *Wupwiini*'s wife was very quickly pregnant again and gave birth to a son who was the very image of her dead *Iro* and who was given the same name.

The opportunities for a "rebirth" are not limitless, but only occur during a person's early childhood. For those who have died in adulthood there is none. Their benevolent spirit double has passed through a stage of development which cannot be revisited.

25.3.12 People with More than One Benevolent Spirit Double

It occasionally happens that a dead child's *ngúnúyééch* is not the only benevolent spirit double remaining to one born later; sometimes at this later birth there is also a different *ngúnúyééch* on hand whom the good ancestral spirits have nurtured over a lengthy period. This child thus has two benevolent spirit doubles during his lifetime influencing his course in a significant way.

Those having more than one benevolent spirit double exhibit great intelligence and notable talents even in childhood. As adults their mana is evident in their ability to make their influence count, and in their acquiring authority and high status. The presence of several spirit doubles leads to a great blossoming of personality and a shaping of the dispositions of their SEIC bringing them great reputation. They become chiefs and experts in the practice of magic, and later in life they may earn the title of sage (*átásór, mwáánesór* etc.). It is common knowledge even in their lifetime that their benevolent spirits of the dead will indeed become *énúúsór*.

A "rebirth" as I have just outlined is not a prerequisite for a person having more than one benevolent spirit double. Moreover, the number even in these extreme cases is restricted to two or three. More than three is indeed conceivable, but does not in the islanders' view actually happen.

What is more, even ethnographers are supposed to have more than just a single *ngúnúyééch*. There was otherwise no explanation of why I was so persistently and eagerly transcribing the islanders' wisdom and trying to understand it.

25.4 A Person's Malevolent Spirit Double (*ngúnúngngaw*)

Notions of a person's malevolent spirit double are, unlike those of benevolent spirit doubles, limited and not well nuanced. Many statements about *ngúnúngngaw* remain obscure and are inferences from characteristics it will possess when it has become a (malevolent) *soope*.

Each person just has a single malevolent spirit double, even if he supposedly has several benevolent ones. It does not pre-exist the person but originates with him, indwelling him throughout his life. The malevolent spirit double and the body are one, indivisible. There is no available understanding of where in the body it resides (i.e. in what specific human organ). Because it cannot leave the body people consider it completely invisible. Not even so-called "seers" (*móngupwi*) and mediums (*waatawa*) can see it. The assumption is that it is not particularly attractive, indeed that it creates rather a gloomy impression. In appearance a person's malevolent spirit is less like him, being rather more like his shadow.

The malevolent spirit double does not have a physical body, but just a form; it is thus literally a spirit-like being. It has all the sense organs (especially a well-developed sense of smell) without ever attaining the capabilities of its benevolent counterpart. When the body is asleep, it too is asleep. It is incapable of speech. It grows up alongside the body but only to the point of death. The spirit of the departed, arising from a child's *ngúnúngngaw*, doubtless remains stunted.

The malevolent spirit double has the ability to think and has willpower, yet its SEIC never reaches the developmental stage of the body's SEIC, but continues to remain dark. It never becomes reasonable and wise (*miriit*). It remains woeful and degenerate in character, being continually in a bad mood, full of envy and rejection. It uses every opportunity to harm the person and ultimately to destroy his physical existence.

Because the malevolent spirit double cannot leave the body its potential for action is limited. It mainly harms the body's SEIC, seeking to draw the person's attention away from impending dangers, so that he fails to recognise them in time.

Chuuk Islanders call this *étúmwúnúngngawa* (making somebody unaware). The *ngúnúngngaw* is able to cause a person climbing a tree to fall to his death, or cause him to neglect a taboo and thus bring disaster upon himself and his family.

Its impact on the person's SEIC is greatest when the benevolent spirit double is absent. The person is then virtually prey to its malevolent mischief. It is capable of unleashing mental and emotional chaos, extreme moods and violent anger without malevolent spirits getting involved from outside. Yet the malevolent spirit double usually fails to achieve its aims, because the benevolent spirit double is superior to it and maintains its guard against it. Chuuk Islanders are not so much worried because a malevolent spirit double exists but rather that their benevolent spirit double might be absent just at the crucial moment.

25.5 The Significance of the Two Spirit Doubles for the Body

The relations between the person and his two spirit doubles are much more nuanced and complex than between objects and their single spirit double.

A person's benevolent spirit double is pre-existent; during the course of the person's development from birth to death it influences his total being – his appearance and his personality. Body and benevolent spirit double are separate entities. The benevolent spirit double is not beholden to the body in any way, and it can exist for an unlimited time without him. Yet the body needs its presence nearby to achieve a fully-rounded life. Only the short-term absence of the benevolent spirit double has no effect. In its determining impact a person's *ngúnúyééch* is the equivalent of the *ngúún* of objects.

The benevolent spirit double is concerned in a broad way with maintaining the body. It behaves in this like a close family member. It exercises its protective functions through keeping malevolent spirit beings at a distance, and through influencing the body's SEIC by encouraging it to behave sensibly and by making it aware of dangers, often in dreams. In this and by virtue of its experiencing dreams it operates as a kind of personification of the subconscious. One of its protective functions is as the voice of conscience; it will often prompt the person to act unwittingly in an ethically appropriate manner. The benevolent spirit double is essentially the personification of a person's instinct for self-preservation.

By contrast, the malevolent spirit double is of much lesser significance for a person. It is not pre-existent; it has a life-long attachment to the body, and it lacks any determining authority over the person's development. It tries to destroy the body by taking the person's attention away from danger, by influencing his SEIC, or else by confusing him; it thereby triggers erratic ways of behaving. In the main the malevolent spirit double is a type of embodiment of a person's urge for self-destruction.

It is thus not accurate to say in respect of Chuuk that "one of the two 'souls' is completely insignificant during a person's lifetime" (H. Fischer 1965:273).

Chapter 26
The Two Spirit Doubles of a Person
after His Physical Death

26.1 The Death of the Body (*máánó*)

Reasons for the body's life becoming extinct can be very wide-ranging. If somebody dies before reaching a great age it is because malevolent spirit beings have caused his death; or because benevolent spirit beings needed to punish him for wicked behaviour; or because of the fatal impact of mana from related magic; or because his benevolent spirit double had abandoned him for an inadmissibly long time. Yet even the most reliable *ngúnúyééch* who knows not to absent himself from the person cannot protect him from a natural death at the inevitable onset of old age. Eternal life is not granted to the physical body; it is only granted to its benevolent spirit double.

As stated above (13.1), a person is considered "dead for ever" (*máánó*) when breathing and heart activity are no longer discernible. His death is a purely physical matter, because his benevolent spirit double is still alongside even after the point of death; it will not leave him in a hurry.

The Chuukese language possesses two synonyms for the concept of death: the commoner word *má* and the rather crude *pe*. Creatures are *má* not just when their breathing and heart activity have ceased, but also when they are no longer conscious, for example after being hit on the head. It is very likely that after this type of "death" they will come to life again. *Má* can also cover a plant with drooping leaves, a car stalling under an excessive load, a worn out battery, a light bulb that has blown, a paralysed or numb arm or leg, a penis failing to achieve erection, in short, everything which has lost its usual potential for moving or working well. When it is clear that a creature cannot be revived the phrase is: he is *máánó* (defunct).

A death is an event impacting on a family group in a particular way, putting their sense of togetherness under the spotlight. Gladwin/Sarason have examined in detail the course of events on somebody's death (1953:161-167), so here I restrict myself to what needs to be understood in relation to a deceased person's two spirit doubles.

As soon as somebody has died people avoid mentioning his name. Any infringement against this counts at most as lack of tact towards those who are bereaved. Informants stress that, unlike with other breaches of a taboo, sanctions are not to be expected. If for any reason the deceased man needs to be mentioned, the word *máawe* precedes his name (and *feefinewe* for a dead woman).

The phrase for referring to a dead person by name is *féngúféngúsootupw* (literally: to awaken the dead), which suggests that in the past there was a lurking fear of sanction from the deceased. Refraining from naming an important dead person may lead people to avoid a commonly used word if it sounds even somewhat like the person's name. Thus since the death of chief *Ráyisom* from the village of *Féwúúp* the word for rice is no longer *ráyis*, but *paraas* (the pattering food) or *mwéngéépwech* (white food). For the same reason in *Wóónipw* the villagers no longer call fresh water *kkónik*, but *appúng* (falling water, rain water).

Another precaution following a man's death is to close off a plot of land, following a woman's death to close off a lengthy strip of reef. These "no go" places are marked by taboo signs. This also happens out of pious respect for the deceased person – generally they were his or her favourite places of work. Again, infringements against the taboo do not carry weighty consequences, but at the most are considered matters of tactlessness and lack of respect.

Areas closed for this reason are called *róóng*, specifically *pwaaw* on land and *mechen* on the fringing reefs. Usually the restrictions are imposed for ecological reasons, so that stocks can revive after overfishing. Closures imposed as the consequence of a death are called *mechenin* or *pwaawun mii má*. If it is the death of a person of status then his sphere of influence, even a whole island, can become *pwaaw*.

The dead person's presence is not a reason for anxiety for those left behind; they have nothing to fear from him and his benevolent spirit double. This seems to be highlighted by the strong reference to the absence of sanctions when a taboo against calling a name or trespassing into a restricted area is broken. The benevolent spirit double cannot punish people's infringement of the taboo, because it has not yet become a spirit of the dead (*énú*); for a few days more it remains what it always was, a spirit double (*ngúún*). Its malevolent counterpart responds quite differently.

26.2 The Malevolent Spirit Double after Physical Death

At the point of death the malevolent spirit double can leave the body. In doing so it has become a malevolent spirit being (*énú, énúngngaw*) and from now on will exist as *soope*. People are afraid of it. It is unlikely that it will make itself visible at this time, because it can only achieve its aims by remaining unknown. Its mental and emotional make-up corresponds to that of a malevolent spirit being. It is irritable; it tries to pick a quarrel with the dead person's benevolent spirit double; it pesters the person's family; it would even desecrate the corpse if the deceased's benevolent spirit double and the attendant benevolent family spirits of the dead did not prevent this. When in the presence of a light lit for the dead person it withdraws into a dark corner and can thus be held in check. At the burial it moves around close to the dead person and then takes up position by the grave. From that moment on it has nothing more to do with the members of the deceased's family.

Precisely how the malevolent spirit double leaves the body is not known. Particular orifices in the body do not play a role here.

26.3.1 The Benevolent Spirit Double after the Body's Death until the Time of Its Transformation into a Spirit of the Dead

Death is a burdensome event for the deceased's benevolent spirit double, and causes it to stay constantly nearby in deep sorrow. If the spirit has caused the body's death by its absence it is now blaming itself harshly. It observes the preparations for the burial (*peyiyas*), sleeps on the deceased's own mat and appears in dreams to those left behind for their consolation. Overall the impression given is that it is in an unstable mental and emotional condition.

Those who have just died are usually laid out in a crudely made coffin draped with cloths. The women of the family sit around and bewail their dead family member loudly; men conceal their pain.

During this period more and more relatives and friends each bring their gift (*oowun ménúmá*). It is meant for the dead person's benevolent spirit double and equates to the first actual offering (*ósór*) to its future benevolent spirit of the dead. Before the Christian gospel was brought to Chuuk these gifts for the dead consisted of the same objects as the offerings (*ósór*) people made to the benevolent spirits of the dead. The gifts were laid with the corpse in the coffin and later on the grave; the dead person's *ngúnúyééch* could take the spirit doubles of the offerings for itself. These days the offerings consist of soap, towels, material for making clothes and similar useful everyday objects. In a Christian burial they are no longer or only partly placed into the grave. His pillow and the clothes left on him are not considered *oowun ménúmá*.

A more detailed description of a Christian burial ceremony is contained in Gladwin/Sarason (1953:161-167).

The grave (*peyiyas*) contains a flat or roof-shaped cement lid which recalls the former traditional coverings of woven coconut palm fronds (Krämer 1935: Table 18).

While the earth is being shovelled back into the grave, and later during the cementing process, a stick is put in the grave, standing upright on the coffin, and is eventually pulled from it. The opening that had been kept open by the stick allows the dead person's benevolent spirit double to leave the grave and return again, because it had allowed itself to be buried alongside him. Without this opening it could only extract itself and return later to the corpse with great difficulty. Similar difficulties would arise if the body was buried too deep.

In the days following the burial the benevolent spirit double revisits the deceased person's home several times. The familiar surroundings supposedly remind it of the person it is mourning – just like any family member. During this time the living relatives continue to lay gifts on the grave and hold secret night vigils nearby. People expect the benevolent spirit double to be recognisable to the dead man's family, emerging from the grave as a faint glimmer of light or a wisp of smoke in human form. It brushes the soil particles inaudibly from its clothing, smoothes its hair, and gets absorbed in the gifts it finds. Those watching need to be absolutely still, because it does not like being observed. Meanwhile the malevolent spirit of the dead is behaving noisily nearby: twigs are cracking as he rummages in the bushes; he is grunting and whistling, and causing his eyes to gleam and blaze in the dark.

The benevolent spirit double stays like this near the dead body for between three and five days. Its mental and emotional bond to him is so strong that it would remain by him forever if it could. The more the corpse decays the less its spirit double tends to return to the grave, and the shorter its visits become. Finally it cannot tolerate the smell of decay any longer. From this point on the benevolent spirit double keeps its distance. This spatial separation essentially runs counter to its wishes. Were it not for the smell of decay the spirit would remain beside him forever.

In the past, because it is the inclination of the benevolent spirit double to want to stay by its body, important people who had died were not just buried but treated so that their bodies (or at least some parts of them) were preserved. So long as they were prevented from decaying by the process of embalming or if the smell of decay could be suitably eliminated, the benevolent spirit double remained close by also as a spirit of the dead. Mummified corpses (or parts of corpses) belonging to high status people were therefore kept in communal housing (*wuut*), but also in private homes. The benevolent spirit of the dead belonging to the body thus stayed particularly close and was able to provide help more easily, particularly if it was an *énúúsór* or had possessed over its lifetime several benevolent spirit doubles.

In 1906-1907 Krämer found on *Etten* island the mummy of the "breadfruit sorcerer" *Valeisom* (Krämer's spelling). Its body's had been preserved because its spirit of the dead was supposed to continue overseeing the ripening of the local breadfruit, just as *Valeisom* himself had done during his own lifetime (Krämer 1932:273).

Sometimes the mortal remains of an important personage were preserved for the same reason in a casket of the *faar* that served as the place of sacrifice for his spirit of the dead.

Proper burial in the house seems for similar reasons to have been the practice, just as the preservation of the mummified corpse or body parts. Sometimes the deceased were particularly cherished.

In the past the common practice among islanders was for most people to be buried or sunk into the sea. In a sea burial (*féwúpacheenó*) the corpse was wrapped in a mat of pandanus leaves, weighted with stones, and lowered on to the reef shoreline. This happened only at the express wish of the deceased, or if the family members owned no plot of land specifically for a burial (Gladwin/Sarason 1953:161). These days the norm is to bury the body in a coffin on a plot outside the home.

Fondness for a deceased person was another reason for leaving the corpse unburied for a longer time, enabling the body fluid to be drained and collected. This was then mixed with herbs to form an "oil of the dead" (*néénúmá*) and processed for those left behind to use as a cosmetic. It is even said that women used to eat parts of the corpse of a particularly beloved child. Such cases seem nevertheless to be too rare for them to be termed examples of endocannibalism. They also have little in common with notions of the deceased's benevolent spirit double.

The dead person's family members wish to know when the benevolent spirit double is finally going to leave the decaying corpse. So, right after the burial, they carefully sprinkle the area surrounding the grave with sand. The benevolent spirit double will leave behind a foot or hand print, to tell the relatives that the moment for its transformation into a benevolent spirit of the dead has all but arrived.

Foot and hand prints can also become visible in the fresh soft cement of the grave cover. The direction they indicate may even sometimes signal yet another imminent death.

Now the *fiirowurow* can take place: the relatives assemble and share out his personal possessions. Anything of little use is burned.

Within the whole tapestry of significant meanings the function of the *fiirowurow* cannot be clearly discerned. The local word suggests that fire plays a role. Informants explain the burning of the person's belongings as a sign that people do not wish to be reminded of his departure. This runs counter to the fact that people keep the better items; they need not be incinerated to be of use in the beyond. Goodenough writes (1963:132) that the soul of the deceased supposedly rises in smoke up to the gods. From Bollig's (vague) information 1927 it seems that the function of the *fiirowurow* used to be more significant than today.

The *fiirowurow* sometimes takes place at the graveside. The ash then fulfils the same function as the scattered sand; the deceased person's benevolent spirit is able to leave its prints in it.

26.3.2 The Transformation of the Benevolent Spirit Double into a Spirit of the Dead (*wutumas*)

The physical separation of the benevolent spirit double from the body is essentially inevitable, brought about by its sense of smell. From a mental and emotional perspective it continues to be bound up with the body. But a law of the beyond also requires it to separate emotionally. No *ngúún* is allowed to remain, but has to become an *énú*. This occurs in a process only accessible to spirit beings. The living know of it partly from dreams. Exact descriptions come from the mediums; their benevolent spirit doubles are sometimes present at these events as observers. The process is called *wutumas* (face washing).

This special term is a combination of *wuti* (to splash, to rinse) and *maas* (eye, face); *wuti* means a gesture where the outside edges of the palms are laid together to form a shallow drinking cup enabling one to fling water at an object.

Many benevolent spirit doubles are reluctant to separate; they do not wish to become an *énú*. An *énúúsór* needs to request them bluntly and occasionally use force. Other benevolent spirits of the dead get the job of dragging obstinate spirit doubles to the place where the *wutumas* is due to take place. The schedule for this is not exact, but it is likely to be between day 4 and 7 after death.

It takes place on the reef's edge of an uninhabited island where sea water is available. Mostly it is a *náán* of the deceased's family. However, there are also places for the *wutumas* of the benevolent spirit doubles of a village or a whole island.

Numerous *neeniyen wutumas* are situated on the small islands of the Chuuk barrier reef. For *Wupwiini*'s family clan it is called *Winiisópw* and it lies on *Wonnang*.

Arriving at the place designated for its *wutumas,* the benevolent spirit double finds a whole number of benevolent spirits of the dead and other *ngúnúyééch*; they accompany it to the reef edge until it is knee-deep in the water. They begin by splashing its face with sea water, but stop this after a while and challenge it with the words *kepwe kékkééri* (you should call) to call out the name of its nearest relatives. If the benevolent spirit double still remembers these names after the first "face washing", the spirits of the dead start splashing again, and after a short while request it to name his family members. After a little while memory lapses occur, and confusion, and soon the benevolent spirit double can no longer remember a single name. The dead spirits present comment on this with the words *esapw chchiwen tipen aramas, aa tipen énú* (it no longer has a person's SEIC, but a spirit being's SEIC). At this point it ceases to be a *ngúún*, but belongs to the world of spirits; it has become an *énú* or *énúúyééch*.

The benevolent spirit double's transformation starts with it forgetting the names of its relatives, that is with a mental and emotional change as understood by the islanders. When the transformation is complete the personality is altered utterly. The benevolent spirit double, which has now become a benevolent spirit of the dead, now has mental and emotional dispositions which it did not have before. The change happens exclusively to its SEIC, and does not affect its external appearance.

The fact that the new spirit of the dead has now forgotten the names of its family members needs a word of explanation. Forgetting a name means for the islanders the break of the emotional bond to those bearing the name. The way they ensure that others do not forget their names has already been described (see 18.3 under *ttong*). The fact that the new benevolent spirit of the dead no longer remembers his clan members' names is proof that its emotional bond to them has altered and become looser. It still recognises them but has become more distant and no longer feels so strongly and personally drawn into their destiny. Now it is above them, even in an ethical respect, because it is even able to punish them for bad actions, especially if it has become an *énúúsór*. That was still prohibited while it was a *ngúúnúyééch* still affiliated to a living person.

The connection between forgetting the name as symbolic of the loosening or breaking of an emotional tie and the transformation of the *ngúnúyééch*'s personality at the *wutumas* is the subject-matter of a striking comparison in the following love song known through the island of *Toon*: *Ennet, koo/nee, repwe chipwang reen aar resin ewiniyey. Ngaang wúsapw tipen énú. Wúpwe chék kkémwéchúnnúk wóón pwopwun itomw* (Truly, my beloved, they [the benevolent spirits of the dead] will try to transform me, but to no avail. They will lose heart. I shall not learn to think and feel like a spirit being. I shall not cease clinging to your name). The desire to cling on to the name signifies the determination to remain true to the beloved, i.e. not to renounce the emotional bond to him or her.

The loosening of the mental and emotional bond in the former *ngúnúyééch* is also clearly evident in that informants describing the transformation use the same terms for SEIC dispositions as those used to describe strong emotions: *pwpwos* (longing), *nuukómmóng* (passionate feelings), and *éwúrek* (anxiety directed towards the future). Such feelings of a benevolent spirit of the dead towards its social group, they say, are not felt ever again, or hardly ever.

A person's way of life has no effects on the fate of his benevolent spirit of the dead. Punishments for wrongdoing (*ttipis*) impacted in his lifetime on his body or his relatives' bodies had been carried out by inflicting some kind of harm (*feyiyangngaw*). After physical death he continues to live as a spirit being in the beyond neither more happily nor less happily than he had done in his lifetime, however frequently the deceased person might have committed *ttipis*. As benevolent spirit doubles those newly transformed spirits of the dead cannot be categorized as "blessed" and "cursed" spirit beings. In the Chuuk Islanders' understanding they are all blessed to the extent that they no longer belong to the world of humans, no longer think and feel like they do, and so are not affected by the vagaries of human fortune. They are distinct solely by virtue of their different status, which they already had when they were still spirit doubles, a status that had a bearing on the status the person they belonged to could achieve. When the personality of somebody leading a bad lifestyle (and thus having a low status) lives on as a low-status spirit of the dead, that is not due to its way of life; it is because its *ngúnúyééch* was from the outset formed in such a way that even as an *énú* it cannot attain any higher status.

Notions of the deceased having suffered a "bad death", such as those described by Sell in Indonesia in 1955, are unknown in Chuuk, with one exception. This special case (*énúúsooso*) is dealt with in 26.6 below.

After the conclusion of the *wutumas* the new *énú* as a benevolent spirit of the dead generally gets a new name. Henceforth it is only visible to those who dream and to mediums. Only at this point can it be contacted, via a medium.

If a person has had several *ngúnúyééch* then each one adopts a particular name after their transformation to an *énú*. So the personality of somebody like this continues to exist separately in several guises. For example both *énú Pwereniinen* (sky invader) and *Tééyéwú* (mast climber) go back to a single person (from the village of *Féwúúp*).

26.4 A Person's Stages of Existence as Body and Spirit

If we compare the developmental course of a person and his two spirit doubles the emerging picture is as follows.

His benevolent spirit double's existence is arranged in three stages. In the first stage before the body's birth it has the form of a baby and lives without a body among the benevolent spirits of the dead of its own social group. The second stage of its existence begins at the birth of the body to which it is assigned; now the body develops in parallel to it and assumes the form of an adult person. The death of the body does not necessarily interrupt the further development of the physical aspects of the benevolent spirit double. Even after the death of the body it is still called by the same term *ngúún* or more accurately *ngúnúyééch*. Some days afterwards it undergoes a transition affecting not its physical aspects at this stage but exclusively its SEIC. From this point on it has become a spirit of the dead and is called *énú* or more exactly *énúúyééch*, *énúúsór* etc.

The existence of somebody's malevolent spirit double is in two stages. Its existence starts with the body, remains closely linked until its death, and is called at this stage *ngúnúngngaw*. When the body dies its first phase of existence comes to an end. It is free and has become a malevolent spirit of the dead. From now on people refer to it by the term *énú*, more accurately *énúngngaw* and specifically *soope*.

26.5 The Problem of Two Spirit Doubles of Animals

Theoretically the Chuuk Islanders find it altogether feasible to imagine animals having a benevolent and a malevolent spirit double, with characteristics and functions mirroring those of humans. In the beyond animals do also exist which are not malevolent spirit beings (*soope*). Many benevolent spirits of the dead are imagined as existing alongside their favourite animal which they always had with them in their lifetime. It must logically be about something like the benevolent spirit double of the relevant animal. Its malevolent spirit double would be a dangerous animal and thus unimaginable as accompanying a benevolent spirit of the dead. The islanders never call animal spirit forms in the beyond by the name *énú*, nor even *ngúnúyééch*, but always by the general word *ngúún*, applicable to objects. Animals like this have a further feature in common with the spirit double of objects, in that people cannot comprehend a transformation of the SEIC as with a person's *wutumas*.

26.6 The Problem of the *énúúsooso*

One phenomenon evidently also related to conceptions about people's two spirit doubles can only be explained and categorized rather imperfectly. This is the concept of "remote magic", which in Chuuk's distant past warring groups used against each other to inflict harm on their enemy.

The central feature of this magic was the *énúúsooso*. People made use of the captured corpse of a defeated foe, disfigured its face to produce a horrifying spectre and tied it upright to a tree or a post so the dead body faced the village that it had once inhabited. Then people brought him offerings calculated to cause horror and anger in each benevolent spirit being: prickly and poisonous fish, shark and skate flesh, nasty tasting herbs etc. Offerings like these accompanied by magic words were supposed to make the *énúúsooso* furious and cause it to bring about calamity, miscarriages and death to the enemy.

Mahony, who studied the *énúúsooso* (1970:168-172) in great detail in the context of the Chuuk Islanders' ideas about medicine, describes two variations; they were used when no corpse was available. He explains the term *énúúsooso* plausibly, translating it as "planted spirit" or "set down spirit".

But there is a problem with this. The misfortune that the *énúúsooso* is supposed to usher in can only be caused by a spirit being. The deceased person whose corpse was used as the *énúúsooso* had two spirit doubles. Which of the two was supposed to have got angry at the offering, its *ngúnúyééch* or its *ngúnúngngaw*? Mahony only mentions the *énúúsooso*'s "spirit"; this can be either. But if it was the benevolent spirit double that brought misfortune, why did it react to the sacrifice parody of an unfamiliar group and turn as a benevolent spirit being against its own group?

The custom of setting up an *énúúsooso* has not been followed for a long time now, so that even very old informants cannot give a fully convincing explanation of what notions lie behind it. A lot of evidence suggests that it was the deceased's benevolent spirit double who was roused to anger; with the result that it had to be treated like a malevolent spirit being having enormous mana (and thus needed to be understood in terms of a "bad death" in Sells's term, 1955).

Yet even this conjecture leaves open a whole range of questions. For example: Could the benevolent spirit double develop these effects on others while still a *ngúnúyééch*, or only after its transformation into an *énú*, as the term *énúúsooso* suggests? And so on.

26.7 Comparing a Person's Two Spirit Doubles with Spirits of the Dead – a Summary

A person's benevolent spirit double (*ngúnúyééch*) practically has all characteristics and functions of a benevolent spirit of the dead: namely a human appearance, intelligence, a friendly temperament that it can like all benevolent spirit beings induce in a person. It differs in principle from a benevolent spirit of the dead only in being mentally and emotionally bound to a physical body.

The malevolent spirit double (*ngúnúngngaw*) is to a great extent its counterpart. Its physical characteristics are only vaguely understood. It differs in principle from a malevolent spirit of the dead only in being bound to a physical body.

Chapter 27
Contacts between the Living
and the Spirits of the Dead

27.1 Introduction

If a few days have passed since the burial of a deceased person it can be assumed that his benevolent spirit double has become a spirit of the dead in the *wutumas* process. Around this time people can attempt to communicate with it via a medium (*waatawa*).

The practice of living people making contact with benevolent spirits of the dead associated with their social circle has become extraordinarily rare on Chuuk. During the Second World War it revived briefly under the pressure of threats to existence. Mediums available these days exercise their craft secretly, imitating their predecessors. The reason for this is mainly to be sought in Christianity, which the islanders have absorbed fully (at least in a formal respect) and whose teachings have no place for any activity of a medium. Further causes for the waning influence of mediums are the phenomena of acculturation, such as the introduction of western medicine, technology and education.

For this reason I was unable to find out about details of practices and processes involving mediums by observing them. The following description of the actions and notions motivating people having recourse to contact with spirit beings are based exclusively on reports by my informants *Apenis* and *Wupwiini*. I am of the opinion that their evidence is reliable, given that both knew the material from direct experience: *Apenis* was previously an active medium, and *Wupwiini* had taken part in numerous sessions involving mediums in his role as a descendant of a family holding the office of chief over many decades, and who had been a chief himself.

27.2 Reasons for the Need for Contacts

In all sorts of areas of life the Chuuk Islanders have repeatedly confronted issues whose solution is problematic. These difficulties do not arise directly from lacking a means to confront them. The islanders partly have astonishingly complex strategies and methods for overcoming their circumstances. For example they can cover long distances of open sea in their outrigger boats and arrive safely without a compass (Gladwin 1970; Lewis 1972). The difficulties occur in the proneness to breakdown of all human ventures, which is more likely the more complicated the undertaking.

Uncertainty facing islanders in the outcome of their endeavours creates a need for protection from possible failure. Recourse to divination (*pwee*) helps pinpoint an auspicious time for the start of a venture or the choice method of proceeding, for example when treating illnesses. Magic practices (*roong*) bring guaranteed effectiveness or heightened potency to any medication. By making offerings and adhering to important taboos and acceptable behaviour people earn the favour of benevolent spirits of the dead; their intervention is reckoned to reduce or guard against the likelihood of a human enterprise coming to grief.

Yet what is to be done when a venture goes wrong despite exhaustive precautions, or when it is unclear what ought to happen, or when an unprecedented problem arises where a remedy (such as for a new disease) is unknown?

The lack of available solutions is mostly a matter of gaps in knowledge, and gaps in knowledge are the stuff of future ventures. Yet in addition, everything that occurs in the present but not immediately near or visible to people remains largely unknown to them. Nobody can, for example, give information about the whereabouts of an overdue boat or the state of its crew. People feel undermined by gaps in their knowledge and feel a strong need to eradicate them. The knowledge that is hidden from them is, the islanders feel, available, but only in the beyond; benevolent spirits of the dead have this knowledge, because they are all-knowing; one of these is always in human company and can give advice, even in seemingly insoluble predicaments. They are very ready to share their knowledge with people; they even feel the need to share, whenever it concerns the wellbeing of their living circle of friends and relatives.

Because it is accessible only in the realm beyond death, it is difficult to get at this knowledge. The transfer of knowledge between spirits of the dead and people needing it can occur by means of dreams. Yet this path is fraught with uncertainties. Dreams cannot be called upon if questions addressed to a spirit are very detailed. In this case a more immediate contact needs to be made between people and the spirits of the dead of former family and friends.

27.3 The Medium (*waatawa*)

27.3.1 The Medium as Intermediary for Contacts

Benevolent spirits of the dead are well known for not conducting conversations with ordinary people, but only with specific people that they select. These particular people they speak to are able to relay to their ordinary fellow men what they hear from the spirits. In reverse, these particular people convey all the questions and requests of their fellows to the spirits of the dead, to get advice and possible sources of help.

The special person through whom messages pass between living people and spirits of the dead is a medium, a mediator in the literal sense.

The medium's activity is closely related to the islanders' notions of a spirit being and the beyond. Its business is not just as an intermediary between living people and spirits of the dead. Yet mediation is the main task for the person concerned. Acquiring vital knowledge is a central concern and motivation.

27.3.2 The Medium as an Intermediary for Knowledge

This function of a medium makes it the most important source of comprehensive and relevant statements concerning the beyond and all related knowledge; and more besides. For the islanders all traditional knowledge that they possess was once unknown; people only became gradually aware of it from the beyond, via mediums. Typical of this knowledge necessary for tackling everyday life are diagnoses of illnesses and treatment, and improvements in growing and getting food, etc. Even what satisfies aesthetic needs such as dances and songs ultimately derives from the beyond. Therefore, regarding innovations at the heart of Chuukese culture, a key role must be ascribed to the mediums (Mahony 1970:136-137, 211, 215, 464).

27.4 The Terms Used to Describe a Medium and Their Significance

A variety of very varied terms describe a medium. Most frequent is a group of words containing the morpheme *wa-*. The concept associated with it embraces transport on water, land and in the air, and animals for riding, water conduits, blood vessels, etc. The medium is conceived of as a means of conveying something.

The terms relating to a medium are *wáán énú* (spirit beings' means of conveying [knowledge]) *wámwmwár* (*mwmwár* shouldered, resting on the shoulder) and the term common on *Toon: waatawa* with its dialect variants (cf. 3.4), the reason why I use it exclusively.

Yet another group of terms indicates areas of activities typical of a medium. These terms are *sowuyénú* (expert in spirit beings), *sowuyawarawar* (expert in summoning spirit beings), *sowuwósoomá* (expert in sacrifices), *sowuyamwééngún* (expert in summoning absent spirit doubles) and *sowupwérúk* (master of dance).

27.5 The Personality of a Medium

27.5.1 Physical Features

Men and women are equally suited to be mediums. The *énú* who choose their medium bear in mind aesthetic considerations and prefer impressive appearance and beauty (*áteyééch* and *niyeyééch*). Old (*chinnap*), frail and ugly people stand little prospect of becoming mediums.

The gender of benevolent spirits of the dead has no bearing on the medium chosen. Female *énú* can use men as their medium and vice versa. Women mediums nevertheless have the disadvantage of not being effective during their period. Pregnancy, on the other hand, is not a reason for being refused by *énú*.

In reality there were always more male *waatawa* than female. The number of mediums within a social group was usually limited to one. Mahony writes "Lineages usually tried to encourage at least one man and one woman to assume the important role of spirit medium ..." (1970:137).

27.5.2 Mental and Emotional Characteristics

The need to relay knowledge presupposes that the mediums are of above-average intelligence; normal talents are not sufficient. Chuuk Islanders take it for granted that no spirit of the dead, least of all an *énúúsór*, would envisage a person as its *waatawa* if he were not to some extent equal in a mental and emotional sense. Mentally abnormal people or epileptics are not considered for this office. As to the personality required for the *waatawa*, he or she needs to have maturity (*miriit*) and a certain experience of life; youngish people under thirty are not suited to being mediums because over a longer term they are not trusted with having due consideration for the sexual taboos that are all part of the function of a medium.

For Mahony the characteristics appropriate for the post of *waatawa* run counter to this completely: "People who had demonstrated some facility in contacting spirits, perhaps by having been eaten or climbed on by a malevolent spirit in the past, usually filled this role" (1970:136).

In the medium's personality type and activity one significant feature is the notion that a person's conspicuous, positive mental and emotional qualities can be traced back to him possessing more than one single benevolent spirit double. Having several *ngúnúyééch* immediately signals his expanded potential for knowing about what occurs in the beyond; of course, the medium cannot himself send out his benevolent spirit doubles for them to collect information, but they do so of their own accord. For example, they accompany the benevolent spirit double of a deceased person to the *wutumas* and witness its transformation into a spirit of the dead. The medium finds out from them what has occurred; they impact (*ámeefi*) on his SEIC, or else they cause the medium to dream about the scenario so that he can report back the details. Yet the medium can no more converse directly with his own benevolent spirit doubles than can normal humans.

His benevolent spirit doubles are important guardians against attempts by malevolent spirit beings to disrupt the *waatawa* while he is actually functioning as a medium. Should symptoms arise caused by his benevolent spirit doubles being absent too long, the medium himself has the capacity to summon them (*amwééngún*, cf. 25.3.9).

27.5.3 Status

The sheer intelligence of the *waatawa*, his unattainable, super-human wisdom and his activity as a medium all amount to personal status and prestige; yet more than that: they establish a particular position of power that he can use for his own ends. In the past there were cases where the village medium was chief (*samwoon*) at the same time; and if not, then at least he could always influence the chief to his way of thinking. Despite the reputation they enjoyed, mediums had to defend themselves from the occasional criticism that they were deceivers, too inclined to dominate people, and supposedly for that reason asserted that what they pronounced was true. In any case, the office of *waatawa* brought status and prestige, and considerable material benefits besides, for him and his clan, because he could expect in return for his services equivalent reward (*niffang, oowun waatawa*). For this reason there was a certain benefit from becoming a medium.

27.6 The Career of a Medium

Essentially, the spirits of the dead determine who becomes a medium; that is, at least one of them. In some cases the initiative can come from the living, but needs to be endorsed by the *énú*. This happens in various ways. An old medium finds out during waking hours, or else in a dream from the life beyond, that after his death a certain younger man or woman is due to take over his office. Any person can dream of this. Sometimes a spirit of the dead names the name of a future medium via a medium who is still practising. Finally a person can try to become a medium by making the corresponding preparations and adhering to the required taboos. In this case the family group stipulates a member they deem to be suitable to oversee the requirements.

This arises if the group intends to communicate with the spirit of the dead of somebody recently deceased and wants to find out (1) whether his *wutumas* has already taken place and (2) what opportunities exist for it as *énú* to gain some benefits for those still living.

A sure indication of whether spirits of the dead want or accept a particular person as their medium is a physical one: the person concerned suddenly feels an unusual revulsion towards every type of food; feels nausea for days and weeks at the very thought of food; and only manages to drink coconut milk. Over this period he loses a considerable amount of weight.

This aversion to anything edible is caused by spirits of the dead, in order to free the future medium from all the food aromas which will be rejected by them, i.e. the foods that are taboo (*pin*) in future for the person concerned. A long-lasting urge to be sick is also a sign that the future *waatawa* needs to avoid sexual intercourse from that point on if he wishes to avoid jeopardising his chance of being chosen. He can decline the opportunity for election by disregarding these taboos, or by rubbing himself with orange peel or sprinkling water on himself in which fermented breadfruit (*épwét*) has been washed. But by doing this he is thwarting the will of the spirits of the dead, and he risks arousing their anger.

After a few days of self-imposed fasting he begins seeing the spirit doubles and *énú,* and he is addressed by them. He is completely conscious throughout this, but has an "abstract and vacant look" about him, because he is not paying attention to what is going on in the mundane world of humans. He knows full well what is happening to him and can give a report about it, for example that a particular spirit of the dead has approached him, declared himself as his medium and informed him that he will shortly be speaking to the living people of his group. Or else he reports that a particular living person's benevolent spirit double has informed him that his body will soon die and that the spirit would be pleased to have him as a medium after his transformation into a spirit of the dead. Even the future medium's dream life gets more intensive, and later the dream takes on special significance for fulfilling his tasks by knowing about events in the beyond.

The environment of the future medium notices nothing of all these procedures. He exhibits no unusual emotional condition, does not fall into a trance, apart from his vacant look, because he is not concentrating on the events of the material world. Furthermore, it never happens that a benevolent spirit of the dead with whom a medium has dealings unexpectedly seeks him out; this means that the medium can never suddenly appear "possessed".

After a certain time the nausea disappears, because the *énú* cannot intend to allow their chosen medium to starve. From that point on the medium can be schooled by an experienced specialist in the required knowledge, the vocabulary (*kkapasen énú*) and the mediating procedures. As a future *sowuyamwééngún* the medium has also to learn the art of making the medicine for benevolent spirit doubles unwilling to return (*amwééngún*), and he has to become intimately acquainted as a future *sowupwérúk* with the art of dance (*pwérúk*). The medium can acquire these skills even before the period when the symptoms of choosing by the spirits of the dead are evident in him.

His choosing can be cancelled at any time by their deciding to stay distant from him. Mostly the fault for this lies with him; either he has not adhered to the required taboos (*pinin waatawa*), or has become *ttipis* by some wrong behaviour and is being punished by the spirits of the dead with the complete loss of his capacities for mediation.

In a medium's activity as a mediator between living persons and spirits of the dead two different aspects are evident; I intend calling them the active aspect and the passive aspect.

27.7 Notions of a Medium's Active Association with Spirits of the Dead

27.7.1 General Remarks

The position and function of the *waatawa* between living persons and his clan's benevolent spirits of the dead rest on a few characteristics which literally make him understandable as a medium.

The medium does not just have dealings with *énúúyééch* but also with the *ngúnúyééch* of living persons; in principle, as spirit beings they are not distinguishable one from another.

A basic prerequisite for a medium's association with these spirit beings is his ability to see and recognize all non-material spirit beings and objects; also, in so far as they are not objects, he is also able to conduct conversations with them,

A *móngupwi* (seer) has abilities, but they are restricted. While awake he can, of course, see spirit beings just like a *waatawa*, but only those who are still *ngúnúyééch*. *Énúúyééch* remain invisible to him. Furthermore, the *móngupwi* cannot converse with them or be used by them as a medium. Apart from his ability to see benevolent spirit doubles he is not in any way different from normal people.

Given the islanders' notion of the limitless quantity of spirit beings, a medium can only properly know a finite number of them. Whenever he wishes to recognise a spirit being he must know the person this spirit belongs to, or once belonged to. Essentially this implies that the medium associates only with those benevolent spirit beings in his own area of experience, i.e. his village or his island. He knows from them of course what their intentions are, where they gather and what they are involved in.

To have active dealings with spirit beings a medium does not need to be tuned in a particular physical or mental and emotional way; further preparations other than adhering to important taboos (*pinin énú* and *pinin waatawa*) are not required. Spirit beings may visit the medium anywhere and at any time. These visits occur without a normal person noticing. The medium does not communicate in speech; their conversation is a dialogue of thoughts, so that nobody can overhear.

27.7.2 The Medium and Benevolent Spirit Doubles

So it is possible for a medium to meet a tearful benevolent spirit double of a living acquaintance and find out that it is weeping because the person is due to die soon. A medium can thus predict for someone still alive when he will die. When someone shows symptoms of illness that indicate his benevolent spirit double is absent, the medium can be asked whether he knows something about the spirit double's whereabouts. It is quite likely that it has given notice of absence and has indicated why it is absent and when it will return. It will leave this information so the group is not unsettled if one of its members exhibits related symptoms.

If a person's benevolent spirit double has disappeared without trace the medium will ask an *énúúsór* or another benevolent spirit double to look for the missing one and induce it to return, if it finds it. Otherwise the only course is for *amwééngún* to fetch him (cf. 25.3.9).

A medium has even got the option of asking a recently deceased child's benevolent spirit double to delay its transformation into an *énú* until the mother has given birth again, so that it can accompany this newborn throughout life.

Many benevolent spirit doubles take leave from their medium when physical death is imminent. Then they tell the medium whether they wish to consider him as their medium or not. In this case they also tell him their situation when they have become *énú*.

To the islanders' way of thinking contacts between a medium and the spirit beings called *ngúún* play a subordinate role. By contrast, his contacts with the spirit beings called *énú* are much more significant.

27.7.3 The Medium and Spirits of the Dead

Because it is not sensible to establish links with malevolent spirits a medium has dealings exclusively with benevolent spirit beings. Only they have the ability to communicate, and only they feel the need for contact and possess the required knowledge.

Énú visit their medium to converse with him and to bring him news of other *énú;* and to communicate the requests he is to pass on to the living. Vice versa, a medium is able to commission the *énú* on behalf of the living to provide food, and to give information or help in particular situations, etc. (*atoow ngeni énú*). A medium can also relay warnings from the benevolent spirits of the dead to any who, by their way of life, risk arousing the anger of an *énúúsór* and thus endanger their community as a whole.

A close emotional bond of friendship may develop between the *énú* and their medium where the *énú* emerge particularly as friends of the medium. This relationship is marked by the *ttong* feeling, which features prominently in personal dealings among the islanders, links that can be very intense and enduring. Many *énú* remain faithful to their medium for his whole life. The more such devoted *énú* maintain relationships with a medium and the more numerous the *énúúsór* are among them, the more the medium gains a reputation as a *wáán énúúsór*, because it can be assumed that the *énú* will do their best to make their statements via their medium appear accurate and reliable. The medium thereby stands to gain in authority.

It may happen that following the death of their medium the spirits of the dead grieve so much as to seek no other, and after that are forgotten. Generally, though, they do look for a new medium, especially those of greater importance, the *énúúsór*.

The relational link expressed in the term *ttong* leads naturally to a medium maintaining contact primarily with the benevolent spirits of the dead belonging to his own group. They are closest to him, and he has a very close personal link to them. He knows in detail about active relationships within the realm of the benevolent spirits of the dead. This is why a village or island medium regularly makes himself available for mutual support and dialogue. He will be concerned about the local place of sacrifice, the *faar*, and will ensure that the required offerings are brought and that those demands laid down by relevant *énúúsór* are fulfilled.

27.8 Notions of a Medium's Passive Dealings with Spirit Beings

27.8.1 General Remarks

In the previous section I described the active role which falls to the medium if he needs to relay messages between living people and spirits of the dead. This rather indirect opportunity exacts little effort from both the living and the spirits themselves.

Yet there are occasions when both parties feel the need to sustain direct conversation. These times do not have to be distinct from those when the medium is an active intermediary. However, the need for a direct conversation is prompted by a particular and troublesome issue, usually a matter of general application for a largish social group, or one arising from the wish of an *énú* to lend weight to his demands for his voice to be heard.

Particular issues arise as follows. A case of family illness cannot be alleviated by the usual familiar means, or is so unusual that the necessary cures are unknown. The procedure is then to find out from the medium whether the reason for the illness resides in an undiscovered crime, who is guilty and how long the unfortunate circumstances will last. In the case of a new disease a spirit of the dead versed in medical skills can name an antidote; another can be asked for further information about where the patient's absent benevolent spirit double is likely to be; and what might stir it to return. The attendant spirits of the dead can be asked where lost relatives are and how they are, and whether they are inclined to return.

For example, significant matters relevant to a sizeable social group may consist of clarifying whether a benevolent spirit double of somebody recently deceased has become an *énúúsór*, and what he is called, etc. Through the medium chiefs can get help in decision-making and information pertinent to resolving a dispute. The possible grounds for a direct conversation between living people and their benevolent spirits of the dead may be extended at will.

A *waatawa* has to consider himself as a medium for all conceivable benevolent spirits; as a rule he cannot give preference to any of them, even when he is particularly drawn to one. The spirit being chooses the medium, not the other way round. Spirit beings feel attachment or antipathy towards a medium; they cannot be compelled to associate with him if he as a medium comes across as unsympathetic. The medium thus has no hold over spirit beings and cannot therefore consider them as personal possessions; they are free at any time to select a different medium. Conversely, a spirit being considers its favoured medium as its own.

A spirit being calls its medium *wááy* (my means of transport). Yet a medium cannot refer to it as *ney* or *ááy énú*, unless he wished to designate the deceased person associated with the spirit of the dead as a genuine relation. Thus one does not need to be *waatawa* to be able to call a spirit being *ney* or *ááy énú*.

In the passive role as a conversation facilitator between a benevolent spirit of the dead and its living group members the *waatawa* is also able to function as a medium if both groups are unknown to it. This is however rather a theoretical possibility.

27.8.2 The Course of Conversation between Living People and One of Their Benevolent Spirits of the Dead

If the initiative for conversation with a benevolent spirit of the dead starts from the living members of a group the responsible medium is asked to make himself available at a particular time and place. If the initiative starts from a spirit of the dead the medium himself can summon the group.

The contacting is not restricted to a specific time of day, and it is seldom out of doors. But even as regards the place there are no hard and fast rules. There is not usually enough space in individual dwellings. Therefore those attending usually go to the community house (*wuut*). Generally people came together with the village or island *énúúsór* in the community house in which the *faar* used for sacrifices to the *énúúsór* was located.

A few days before the event the medium starts the physical preparations. He follows the taboos regarding food and sexuality (*pinin waatawa*) which he had not been so strict about the rest of the time. He does not carry out any tasks which might require him to come into contact with taboo foods or strong odours. He refrains, for example, from slaughtering animals; a pig's gall bladder with its bitter contents might cause the benevolent spirit of the dead he has yet to summon to stay away.

Scrupulous body hygiene is part of his preparations. The medium bathes frequently and uses plenty of aromatic lotions (*néé*), yellow turmeric (*teyik*) and coconut cream (*arúng*) to treat his body.

Shortly before the beginning of the event he puts on his ornamentation (*mwárámwár* etc.) and clean clothing. He has been refraining from eating since the morning, to avoid smelling of food. (Later in his career as a medium he is not obligated to observe food taboos as fully as at the beginning.)

Making contact with a spirit of the dead is a sensational event. While the medium makes the final preparations those taking part and other onlookers assemble in the community house. On the *faar* recent sacrificial offerings are hanging and lying, including medicine for enlightenment (*sáfeen asaram*), because even the spirit of the dead is required to have a bright SEIC when he speaks. An offering is not an absolute requirement.

If important and well-known *énúúsór* were due to be summoned to the event then dances were held in their honour, but only in exceptional circumstances.

Those present who are not under such strict taboos have also put on their finery and their perfumes and are sitting along the walls inside the community house. The medium sits cross-legged in the middle on a *kiyeki*, a mat of woven pandanus leaves. Everybody waits until the last person has arrived and calm has descended. Only whispers are permitted, because benevolent spirit beings usually feel disturbed by noise and keep away from crowds. During the time the spirit of the dead is with the medium nothing must happen to shock it and drive it away.

On an occasion such as this no musical instruments are evident; nor must the medium be drawn into any usual mental or emotional panic. He is sitting there waiting. In the islanders' view it is not the medium who is active, but the spirit of the dead speaking through him.

When calm has come over the assembly one of the participants calls the name of the spirit of the dead and bids it attend; typically: "*Epweniisór, kepwe feyitto!*" If the name of the spirit is as yet unknown (because it is the spirit of a deceased person who has only recently died) it is the name he had as a person. The call is made by the most senior man (*mwáániichi*) of the social group that considers it their *énú*. The chief usually calls the area's *énúúsór*. It is never the medium himself who calls the *énú*.

The summoning process is known as *apaapa* (to entice, attract) or *afééfé* (to tie), and the caller himself is *chóón apaap énú* (the one attracting the spirit).

It is generally assumed that the spirit of the dead will not refuse; indeed, that it will be close by and aware of all the preparations being made. Sometimes it is already taking the offerings spread out for it on the *faar* and consuming them. This is evident from whether it is hovering there calmly or whether it is vacillating. Sometimes the request to attend needs to be made several times.

It is not easy to be definite about the time when the unseen spirit being will contact the medium. If the medium begins to get unsettled people know that the spirit is close to him. The medium now moves his fingers as though folding both hands, but instead leaves them open and begins to beat rhythmically with the inner hands on the pandanus mat. The steady beating sound is meant to have a stimulating influence on the spirit being. This movement is called *oruworu* (possibly meaning to cause to jump up). It can also be done with palms alongside and thumbs linked. The *oruworu* continues until the spirit of the dead has come down.

Gradually the signs of physical excitement in the medium get more intense. He begins to breathe more deeply, then tremble and groan (*ngúúngú*). If he sneezes or coughs those present know that the spirit being is in physical contact with him and is climbing on his shoulders (*téétá*).

The process has reached a climax. Nobody knows precisely whether it really is the right spirit of the dead/ancestral spirit which is climbing on the medium. As well as attracting benevolent spirits of the dead the event lures a number of malevolent spirit beings keen to harass the medium. But the medium can also reckon on his own benevolent spirit double and its family ancestral spirits to keep the malevolent spirits at bay. Nevertheless, if malevolent spirit beings manage to get to the medium it will then be assumed that his guardian spirits have been absent or inattentive. In these circumstances not only is the medium in great danger, but the others attending as well. If a malevolent spirit has physically contacted the medium the situation changes drastically.

Signs of physical agitation increase dramatically in the medium. He gets goose bumps (cold body temperature typical of malevolent spirit beings!) and rolls his eyes. His SEIC gets darker and his behaviour turns extreme: he jumps up; raves, utters animal noises and shouts at those present; and seeks to threaten them, grimacing and glancing angrily at available sticks or knives. People shriek and run off. Some bold ones eventually manage to subdue the medium and help him to shake off the malevolent spirit beings. In the general chaos it is impossible to continue with the event. This kind of spirit possession is considered by all those attending as dangerous and destructive, not just undesirable but also quite meaningless; this is because malevolent spirit beings are not able to speak normally, nor can they be approached for advice and help (cf. 24.10.6).

If, instead of a malevolent spirit being, a benevolent spirit has made physical contact with the medium, all signs of physical agitation quickly disappear: the medium calms down, his features lose their harshness and his mental and emotional disposition is *pwaapwa* (joy), *kinamwmwe* (contentment, serenity, happiness), *miriit* (mild-mannered behaviour). He sits there cross-legged, his torso rocking rhythmically forward and back (*mwéwúchúúch*). He resumes his hand movements (*oruworu*).

The *waatawa* always has a particularly bright SEIC when one of the ancestral, close-family spirits mounts his shoulders or when it is a benevolent spirit of the dead of a deceased child such as mediums especially like dealing with.

Nevertheless even benevolent spirit beings occasionally signify quite some physical effort for the medium. It is quite obvious from his bearing when an adult's spirit of the dead is on his shoulder bowing him down with its weight. The medium can carry children's spirits of the dead with an erect posture; with adult spirits of the dead the medium can be heard groaning (*ngngú*) and beginning to sweat (warm body temperatures typical of benevolent spirit beings!). It sometimes happens, though, that the medium carrying a spirit being on his shoulders stands up, walks around and demonstrates the dance steps that the spirit wants to teach those present!

Many spirits of the dead allow themselves longer before they climb on the medium. They may then need to be encouraged to do so by the speaker (*chóón apaap énú*) who summoned them at the outset.

For this to happen he can say the following formula: "*Mwetetá, mwetetá, sipwe rongorong mweniyomw*", or "*Téétá, téétá, sipwe rongorong menginomw*" (Jump up/climb up, we wish to hear what you have to say).

The conversation between the speaker and the spirit of the dead cannot begin until it has taken up position on the medium's shoulder. Only then is the medium literally "possessed". The islanders do not exclude the possibility that an *énú* is well able to get inside a person's body. But they do not link possession with the notion that a spirit has "gone into the medium". The spirit of the dead just sits astride him and determines from this position how the medium behaves.

Yet the medium still has not said a word. Now comes the moment when the speaker can ask the spirit to call out its name, with the question: "*Ese iyéén*" (who is that)? Quite possibly he will have to put the question to it several times.

In general parlance the question is not worded *ese iyéén*, because it contains a negative which makes it incomprehensible (who isn't that?).

If the spirit of the dead already has a name familiar to those present they discover at this naming which deceased person is meant. The spirit of a deceased person who is reported via a medium for the first time has to explain what his name was as a person if his name as an *énú* was different. Once he has been identified in this way he is invited to speak by the *chóón apaap énú*.

This invitation is formulaic, containing unusual metaphors: "*Wáási menginomw* or *mweniyomw* (roughly: make a breach for your word), *wáási* or *suuki sópwun waa*" (roughly: make the bow of the boat free or open), or *kepwe memmengin*" (you should speak), etc.

The invitation to speak is never addressed to the medium but always to the spirit of the dead that is using – as all those attending notice – the medium's own vocal chords and mouth. Together they form in this situation a mental and emotional whole. The medium himself uses the first person "I" when the spirit of the dead speaks.

The spirit immediately adopts a formal style with courteous phrases well known to the islanders. Among these are thanks for the offerings ("*Kinissow ngenikemi ...* "), for the honour of receiving the invitation, etc. There is no special language for this, apart from the somewhat unusual metaphors that people commonly associate with spirits of the dead. Some of them speak Japanese or English, but only in exceptional circumstances. For example, if the deceased person spoke English the spirit would have to be able to as well.

It can be asked to speak clearly for all to understand. A medium's voice sounds as though it has undergone a change, so that now the deceased person is recognisable from it, particularly if the spirit is a child's.

The more clearly and coherently an *énú* speaks, the more it is considered an *énúúsór*. Proof of this only comes later when what he has foreseen proves true or stands up to scrutiny, i.e. when animals he has forecast in a particular spot can indeed be found there by the hunters, or when ingredients for medicine he was asked about are actually effective. An *énúúsór* does not lie. He loves the truth above all. His utterances are viewed as particularly reliable. Because young children have not yet learnt to lie their spirits of the dead are considered more reliable than others'. Children's spirits are thus reckoned to be *énúúsór*.

Spirits of the dead don't just speak; some sing and teach listeners a new song. Others weep, for example when they bring news that a fellow departed spirit will not be returning.

Usually it can be expected that the spirit of the dead will speak in a friendly, calm and thoughtful manner, examining all the questions that are put to it. It may become angry because its wishes have not been granted, or because it has to report that somebody has committed a wrongdoing. It will then angrily require those left behind listening to change their behaviour; it will threaten consequences if people are not compliant. When something like this happens spirit beings that are essentially reckoned to be benevolent will behave like malevolent spirit beings.

If those present do not wish to ask any more questions the session draws rapidly to a conclusion. The speaker expresses his admiration for the spirit being's knowledge, thanks it for willingly sharing its expertise and bids it farewell with a phrase such as: "*Ke nee nó.*" The spirit being itself can also say that it has no more to say and no further questions or wishes to present.

Contacts with a spirit of the dead vary in their duration, but they are seldom shorter than two hours. Sometimes it is the case that several are summoned in succession. That will depend on the medium's ability to cope with stress, given that the process is demanding.

It is evident from the medium's body that the spirit being is climbing off his shoulders. The medium's movements eventually stop completely.

When the *énú* says that it wants to come to an end it again uses unusual phrases, such as: *"Wúwa sókupw, aa sókupw menginey* and *aa sópw menginey"* (I have finished speaking), or it simply says: *"Wúpwe téétiw me wóón wááy eey"* (I wish to get off my medium).

27.9 Conclusion

As a medium, the *waatawa* is the mediator in bilateral contacts between members of a social grouping comprising living people and the benevolent spirit beings (*énúúyééch, énú aramas, énúúsór*); these are understood to be the continuation of the personalities of deceased group members. The medium has already been in relationship with these spirit beings since the time they were assigned (as *ngúnúyééch*) to a living person. He can in his waking state see all kinds of spirit beings and have direct conversations with them, something that is only possible for normal people indirectly in a dream. In this way he mediates the will of earth-bound people to those in the beyond, and vice versa. That is the active part of his mediation work.

The medium is active also as a specialist in diagnosis and therapy (*amwééngún)* for illnesses caused by the absence from the living person of benevolent spirit doubles.

When living people feel the need to speak directly to a clan member in the beyond (and vice versa) the *waatawa* has to act as a go-between. In the forefront, though, is the notion that it is not the medium who is active, but that something is happening to him. This represents the essentially passive nature of mediating.

The medium's personality is characterised by intelligence and a specific artistic talent (as dancing master). Unusual mental and emotional traits or abnormalities are absent from his make-up. In his work as a medium there is no role for specific physical or mental and emotional conditions, or else they are secondary phenomena without any function. The medium has his full faculties, is fully conscious, and can experience what is going on around him.

General Results

My study of the concepts of body, mind, soul and spirit among the Chuuk Islanders was basically aimed at discovering their overall concept of man, of the person. During fieldwork my focus was the concept of soul. I started from a preconception that there are two defining features of soul: (1) that soul is the seat of the mental and emotional capacities and operations in a person, and (2) that soul is the being that survives the body's death and continues the body's personality. The understanding that was expressed at the outset, namely that for Chuuk Islanders these two features might be spread over each of two distinct conceptual realms, has been fully confirmed. I called the first realm SEIC (Seat of the Emotions, Intellect and Character), and the second realm spirit double.

Broadly speaking, for the Chuuk Islanders a person consists of a body and two spirit doubles – one good and one bad. The three have one SEIC each.

The body's SEIC is located in a part of the upper stomach cavity but is not related to a particular organ. The SEIC has characteristics that I have called SEIC dispositions. SEIC dispositions are either permanent or temporary. A person's character traits and intellectual abilities represent largely permanent SEIC dispositions. Temporary dispositions are SEIC movements, comprising thought processes, emotions, and impulses of the will.

During the course of a person's physical development his SEIC displays age-related dispositions. The SEIC of a newborn baby is small, soft and closed; associated with this are unsophisticated character traits and expressions of feeling and willpower, and a lack of intelligence, consciousness and understanding. As the years go by the person's SEIC gets larger and harder and opens out. These changes mean that at different ages the human personality exhibits various marks of character. Some SEIC dispositions are so typical of a particular age that the relevant age is called by that disposition.

The Chuuk Islanders' language includes a wide-ranging vocabulary for expressing SEIC dispositions. The nuanced structure of this vocabulary reveals that mental and emotional concepts are conceived in a diverse way. The scope and complexity of language categories relating to the intellect and to the emotions lead us to conclude that this realm expresses a core focus for the interests and requirements of the Chuukese culture.

The SEIC itself has no autonomous substance; on the death of the body its functions cease, and it ceases to exist immediately.

A person's two spirit doubles are quite different, having human attributes, the ability to think, feel, and express volition, thus also having a SEIC. They are spirit beings, one of which constitutes a person's second, spirit existence.

This second form of a person's existence – his benevolent spirit double – is not actually understood as being of human origin and classification. It is part of a world view according to which each material thing possesses a spirit double ready to add full value and functional competence to its material existence. Thus a human exists in two simultaneous worlds, with his body in the material one (the here and now) and his benevolent spirit double in the world of spirit doubles attaching to all objects and beings (the world beyond).

A person's benevolent spirit double is not linked to his body, and does not dwell inside his body (although this is not excluded), but on his body or very close by. It is able to leave the body for a short while without there being consequences. However, after a few hours the body starts showing signs of deterioration which could lead to its death if the benevolent spirit double does not return in time. Both objects and human beings only have complete value and viability when their spirit double is present.

It has emotional ties just like a close relative. It is his guardian spirit in the fullest sense of the word. Sleep is not a result of any absence of the benevolent spirit double from the body. Dreams are short extracts from the continuum of what his benevolent spirit double (in the beyond) is experiencing.

A person's death is something purely physical. His benevolent spirit double does not leave him finally at that time; it remains by the corpse and is even buried with it. Actually it never ultimately leaves the body, but stays in the neighbourhood where the person has lived and has been buried. A few days after the death of the body the benevolent spirit double needs to change into a benevolent spirit of the dead. This transformation occurs exclusively in its SEIC. Its outer appearance and its spirit aspect remain unaffected by it. After its transformation living people are able to communicate with it via a medium. Until the time of its transformation the benevolent spirit double is called *ngúnúyééch*, thereafter *énú*. In principle it remains what it always was, a spirit being. It is therefore not the case that a person's benevolent spirit double after death "goes into the beyond", for the beyond was – even in the lifetime of the person – its habitual dwelling.

This benevolent spirit being (called *ngúnúyééch* during the person's lifetime) is identifiable by three significant features: (1) It is a being that is experienced in a person's dreams; (2) only if it is present near the body, or at least available, can it possess its complete functioning potential; (3) it perpetuates the human's personality after the death of its body.

Having these characteristics, the *ngúnúyééch* equates to what H. Fischer 1965 has termed the "dream ego".

The malevolent spirit double on the other hand originates with the body, remains bound to it throughout its life and seeks its ruin. For the malevolent spirit being the body's death signifies a severing of emotional ties. At this point the spirit is free, is no longer called *ngúnúngngaw* but *énú*, specifically *soope*, and has become a malevolent spirit of the dead; it has nothing more in common with the human's personality.

Notions of a person's malevolent spirit double are so vague that the impression is conveyed that acceptance of its existence over a lifetime may have arisen subsequently, in order to furnish a plausible explanation for the occurrence of malevolent spirit beings.

I conclude with a few remarks about the evolution of the Chuuk Islanders' concepts of the soul, arising from cultural contacts and particularly from Christian concepts. Soul as the centre of human mental and emotional capacity is a conceptual realm where Christian ideas could only cause change at the margins. Quite different is the conceptual realm of soul as the being that survives a human's dying and perpetuates his personality. Considerable changes have occurred in this aspect of the concept of the soul to the extent that its visible manifestations such as places of sacrifice/offering, activities of mediums, etc. have practically disappeared. Yet the conceptual structure – the cognitive categories that underpinned these visible phenomena – has largely remained evident and intact. The conceptual interference resulting when the notion of Christian sacrifice/offering meets indigenous thought categories does indeed become visible and unsettling. However, several aspects of the Christian interpretations of soul and spirit can be more easily embraced and understood by Chuuk Islanders than by Europeans and other Westerners. The concept of the Holy Spirit as a person is less foreign for them than for their missionary visitors.

In researching the ideas of the body and the soul among Chuuk Islanders I have in any case acquired the same impression as Goodenough with respect to their social organisation (1951:26): despite far reaching changes in the islanders' material culture in the aftermath of cultural contacts, their abundant and imaginative notions of soul seem only slightly modified by the events of the past one hundred and fifty years.

Index of Chuukese Terms
(Alphabetical order after Goodenough/Sugita 1980)

Bibliography

Badenberg, Robert: The Body, Soul and Spirit Concept of the Bemba in Zambia. Fundamental Characteristics of Being Human of an African Ethnic Group. (edition afem - mission academics, Band 9. Verlag für Kultur und Wissenschaft) Bonn 1999.

Badenberg, Robert: Sickness and Healing. A Case Study on the Dialectic of Culture and Personality. (edition afem - mission academics, Band 11. Verlag für Theologie und Religionswissen-schaft). Nuremberg 2003.

Badenberg, Robert: The Concept of Man in Non-Western Cultures. A Guide for One's Own Research. Handbook to Lothar Käser's Textbook: Animism – A Cognitive Approach. Nürnberg 2014.

Barthel, Thomas S.: Ethnolinguistische Polynesienforschung. Anthropos 59.1964:920-26.

Berlin, Brent; Breedlove, Dennis E.; Raven, Peter H.: Folk Taxonomies and Biological Classification. In: Tyler 1969:60-66.

Bierbach, Annette; Cain, Horst: Soomá – Soope. Good and Malevolent Spirits in Chuuk. Baessler-Archiv, Neue Folge, Band XLV (1997):237-258.

Blacking, John (ed.): The Anthropology of the Body. New York 1977.

Böhme, Hans Heinrich: Der Ahnenkult in Mikronesien. Studien zur Religionswissenschaft Band 2. Leipzig 1937.

Bollig, Laurentius: Die Bewohner der Truk-Inseln. Religion, Leben und kurze Grammatik eines Mikronesiervolkes. Anthropos Ethnologische Bibliothek, Band 3, 1. Heft. Münster 1927.

Cain, Horst: Aitu. Eine Untersuchung zur autochtonen Religion der Samoaner. Wiesbaden 1979.

Carroll, John B. (ed.): Language, Thought, and Reality. Selected Writings of Benjamin Lee Whorf. Cambridge, Massachusetts 2000.

Caughey, John L.: Fáánakkar. Cultural Values in a Micronesian Society. University of Pennsylvania Publications in Anthropology no. 2. Philadelphia, Penn.1977.

Chang, Kwang-chi; Grace, George W.; Solheim II, Wilhelm G.: Movement of the Malayo-Polynesians 1500 B.C. to A.D. 500. Current Anthropology 5.1964:359-406.

Coppel, William George: Catalogue of Theses and Dissertations Relating to Micronesia. The University of the South Pacific Library. Suva, Fiji 1980.

Crawley, A. Ernest: The Idea of the Soul. London 1909.

Crawley, A. Ernest: „Doubles". In: Hastings 1911, 4:853-860.

Damm, Hans: Völkerkundliche Bibliographie ab 1928, Südsee. Ethnologischer Anzeiger 3.1932/35:118-167.

Damm, Hans: Mikronesische Kultboote, Schwebealtäre und Weihegabenhänger. Jahrbuch des Museums für Völkerkunde 13. Leipzig 1954:45-72.

D'Andrade, Roy: The Development of Cognitive Anthropology. Cambridge et al. 1995.

Dickson, Diane; Dossor, Carol: World Catalogue of Theses on the Pacific Islands. Pacific Monograph Series Nr. 1. Honolulu, Hawaii 1970.

Dyen, Isidore: On the History of Trukese Vowels. Language 25.1949:420-436.

Dyen, Isidore: A Sketch of Trukese Grammar. American Oriental Society, Essay 4. New Haven, Conn. 1965.

Elbert, Samuel H.: Trukese-English and English-Trukese Dictionary. U.S. Naval Military Government. Washington D.C 1947.

Feest, Christian F.: Beseelte Welten. Die Religionen der Indianer Nordamerikas. Freiburg, Basel, Wien (Herder) 1998.

Finsch, Otto: Ethnologische Erfahrungen und Belegstücke aus der Südsee. Annalen des K. K. Naturhistorischen Hofmuseums in Wien, Band 3-8, Jahrgang 1888-1893. Wien 1893.

Firth, Raymond: The Analysis of Mana: An Empirical Approach. In: Harding/Wallace (1940) 1970:316-333.

Fischer, Ann: The Role of the Trukese Mother and its Effect on Child Training. Harvard University, Ph.D. (Manuscript) Cambridge, Massachusetts 1956.

Fischer, Hans: Studien über Seelenvorstellungen in Ozeanien. München 1965.

Fischer, Hans (Hrsg.): Ethnologie. Eine Einführung. Hamburg 1983. Neufassung: Fischer/Beer 2003.

Fischer, Hans; Beer, Bettina (Hrsg.): Ethnologie. Einführung und Überblick. Neufassung. Berlin (Dietrich Reimer) 2003.

Fischer, John L.; Fischer, Ann: The Eastern Carolines. New Haven, Conn. 1970.

Frake, Charles O.: The Diagnosis of Disease Among the Subanun of Mindanao. In: Hymes 1964:193-211.

Freilich, Morris (ed.): Marginal Natives - Anthropologists at Work. New York 1970.

Girschner, Max: Die Karolineninsel Namoluk und ihre Bewohner I. Bäßler-Archiv 2.1911:123-225. Leipzig/Berlin 1911.

Girschner, Max: Die Karolineninsel Namoluk und ihre Bewohner II. Bäßler-Archiv 3.1913:165-190. Leipzig/Berlin 1913.

Gladwin, Thomas; Sarason Seymour B.: Truk: Man in Paradise. Viking Fund Publications in Anthropology Nr. 20. New York 1953.

Gladwin, Thomas: East is a Big Bird. Navigation and Logic on Puluwat Atoll. Cambridge, Mass. 1970.

Goetzfrid, Nicholas J.; Wuerch, William L.: Micronesia 1975-1987. A Social Science Bibliography. New York, Westport, London 1989.

Goodenough, Ward Hunt: Property, Kin and Community on Truk. Yale University Publications Nr. 46. New Haven, Conn. 1951 and Hamden, Conn. 1966.

Goodenough, Ward Hunt: Cooperation in Change. New York 1963.

Goodenough, Ward Hunt: Notes on Truk's Place Names. Micronesica (Journal of the College of Guam) 2.2.1966:95-129.

Goodenough, Ward Hunt: A Similarity in Cultural and Linguistic Change. In: Kinkade/Hale/Werner 1975:263-273.

Goodenough, Ward Hunt; Sugita, Hiroshi: Trukese-English Dictionary. Memoirs of the American Philosophical Society, vol. 141. Philadelphia, Penn.1980.

Goodenough, Ward Hunt; Sugita, Hiroshi: Trukese-English Dictionary. Supplementary Volume: English-Trukese and Index of Trukese Word Roots. American Philsophical Society, Vol. 141 S. Philadelphia, Penn.1990.

Goodenough, Ward Hunt: Under Heaven's Brow. Pre-Christian Religious Tradition in Chuuk. Philadelphia 2002.

Haekel, Josef: Religion. In: Trimborn 1971:72-141

Hambruch, Paul; Sarfert, Ernst; (Damm, Hans): Inseln um Truk. Ergebnisse der Südsee-Expedition 1908-1910. II. Ethnographie: B. Mikronesien, Bd. 6. 2. Halbband. Thilenius, Georg (Hrsg.) Hamburg 1935.

Harding, Thomas G.; Wallace, Ben J. (eds.): Cultures of the Pacific. New York (1940) 1970.

Hastings, James (ed.): Encyclopaedia of Religion and Ethics. Edinburgh 1911.

Heintze, Dieter; Didoni, Ursula: Bilder des Menschen in fremden Kulturen. Beispiele aus Afrika und der Südsee. Stuttgart 1973.

Hiery, Hermann Joseph (ed.): Die Deutsche Südsee 1884-1914. Ein Handbuch. Paderborn, München, Wien, Zürich (Schöningh) 2001.

Hirschberg, Walter (Hrsg.): Wörterbuch der Völkerkunde. Stuttgart 1965.

Hirschberg, Walter (Hrsg.): Neues Wörterbuch der Völkerkunde. Berlin 1988.

Howard, Irwin; Vinacke, W. E.; Maretzki, T.: Culture and Personality in the Pacific Islands: A Bibliography. Honolulu, Hawaii 1963.

Hymes, Dell (ed.): Language in Culture. New York 1964.

Hymes, Dell: Comment. In: Chang/Grace/Solheim II 1964:392.

Jaspers, Reiner: Die missionarische Erschließung Ozeaniens. Münster 1972.

Käser, Lothar: ... und bliebe am äußersten Meer. Bad Liebenzell 1972.

Käser, Lothar: Der Begriff "Seele" bei den Insulanern von Truk. Diss. Freiburg i. Br. 1977.

Käser, Lothar: Durch den Tunnel. Bad Liebenzell 1989.

Käser, Lothar: Die Besiedlung Mikronesiens: eine ethnologisch-linguistische Untersuchung. Berlin 1989.

Käser, Lothar: The Concept of the Sacred in the Islands of Truk. NAOS (Notes and Materials for The Linguistic Study of the Sacred) 7. No. 1-3 (1991):33-36.

Käser, Lothar: The Concepts of Sin and Curse in Chuuk, Micronesia. NAOS (Notes and Materials for The Linguistic Study of the Sacred) 10. No. 1-3 (1994):29-32.

Kinkade, M. Dale; Hale, Kenneth L.; Werner, Oswald (eds.): Linguistics and Anthropology. Lisse, Belgium 1975.

Kiste, Robert C.; Marshall, Mac (eds.): American Anthropology in Micronesia. An Assessment. Honolulu, Hawaii 1998.

Klieneberger, H. R.: Bibliography of Oceanic Linguistics. London Oriental Bibliographies Volume 1. London 1957.

Kohl, Manfred W.: Lagoon in the Pacific. The Story of Truk. Schooley's Mountain, N.J. 1971.

Krämer, Augustin: Truk. Ergebnisse der Südsee-Expedition 1908-1910. II. Ethnographie: B. Mikronesien, Bd. 5. Thilenius, Georg (Hrsg.). Hamburg 1932.

Krämer, Augustin: Inseln um Truk (Centralkarolinen Ost). Ergebnisse der Südsee-Expedition 1908-1910. II. Ethnographie: B. Mikronesien, Bd. 6, 1. Halbband. Thilenius, Georg (Hrsg.). Hamburg 1935.

Kubary, Johann: Die Bewohner der Mortlockinseln (Karolinen, nördlicher Großer Ozean). Mittheilungen der Geographischen Gesellschaft in Hamburg 1878-1879.1880:224-299.

Laufer, P. Carl: Das Wesen des Menschen im Denken der Gunantuna (Neubritannien). Wiener völkerkundliche Mitteilungen 5.1957.2:127-160.

LeBar, Frank M.: The Material Culture of Truk. Yale University Publications in Anthropology Nr. 68. New Haven, Conn. 1964.

Leeson, Ida: A Bibliography of Bibliographies of the South Pacific. Oxford 1954.

Lehmann, Friedrich R.: Mana. Eine begriffsgeschichtliche Untersuchung auf ethnologischer Grundlage. Dresden 1915.

Lehmann, Friedrich R.: Mana. Der Begriff des „außerordentlich Wirkungs-vollen" bei Südseevölkern. Leipzig 1922.

Lehmann, Friedrich R.: Die polynesischen Tabusitten. Eine ethnosoziolo-gische Untersuchung. Veröffentlichungen des Staatlich-sächsischen Forschungsinstituts für Völkerkunde in Leipzig, Bd. 10. Leipzig 1930.

Lewis, David: We, the Navigators. The Ancient Art of Landfinding in the Pacific. Honolulu, Hawaii 1975.

Mahony, Frank J.: A Trukese Theory of Medicine. Stanford University, Ph. D. (Manuscript) 1970.

Marshall, Mac; Nason, James D.: Micronesia 1944-1974. A Bibliography of Anthropological and Related Source Materials. New Haven, Conn. 1975.

Moral Ledesma, Beatriz: Conceptualizacion de la mujer, del cuerpo y de la sexualidad en Chuuk (Micronesia). Tesis Doctoral (Manuscript), Universidad del Pais Vasco 1996.

Müller, Klaus E. (Hrsg.): Menschenbilder früher Gesellschaften: ethnologische Studien zum Verhältnis von Mensch und Natur. Gedächtnisschrift für Herrmann Baumann. Frankfurt/Main 1983.

Müller, Klaus W.: The Protestant Mission on the Chuuk Islands in Micronesia: History, Strategy and Methods, Theology, 1873-1979. Nürnberg 2014. (German version: Evangelische Mission in Mikronesien (Trukinseln). Ein Missionar analysiert sein Missionsfeld. Missiologica Evangelica. Bonn (Verlag für Kultur und Wissenschaft) 1989.

Reichardt, Anna Katharina; Kubli, Erich (Hrsg.): Menschenbilder. Bern et al. 1999.

Renner, Egon: Die kognitive Anthropologie. Aufbau und Grundlagen eines ethnologisch-linguistischen Paradigmas. Forschungen zur Ethnologie und Sozialpsychologie 12. Berlin 1980.

Renner, Egon: Die Grundlinien der kognitiven Forschung. In: Fischer 1983:391-425.

Sell, Joachim: Der schlimme Tod bei den Völkern Indonesiens. S'Gravenhage 1955.

Streit, Robert; Dindinger, Johannes: Bibliotheca Missionum, Band 21: Rom 1955; Band 22: Rom 1963; Band 24: Rome 1964.

Suchan, Erika: Die deutsche Wirtschaftstätigkeit in der Südsee vor der ersten Besitzergreifung 1884. Leipzig 940.

Swartz, Marc J.: Personality and Structure: Political Acquiescence in Truk. In: Force, Roland W. (ed.): Induced Political Change in the Pacific. Honolulu, Hawaii 1965:17-39.

Taylor, Clyde R. H.: A Pacific Bibliography. London ^{5}1965.

Treue, Wolfgang: Die Jaluit-Gesellschaft auf den Marshall-Inseln 1887-1914. Ein Beitrag zur Kolonial- und Verwaltungsgeschichte in der Epoche des Deutschen Kaiserreichs. Berlin 1976.

Trimborn, Hermann (Hrsg.): Lehrbuch der Völkerkunde. Stuttgart 1971.

Tyler, Stephen A. (ed.): Cognitive Anthropology. New York 1969.

Ushijima, Iwao: The Afterworld View and its Underlying Ideas among Micronesians. Minzokugaku-kenkyu (The Japanese Journal of Ethnology, Tokyo) 32/1 1967.6:24-37.

Utinomi, Huzio: Bibliography of Micronesia. Pacific Area Bibliographies. Honolulu, Hawaii 1952.

Venz, Oliver: Die autochthone Religion der Benuaq von Ost-Kalimantan. Eine ethnolinguistische Untersuchung. Diss. Freiburg i. Br. 2012 (a).

http://www.freidok.unifreiburg.de/volltexte/8977/pdf/DIE_AUTOCH-THONE_RELIGION_DER_BENUAQ.pdf

Venz, Oliver: "A first look at *asakng* as part of the concept of person among the Benuaq in East Kalimantan". In: *Borneo Research Bulletin* 2012.43:225-244 (b).

Wolters, Gereon: Darwinistische Menschenbilder. In: Reichardt/Kubli 1999:95-115.

Animism
A Cognitive Approach

An Introduction to the Basic Notions Underlying the Concepts of the World and of Man Held by Ethnic Societies, for the Benefit of Those Working Overseas in Development Aid and in the Church

by Lothar Käser

Textbook
to Robert Badenberg's Handbook
The Concept of Man in Non-Western Cultures

In European and other western societies animism is often equated with occultism, spiritism and even with satanism, is evaluated according to European and Christian criteria, and is consequently misunderstood. Such an approach, together with lack of knowledge of the conceptual foundations of animistic thought forms, proves to be a particular impediment when foreigners from European and western cultures come to work in animistically oriented societies to offer development aid, to get involved in NGOs, whether under secular government auspices or the church, as doctors, soldiers, engineers, lecturers, teachers, or in specifically Christian mission. This is because animism not only contains religious elements, but with its particular concept of the world and of man constitutes an all-embracing system of orienting oneself, serving that society as a way of shaping and coping with existence. One has to have some knowledge of this in order to understand the people among whom one is working and for one's work to have successful outcomes.

This textbook does not present animism from a European and western perspective but from that of the people who live it out. The sequence of the individual chapters is arranged in such a way that the reader can learn step by step what animism is, in order finally to understand those characteristic functions that belong to the medium and the shaman in animistic societies.

The author, a professor of ethnology, has considerable experience in this field. He has worked for five years in Oceania and has also undertaken numerous research expeditions in Africa, Asia and South America.

Pb. • pp. 284 • £ 22.50 • $ 37.50 • € 29.95
ISBN 978-3-95776-111-8

VTR Publications • Gogolstr. 33 • 90475 Nürnberg • Germany
info@vtr-online.com • http://www.vtr-online.com

The Concept of Man in Non-Western Cultures
A Guide for One's Own Research

by Robert Badenberg

Handbook
to Lothar Käser's Textbook
Animism – A Cognitive Approach

If we want to understand the animistic cognitive system we must focus particularly on its concept of man. Access to it can only be achieved by proceeding systematically. A basic prerequisite for this is a knowledge of the language spoken by the people whose culture is shaped by such an animistic system of thought. Incidentally acquired knowledge is not enough to give the outsider, whether missionary, teacher, doctor or nurse, the necessary insights for operating effectively within a society governed by an animistic cognitive framework.

Why a textbook and a handbook on the same subject? A textbook seeks to address foundational issues and to ask general questions. A handbook on the other hand is concerned to deal with qualitative and quantitative research. This book is the companion volume of Lothar Käser's textbook on Animism – A Cognitive Approach and provides the interested researcher a tool to guide one's own research into the cognitive aspects of a particular dimension of animism, namely, the concept of man.

Robert Badenberg, qualified in mechanical engineering, trained at the Theological Seminary of the Liebenzell Mission (1982-1987). Further study at the Columbia International University (CIU), German Branch, Korntal, awarded M.A. in Missiology (1999). Doctorate in Missiology at the University of South Africa (2001). As author, missionary (he worked in Africa from 1989 to 2003) and mission ethnologist he commands much experience in this field.

Pb. • pp. 116 • £ 9.80 • $ 15.99 • € 12.80
ISBN 978-3-95776-115-6

VTR Publications • Gogolstr. 33 • 90475 Nürnberg • Germany
info@vtr-online.com • http://www.vtr-online.com

Foreign Cultures

by Lothar Käser

An Introduction to Ethnology
for Development Aid Workers and Church Workers Abroad

In recent decades foreign cultures have not just loomed large for Europeans seeking holiday destinations. Since the 1960s increasing numbers of professionals such as teachers, doctors, agronomists, and other professional workers and missionaries from Europe and America have been partnering local churches in Africa, Asia and Latin America whose fellowships are often very differently organised. When preparing these specialists, development agencies and missions often overlook the knowledge and insights that ethnology and cultural anthropology have to offer, help that makes it easier for professionals to take their bearings, to be well integrated, and to go about their work more effectively. This book deals with such issues.

For future theorists dealing with foreign cultures (ethnologists, anthropologists, etc.) there is now a whole range of brilliantly written textbooks. However, for development aid practitioners, whether secular workers or church workers, these introductory works are overloaded with theory and are thus difficult to digest. What has been missing until now is a simple introduction to the basic concepts which could enable a European working in foreign surroundings to come to terms with the ethnological literature relevant for his activities overseas, to recognise these essential concepts woven into the daily cultural reality of life and work, and to work with them and to bring to bear his or her own analysis. This book is a simplified introduction along these lines, not just written for the target readers just mentioned, but also for students of ethnology/cultural anthropology and for those who frequent ethnological museums.

The author is a professor of anthropology with relevant experience of the issues. He spent five years working in the South Pacific, and has visited Africa, Asia and South America on many occasions for research.

Pb. • pp. 290 • £ 22.50 • $ 37.50 • € 29.95
ISBN 978-3-95776-113-2

VTR Publications • Gogolstr. 33 • 90475 Nürnberg • Germany
info@vtr-online.com • http://www.vtr-online.com